THE HANNIBAL FILES

THE
HANNIBAL
FILES

THE UNAUTHORISED GUIDE TO THE
HANNIBAL LECTER PHENOMENON

DANIEL O'BRIEN

Reynolds & Hearn Ltd
London

This edition first published in 2008 by
Reynolds & Hearn Ltd
61a Priory Road
Kew Gardens
Richmond
Surrey TW9 3DH

A CIP catalogue record for this book
is available from the British Library.

ISBN 978 1 905287 70 3

Designed by James King

Printed and bound in Great Britain by MPG Ltd, Bodmin, Cornwall

ACKNOWLEDGEMENTS

Grateful thanks to Marcus Hearn, Mark Lonsdale, Raymond O'Brien, David O'Leary, Richard Reynolds and Beth Richards. Special thanks to the British Film Institute for invaluable stills research.

NOTE

The spelling of two of the characters' names from the novel *Red Dragon* is altered in the movie *Manhunter*. 'Francis Dolarhyde' of the novel becomes 'Francis Dollarhyde' in the film, while 'Hannibal Lecter' of the novel becomes 'Hannibal Lecktor' in the film. *The Hannibal Files* uses the appropriate spelling, depending on whether the reference is to the novel or film character.

CONTENTS

ACKNOWLEDGEMENTS   5

INTRODUCTION   8

PART ONE:
RED DRAGON AT NIGHT, PSYCHO'S DELIGHT   14

PART TWO:
STARLING, LECTER AND GUMB   73

PART THREE:
HANNIBAL COOKS   142

PART FOUR:
TWIN DRAGONS   186

PART FIVE: FINE YOUNG CANNIBAL   199

FILMOGRAPHY   219

BIBLIOGRAPHY   227

INDEX   230

INTRODUCTION

Threatened by the late twentieth century produced more than its share of bizarre cultural phenomena, yet only the most jaded observer would have tipped a fictional cannibalistic serial killer as one of the era's prime popular icons.

Created by author Thomas Harris for the thriller *Red Dragon* (1981), Doctor Hannibal Lecter's combined character traits do not at first glance suggest wide appeal. While few would be particularly hostile towards Lecter the psychiatrist, scholar, aesthete and wine connoisseur, many would draw the line at Lecter the cold, calculating manipulator and inveterate snob. Surely nobody could admire Lecter the mass murderer and consumer of human livers (with or without a nice bottle of Chianti)?

Hannibal Lecter's extraordinary success is a tribute to the enduring appeal of the charismatic anti-hero. Paying customers the world over have long demonstrated an appetite for cultured, articulate supervillains who dispatch their victims with a casual witticism. Anthony Hopkins, the best-known film incarnation of Lecter, argues that mankind has an enduring fascination with its own capacity for violence, terror and outright evil. Doctor Lecter embodies some of the very worst human qualities in an acceptably detached, mythologised form, his gory deeds offering vicarious, guiltless thrills rather than disgusted fear and loathing.

By the time of the sequel, *The Silence of the Lambs* (1988), Lecter had his own official nickname. The Doctor was dubbed 'Hannibal the Cannibal' by *The National Tattler*, a fictional tabloid rag in no way based on any real-life publication. It is frequently forgotten that Lecter's cannibalism, his best-known trait, was not mentioned by Harris in the first book. Described in *Red Dragon* as a small man, with distinctive white teeth and maroon eyes, Lecter acquired the human flesh-eating habit (along with a six-fingered left, or 'sinister', hand) in *Silence of the*

Lambs. Though arguably not playing fair, this extra detail befitted the character's growing celebrity. A show-stealing supporting player in *Red Dragon*, Lecter assumed co-star status for *Silence of the Lambs*, before emerging as the undisputed hero of the much-awaited, much-delayed *Hannibal* (1999).

Peter Guttmacher, author of *Legendary Horror Films*, rates Hannibal Lecter as 'the real king of killers', the one true heir to *Psycho*'s Norman Bates and *Halloween*'s Michael Myers. This is fair praise, yet Lecter's serial killer status is in many ways his least interesting characteristic. Ted Tally, screenwriter for the 1991 film version of *Silence of the Lambs*, compares Lecter to Professor Moriarty, the larger-than-life arch villain of Arthur Conan Doyle's Sherlock Holmes stories. Brilliant intellect is combined with diabolical cunning, limitless greed and ruthless amorality to create a near unstoppable foe, though Moriarty still ends up at the bottom of the Reichenbach Falls. More adept at self-preservation, Lecter plays on common fears and suspicions of psychiatry – the probing and manipulation of the human mind which, normally being based on trust, provokes terror when used for ruthless, systematic abuse.

For all the acres of newsprint debating the parallels between Hannibal Lecter and real-life serial murderers, Doctor Lecter is at heart a supernatural creature on a par with Bram Stoker's Count Dracula. Significantly, Anthony Hopkins based part of his Lecter performance on one of the celebrated vampire's numerous film incarnations. The famous fava-beans-and-chianti slurp in *Lambs* derived from a childhood memory of the 1930 movie version of *Dracula*, starring Bela Lugosi. The scene where Dracula reacts to a cut on Renfield's finger with undisguised animal craving left an indelible impression on the young Hopkins, though his recollection of the overall film is understandably hazy. Having dropped hints in *Red Dragon* and *Silence of the Lambs*, Thomas Harris openly suggests in *Hannibal* that Lecter is the Devil himself. Unfortunately, Harris then performs a complete turnaround, sketching in both background and motivation for Lecter's evil habits.

Thomas Harris, though an entirely law-abiding citizen, shares some of his best known character's love of elusiveness and game-playing. Undeniably gifted, Harris aims fair to be the Stanley Kubrick of popular crime fiction. Like the late movie *auteur*, Harris is a cultivated recluse producing minimal output, publishing just four books in 24 years. Having made his name in the political thriller genre with *Black Sunday* (1975), Harris evidently felt no pressing need to rush out a sequel. As with Kubrick, the gaps between each new work have steadily grown: six years, then seven, then eleven. Though frustrating to both publishers and fans, this increases the mystique that surrounds Harris and Lecter. Originally expected to deliver *Hannibal* at the end of 1993, Harris denied readers any further adventures of Doctor Lecter for another six years.

Refusing to give interviews, Thomas Harris has kept the amount of readily available information on himself to the barest minimum. Born in Mississippi, he began his writing career covering crime stories in both the United States and Mexico. He subsequently worked as a reporter and editor for the Associated Press in New York City. Depending on the source, Harris's year of birth is listed as both 1940 and 1941, and his birthplace relocated to Jackson, Tennessee. He is said to have studied English at Baylor University, Texas, while working the night-shift at the *Waco News-Tribune*. Shunning the standard media tours, Harris has appeared in a video, specially shot for his publisher's staff. Referring to Hannibal Lecter as 'immensely amusing company', Harris nevertheless regards his best-loved character as an embodiment of Absolute Evil: 'He is the adversary for anything like kindness and hope... he's the dark side of the world.'

During the course of writing *Hannibal*, Harris appears to have softened towards his creation. Cruelly forsaken by God as a child, young Hannibal Lecter realised that the cruelties perpetrated by man were as nothing to the Supreme Being's whimsical malice. While no-one has ever suggested that the author identifies with Lecter, Harris's garden at his home in Sag Harbor, Long Island, New York, contains a sculpture of a mutilated, limbless woman. Curiously, for a man so committed to privacy, Thomas Harris appears unconcerned about being identified. The British paperback editions of Harris's books feature a full-page colour photograph of the author on the inside back cover. The bespectacled writer appears an affable enough figure, with a broad face, receding grey hair and a near white beard, more Santa Claus than Serial Cannibal.

Praised by his admirers for effortlessly erasing the boundary between popular fiction and serious literature, Thomas Harris is certainly a canny storyteller. The Hannibal Lecter trilogy operates in both thriller and horror territory, blending detailed, authoritative police procedural with equally unflinching explorations of terrifying psychosis. Harris also has a gift for sympathetic, if troubled lead characters, whose encounters with Demon King Lecter are as cathartic as they are traumatising. While *Red Dragon*'s Will Graham is ultimately destroyed by Lecter's world, Clarice Starling, heroine of *Silence of the Lambs* and *Hannibal*, ends up embracing it. That said, the finale of *Hannibal* veers sharply into a realm where our disbelief becomes difficult to suspend.

Having incorporated the real-life Palestinian terrorist group Black September into the plot of *Black Sunday*, Thomas Harris had few qualms about drawing on real-life serial killers for his subsequent books. Mass murderers have surfaced at depressingly regular intervals throughout history, including such famous examples as Countess Elizabeth Bathory, Gille de Rais (better known as Bluebeard), and the notoriously unidentified 'Jack the Ripper'. A number of the more debauched Roman emperors, notably Nero and Caligula, would probably also qualify. The most infamous modern-day examples include Ed Gein, the inspiration for *Psycho*, Albert DeSalvo, Charles Whitman, Ted Bundy, John Wayne Gacy, Henry Lee Lucas, Peter Sutcliffe and David Berkowitz.

Hannibal Lecter is placed apart from these unpleasant real-life specimens, who supply the raw ingredients for Harris's secondary psychopaths, *Red Dragon*'s Francis Dolarhyde and *The Silence of the Lambs*' Jame Gumb. Both these characters conform to the standard serial killer profile: white males in their thirties, loners, sexually confused, with backgrounds of traumatic childhood neglect and abuse. Dolarhyde also follows the common trait of early violence, torturing and killing animals. Gumb, however, loves his little dog 'Precious', and regards butterflies and moths as his role models, emerging from their cocoons transformed into 'new' creatures. That said, Gumb also murdered his grandparents at the age of 12.

There seems to be a feeling that Hannibal Lecter's cannibal habits represent some form of regression down the evolutionary scale. Reviewing the film version of *Silence of the Lambs* in the *Evening Standard*, Alexander Walker suggested that 'It's the combination of high intelligence and primitive appetite that makes Lecter such an uncomfortable character.' *Financial Times* critic Nigel Andrews described Lecter as 'Stone Age man and Renaissance man rolled into one.' Put another way, Doctor Hannibal Lecter is Henry Jekyll and Edward Hyde simultaneously, his baser appetites long acknowledged, embraced and indulged with relish.

Compared to the Thomas Harris novels, the Hannibal Lecter films are relatively restrained in their graphic horrors, though *Hannibal* (2001) doesn't shy away from the book's lovingly detailed brain-eating. Whatever place *Hannibal* finds for itself in movie history, *Silence of the Lambs* will remain the pivotal film of the series, at least in terms of cultural impact. A decade after Hannibal Lecter first appeared in print, acclaimed stage actor and jobbing film star Anthony Hopkins delivered an Academy Award-winning performance as the bad Doctor. Never the most popular screen subject, cannibalism had occasionally featured in movies over the years, from Will Hay's comedy *Windbag the Sailor* (1936), through Tobe Hooper's Deep South cookout *The Texas Chain Saw Massacre* (1974), to the much-banned Italian mock-shockumentary *Cannibal Holocaust* (1979). *Silence of the Lambs* offered something new, a fascinating leading character who chewed on human flesh yet drew audience admiration and even a measure of sympathy. *Lambs'* massive box-office success and comprehensive Oscar-sweep elevated the previously despised serial killer genre to the Hollywood mainstream. In all the excitement, only a few lonely voices pointed out the existence of *Manhunter* (1986), an earlier, superior film version of *Red Dragon* which died at the box-office.

The figure of veteran movie producer Dino de Laurentiis hovers large over the Lecter movies, mainly because he cannily bought the rights to first refusal on all Thomas Harris's books from *Red Dragon* onwards. It is ironic that de Laurentiis chose to pass on *Silence of the Lambs*, owing to *Manhunter*'s commercial failure and his own financial difficulties. Declining to even read the book, de Laurentiis could only watch and fume as *Lambs* went on to win five Academy Awards and gross over $250 million worldwide. Needless to say, the producer clung onto the *Hannibal* film rights with all the tenacity of Doctor Lecter biting into a human face. Directed by two noted visual stylists, Michael Mann and Ridley Scott, *Manhunter* and *Hannibal* are both elegant, meticulously crafted pieces of work, though Scott's emphasis on black humour renders *Hannibal* a less unsettling, if bloodier viewing experience. *Lambs* director Jonathan Demme, who made his name with quirky, character-based comedy dramas, takes a more sober, low-key approach, determined to stamp quality and integrity on every frame of his movie.

Thomas Harris had appeared to have minimal interest in the film versions of his work, other than the obvious financial benefits and sales-friendly extra publicity. He is reputed to dislike *Manhunter*, Brian Cox's ice cold Hannibal 'Lecktor' aside, and has supposedly never even watched *The Silence of the Lambs*. That said, Harris sent copies of the *Hannibal* manuscript to Jonathan Demme, Anthony Hopkins and Jodie Foster, the first screen incarnation of Clarice Starling. He also advised on the film adaptation and visited the set. In the past, Harris's attitude to the movie world seemed to echo that of Freddie Lounds, the fame and fortune hungry tabloid journalist in *Red Dragon*: 'He had heard that Hollywood was a fine place for obnoxious fellows with money.' Having grown to love Hannibal Lecter, Thomas Harris now seems quite partial to the character's film incarnation as well.

There will always be those who claim that the rise of Hannibal Lecter marks another step in the moral decline of Western civilisation, desensitised audiences being thrilled on by a cannibal hedonist who glorifies the act of murder. It seems just as valid to argue that the Lecter saga represents a modern equivalent of the Grimm fairy tale, reflecting back universal fears of the dark in a fantastical, manageable form. Perhaps the last word should go to American journalist and short story writer Ambrose Bierce, who vanished from the face of the earth a good 67 years before Hannibal Lecter's first appearance. As a Union Army volunteer during the American Civil War, Bierce had seen soldiers' corpses devoured by wild pigs. It's unlikely he would have been bothered by *Hannibal*'s fictional man-eating swine. Responding to criticism of his own ghoulish tales, Bierce had a simple reply: 'If it scares you to read that one imaginary person killed another, why not take up knitting.' Just watch those sharp needles.

PART ONE

RED DRAGON AT NIGHT, PSYCHO'S DELIGHT

*Dr Lecter is not crazy, in any common way we
think of being crazy. He did some hideous
things because he enjoyed them.*
WILL GRAHAM, *Red Dragon*

*We live in a primitive time – don't we, Will? –
neither savage nor wise. Half measures are the curse of it.
Any rational society would either kill me
or give me my books.*
HANNIBAL LECTER, MD, *Red Dragon*

Thomas Harris's *Red Dragon* was first published in the United States by GP Putnam's Sons in 1981, with a Bantam paperback edition following in 1982, also the year of the first British publication. Stephen King, mega-selling writer of the horror hits *Carrie* (1974), *Salem's Lot* (1975), *The Shining* (1977) and many more, acclaimed Harris's book as 'The best popular novel published since *The Godfather.*' While *Black Sunday* had been a highly successful literary debut, *Red Dragon* turned Thomas Harris into a publishing phenomenon.

The title derives from a painting by visionary British artist William Blake (1757-1827): 'The Great Red Dragon and the Woman Clothed with the Sun' (circa 1803-5). Inspired by a passage from The Bible's Book of Revelations, Chapter 12, Verses 1-4, the picture is an object of worship and inspiration for *Red Dragon*'s deeply insane killer, Francis Dolarhyde. Harris prefaces his narrative with parallel quotes from two of Blake's own literary works, *Songs of Innocence* (1789) and *Songs of*

Experience (1794). The intent here is clear enough, the positive human qualities outlined in the former contrasted with the negative attributes of the latter. Mercy becomes Cruelty, Pity becomes Jealousy, Love becomes Terror and Peace becomes Secrecy. Harris appears to be citing Blake as a pioneering chronicler of the psychopathic personality. The quote concludes with four more lines from *Songs of Experience*:

> The Human Dress is forged Iron,
> The Human Form a fiery Forge,
> The Human Face a Furnace seal'd,
> The Human Heart its hungry Gorge.

The image of the forge, where common materials are melted and transformed into new forms, is particularly appropriate to Dolarhyde, who sees his victims merely as 'elements undergoing change' as he follows his goal of transformation or 'Becoming'. As the people who previously ignored or despised Dolarhyde grovel before him with fear and trembling, Dolarhyde is reborn immortal and terrible in the red-hot fire of his own awesome majesty.

Red Dragon is, nominally, the narrative of Will Graham, a former FBI investigator who retired after tracking down Dr Hannibal Lecter, esteemed psychiatrist and murderer of at least nine people. Blessed, and cursed, with the ability to empathise so deeply with psychopaths that he can duplicate their way of thinking, Graham quit his job for the sake of his sanity. Now based in Sugarloaf Key, Florida, Graham works as a humble, largely untroubled motorboat mechanic, living on the beach with his wife, Molly, and stepson, Willy.

This apparent idyll is disrupted by that old narrative standby: the troubled veteran drawn out of retirement for One Last Job. Jack Crawford, Graham's former FBI boss and mentor, approaches Graham to seek his assistance in solving a series of brutal murders across the South East of the country. Someone is wiping out entire families, slaughtering first the parents, then the children. Against his better judgement, and Molly's wishes, Graham agrees to help sift through the evidence, building up a profile of the killer.

An astute combination of detective fiction and character study,

Red Dragon is taut, well-paced, scrupulously researched and persuasively detailed. Harris based his story on real-life murder cases, including several that occurred in and around the Atlanta area. The characters of Crawford and, to a lesser extent, Graham were supposedly inspired by two genuine FBI investigator-profilers, John Douglas and Robert K Ressler. Drawing on his background as a crime reporter, Harris does not flinch from the unsavoury details of Dolarhyde's killings. Evidence left behind at the crime scenes includes saliva and semen, the latter detail dropped from the subsequent film version. As Crawford coolly puts it: 'He's a secretor.' Dolarhyde's artful use of mirror shards, which enables him to see himself reflected back from his victims, includes a piece wedged in a victim's labia.

Hannibal Lecter, now confined to a maximum security hospital for the criminally insane, boasts an equally impressive track record. Attacked by Lecter with a linoleum knife, Graham has been left with a prominent scar, described by Harris in clinical detail: 'It was finger-width and raised and it never tanned. It ran down from his left hip-bone and turned up to notch his rib-cage on the other side.' After the attack, Graham needed a temporary colostomy bag during his hospital treatment. Adding insult to injury, tabloid reporter Freddie Lounds snapped a picture of the prone Graham, which subsequently appeared on the front page of *The National Tattler*.

Though a victim both of other people's brutality and his own haunted mind, Graham remains a strong character. He has enough self-confidence to engage in blackly amusing self analysis: 'He viewed his own mentality as grotesque but useful, like a chair made of antlers.' It becomes clear early on in *Red Dragon* that Graham will never be able to suppress his empathic abilities: 'Often in intense conversation Graham took on the other person's speech patterns.' During his first lonely expenses-paid night in a hotel room, Graham has a disturbingly vivid vision of murder victim, Mrs Leeds, lying next to him on the double bed: '...bitten and torn, mirrored eyes and blood like the legs of spectacles over her temples and ears.'

Graham's investigation into the 'Tooth Fairy' murders, named after the killer's tendency to bite his victims, leads him back to Hannibal Lecter, a potential source of both information and inspiration. Confined to his high security cell for three years, Dr Lecter seems in good spirits. Small and lithe, with neat white teeth, the Doctor's most distinguishing features are his diabolical maroon eyes, which 'reflect the light redly in tiny points'. Dubbed a 'sociopath' by the supposed experts who do not know what else to call him, Lecter might as well be regarded as a creature from the infernal depths, for all the insight it sheds upon him.

Graham's fragile mental state leaves him vulnerable to emotional manipulation, especially by Lecter. After Freddie Lounds's horrible death, burned alive by Dolarhyde, Lecter sends his captor a letter: 'A brief note of congratulations for the job you did on Mr Lounds'. Lecter asserts that Graham deliberately set Lounds up as a target for the Tooth Fairy, posing with the reporter for pictures in *The National Tattler*. Unsure himself why he put his hand on Lounds's shoulder for the 'buddy' photograph, Graham is momentarily swayed by Lecter's attitude. Aside from the usual mind games, the letter exhibits the Doctor's vanity, Lecter putting the initials M.D. after his name. One of Lecter's biggest trumps in his contest with Graham is that he's already suffering the worst punishment society can inflict upon him. Casually obtaining Graham's home address over the telephone, Lecter hands it on to Dolarhyde with the advice: 'Save Yourself. Kill Them All.' Lecter's punishment for this very personal incitement to murder is the temporary loss of his books.

Introduced in his work environment, awkwardly moving among colleagues who regard him with a mix of derision and wariness, Francis Dolarhyde cuts a sympathetic figure much of the time. The red goggles he insists on wearing outside the darkroom, to conceal his yellow eyes, are put to more sinister use during his leisure hours. Dolarhyde's background, especially his appalling childhood, is related in detail over several chapters and has distinct echoes of *Psycho*. The only child of an impoverished single mother, Dolarhyde was born with severe facial deformities: a cleft upper lip and palates. The presiding doctor, short on sensitivity, describes the infant as 'more like a leaf-nosed bat than a baby'. Abandoned by his mother, who screams at the sight of him, Dolarhyde is nicknamed 'Cunt Face' by the other boys at the orphanage. This bad start in life is soon made even worse. Raised from the age of five by his eccentric, borderline insane Grandmother, Dolarhyde grows up in her vast, isolated house, which also serves as a nursing home.

Terrified of the dark, he wets the bed rather than go to the lavatory. Grandmother's response is to grip his penis between a pair of scissors and threaten to castrate him if he misbehaves again. Even Dolarhyde's brushes with normal childhood curiosity become tainted with fear and loathing. While playing doctor and nurse with a girl neighbour behind his grandmother's chicken shed, Dolarhyde is rudely interrupted. A passing headless chicken, freshly decapitated for the pot, runs past, spattering the girl with blood just as Dolarhyde is examining her private parts.

Dead for ten years, Dolarhyde's grandmother still dominates both her house and her grandchild. The woman's clothes, hairbrushes and false teeth are treated as holy relics (the brushes still contain strands of her hair). The teeth are of special significance, 'an imprimatur flecked with old blood'. Under the circumstances, it's not too surprising that Francis Dolarhyde's first human victims are elderly women. Harris's depiction of Grandma Dolarhyde borders on the risible at times, the old lady bearing a striking resemblance to President George Washington, especially when her teeth are in place.

Like Norman Bates, Dolarhyde still sleeps in his childhood bedroom, where a print reproduction of Blake's 'The Great Red Dragon and the Woman Clothed with the Sun' has pride of place. 'Never before had he seen anything that approached his graphic thought.' Dolarhyde is also inspired by The Book of Revelations, which also inspired large chunks of David Seltzer's screenplay for *The Omen* (1976). Details of the forthcoming apocalypse are laid down by the apostle John in impressive, if confusing detail. The section which inspired Blake's painting runs as follows in the revised standard version of the Bible:

> And a great portent appeared in heaven, a woman clothed with the sun, with the moon under her feet, and on her head a crown of twelve stars; she was with child and she cried out in her pangs of birth, in anguish for delivery. And another portent appeared in heaven; behold, a great red dragon, with seven heads and ten horns, and seven diadems upon his heads. His tail swept down a third of the stars of heaven, and cast them to the earth. And the dragon

stood before the woman who was about to bear a child,
that he might devour her child when she brought it forth.

According to the standard interpretation, the pregnant woman stands
for Israel, about to bring forth a male child who will grow to rule all
nations from his throne in heaven. The woman also represents the
Christian Church.

Bearing in mind William Blake's penchant for spectacular, bizarre,
sometimes grotesque allegorical images, his interest in the monsters
from the Book of Revelations makes sense, despite the artist's nominal
rejection of all conventional religion. Working with pen, black chalk
and watercolour, Blake produced a startling rendering of the Great Red
Dragon. Abandoning the traditional image of the mythical creature, a
reptilian quadruped with fiery breath, he gives the monster a humanoid
form, though the image is framed and dominated by its vast, outstretched
bat-like wings. Even less expectedly, Blake presents the spectator with
the Dragon's back, foregoing the opportunity to render its terrible
face(s). Arguably, the smooth, featureless back of the Dragon's main
head, flanked by two curling ram's horns, is far more sinister than the
usual glowing red eyes, gnashing teeth and flaring nostrils. This rear
view gives special prominence to the Dragon's tail, a detail not lost
on Francis Dolarhyde, who has his own tattooed dragon-tail in homage
to his inspiration.

The Woman Clothed with the Sun lies prone at the Great Red
Dragon's feet, entwined in his powerful tail. Partially blocked from
view by the Dragon's legs and tail, the pale, delicately rendered woman
looks appallingly vulnerable, her hands clasped in prayer, her face raised
to heaven. Positioned between the spectator and the crouching woman,
the Dragon dominates the picture and his intended prey.

While not an entirely faithful rendering of the description
in Revelations – the number of heads, horns and diadems has
understandably been reduced – Blake's Great Red Dragon captures
its essence superbly. Given the power of even the most indifferent
reproductions, the actual picture is surprisingly small, a mere 43.5
centimetres by 34.5 centimetres, a point raised by Harris in his book.
Blake liked the Red Dragon enough to feature him in three more

pictures. For the record, both the woman and child escape the jaws of the Dragon.

In best serial killer tradition, Francis Dolarhyde keeps a scrapbook of his crimes, a 100-year-old leather business ledger purchased at a bankruptcy sale. Aside from the expected newspaper and magazine clippings, there are more intimate souvenirs: 'Fastened in the margins, ragged bits of scalp trailed their tails of hair like comets pressed in God's scrapbook.' Employed by a film laboratory that develops home movies – *Red Dragon* appeared before video tape became the dominant recording medium – Dolarhyde collects and shoots eight-millimetre footage of his victims (a plot device used in Michael Powell's 1960 thriller *Peeping Tom*). Not just a passive voyeur, Dolarhyde makes guest appearances in his special home movies, dancing naked among the dead while the camera rolls. Needless to say, his gloves and goggles remain firmly in place. There is more than a hint here of necrophilia, though Harris declines to spell out the exact nature Dolarhyde's relationship with the deceased Mrs Jacobi and Mrs Leeds.

Not one to leave loose ends, Harris neatly ties together Dolarhyde's lethal fixation on his late grandmother with his worship of the Dragon. The Dragon 'speaks' to Dolarhyde in the voice of his grandmother, the words emanating from Dolarhyde's own mouth. The 'Dragon's teeth' used on his victims are exact replicas of his grandmother's dentures, custom made for Dolarhyde during a trip to Hong Kong. Attracted to blind co-worker Reba McLane, Dolarhyde is tempted to stray from the path of the Dragon, invoking its terrible wrath. Holding his genitals in the vice-grip of the Dragon's teeth, Dolarhyde/Red Dragon shouts abuse at himself:

> YOU ARE OFFAL LEFT BEHIND IN THE BECOMING.
> YOU ARE OFFAL AND I WILL NAME YOU.
> YOU ARE CUNT FACE. SAY IT.

Rather than sacrifice Reba to the Dragon, Dolarhyde contemplates suicide by hanging, before deciding on a more ingenious, if bizarre course of action. Posing as a researcher, he travels to the Brooklyn Museum, New York, where the Blake painting is stored. As Harris helpfully explains, watercolour paintings fade under light and 'The Great Red Dragon...' is rarely on display. Noting that the woman in the painting has the same hair colour as Reba, Dolarhyde chloroforms two female gallery attendants and eats the picture. Impressed by this bold display of rebellion, the Dragon announces that he and Dolarhyde are now closer than ever.

The finale of *Red Dragon*, while action-packed, is protracted, overly elaborate and ultimately unsatisfying. Still trying to save the imprisoned Reba from the Dragon's bite, Dolarhyde sets his bedroom on fire and aims his gun at her. With a cry of 'Oh, Reba, I can't stand to watch you burn' – not Harris' finest line of dialogue – he apparently shoots himself instead. Feeling her way out of the blazing room, Reba certainly locates convincing evidence: 'she found hair... put her hand in something soft below the hair. Only pulp, sharp bone splinters and a loose eye in it.' Harris seems partial to detached eyeballs, vital, vulnerable and soft as jelly. Hannibal Lecter has bitten out at least one during his period of incarceration and gets to chomp on another during his successful escape in *The Silence of the Lambs*.

With the Dolarhyde case closed, Will Graham returns home to Sugarloaf Key, realising that his personal life is in poor shape. The case has driven him and Molly apart, despite her efforts to support him, and Willy's possessive grandparents want the boy to live with them. The big, big twist comes when Dolarhyde, still very much alive, literally jumps Graham on the edge of the beach, rupturing his spleen and driving a knife blade deep into his cheekbone. Rendered helpless, just as he'd been by Lecter's attack three years earlier, Graham is rescued by Molly, who hooks Dolarhyde with a fishing rod. Pursued back to the beach house, Molly shoots Dolarhyde four times in the face, leaving the Tooth Fairy with '...scalp down to his chin and his hair on fire'. It later transpires that Dolarhyde fled his burning house, substituting the body of a murdered gas station attendant, whom he'd previously checked out for evidence-friendly dentures.

Though efficiently handled by Harris, the twist finale feels like a cheap trick, a case of not playing fair with either the reader or the characters. Having put his health, marriage and sanity on the line to track down Dolarhyde, Graham is once again denied the chance to be a 'true' hero, crawling in the bloody sand with a face full of sharp metal. Harris's decision to make Molly Graham Dolarhyde's righteous executioner could be lauded as both anti-cliché and pro-feminist, an admirable precedent for Clarice Starling's pursuit of Jame Gumb (aka Buffalo Bill) in *Silence of the Lambs*. Yet there is little sense of catharsis, or even resolution, to *Red Dragon*'s beach finale. Confrontation with Dolarhyde does nothing to alter Molly's appreciation of Will's return to active duty. Dolarhyde's grand delusory schemes of cosmic transmutation are reduced to a much more mundane level: self preservation and petty revenge. Dolarhyde had previously fantasised about breaking Graham's back: 'the Dragon will snap your spine', yet doesn't even try during the beach attack. The Great Red Dragon would not approve.

Back in hospital for major reconstructive surgery, Graham receives an ironic letter of commiseration from Lecter: 'I wish you a speedy convalescence and hope you won't be very ugly.' Graham never sees the note, which is intercepted and burnt by Jack Crawford. By the end of the book, Graham sees little future for himself, either on a professional or personal level. 'He could hold Molly for a while with his face... That would be a cheap shot. Hold her for what?' Having courageously re-entered the lower circles of hell for the benefit of his fellow man, putting both mind and body in extreme peril, Will Graham surely deserves better.

On the surface, the bestselling *Red Dragon* seemed an obvious choice for screen adaptation: an ingenious, highly detailed psychological thriller with an intriguing, non-stereotypical hero and not one but two fascinating psychotic killers pitted against him. Mainstream Hollywood filmmakers tend towards caution, however, and the Thomas Harris book-to-film track record was both short and unimpressive. Six years prior to *Red Dragon*, Harris made his literary debut with the bestselling thriller *Black Sunday* (1975). First published in hardback by GP Putnam's Sons, with a Bantam paperback reissue the following year, *Black Sunday* centres on an Arab terrorist plot to detonate a huge bomb during the American Football Super Bowl Championship game, wiping out the entire crowd. If this monstrous assault on a cherished national institution wasn't crime enough, the explosion would be launched from the Goodyear Blimp airship above the stadium, one American icon destroying another.

The Black September movement in the story was a real, active Palestinian terrorist group, which lent a highly topical edge to the proceedings. By using the Black September name, Harris underlined his narrative's strong sense of carefully researched realism, but left himself open to accusations of both bad taste and cynical exploitation. A splinter group from the Palestine Liberation Organisation, formed in 1970, Black September had grabbed the international headlines only three years earlier by taking Israeli athletes hostage at the 1972 Munich Olympics. The bungled kidnap and equally botched rescue attempt left eleven Israelis dead. While the book escaped any serious protests, a high profile film version intended for international release might not be so fortunate.

The screen rights to *Black Sunday* were snapped up by industry giant Paramount and producer Robert Evans. A former head of the studio, Evans was now a red-hot independent filmmaker affiliated to his one-time employer, giving Paramount major commercial and critical success with *Chinatown* (1974) and *Marathon Man* (1976). John Frankenheimer, similarly hot from the success of Twentieth Century Fox's *French Connection II* (1975), agreed to direct the film on a healthy $8.0 million budget. Looking for some location realism, not to mention a piece of canny cost-cutting, Evans obtained permission to shoot *Black Sunday*'s climactic sequence at the year's actual Super Bowl (Pittsburgh versus Dallas), held at the Miami Orange Bowl. The cast was headed by respected British actor Robert Shaw, regarded by many as a major Hollywood star following his participation in the surprise, or shock, mega-hit *Jaws* (1975). The supporting cast featured veteran screen crazy-man Bruce Dern, recently seen in Alfred Hitchcock's *Family Plot* (1975), alongside Swiss leading lady Marthe Keller and stage actor Fritz Weaver. Both Keller and Weaver had appeared in *Marathon Man*, and the producers of *Black Sunday* (1977) were confident of a hit on the same level.

Discussing the film in his autobiography, Robert Evans recalls there being a huge buzz around *Black Sunday* prior to its release, industry pundits claiming that the film would be 'bigger than *Jaws*'. Adapted from a bestselling novel, with major studio backing, top-drawer behind-the-camera talent, and a star from the highest grossing film of all time, *Black Sunday* came as close as is possible to being a surefire hit. In the fickle world of movies, however, this isn't particularly close. Despite a fair smattering of favourable reviews, *Black Sunday* proved a major box-office disappointment. Audiences appeared utterly underwhelmed by Shaw's Israeli Mossad agent, Keller's committed terrorist and Dern's brainwashed Vietnam veteran turned Blimp pilot. The film's commercial chances were undoubtedly hurt by the near simultaneous release of Universal's *Two Minute Warning* (1976), which featured a sniper loose in a crowded football stadium – the Los Angeles Coliseum – during another Super Bowl game. Charlton Heston's harassed police chief and John Cassavetes's SWAT team leader provided a small measure of star *gravitas*, yet the collection of wafer-thin characters didn't hold the attention for the two long hours before the shooting commenced. Discussing *Two Minute Warning*'s failure in his autobiography, Heston offered a fair explanation for the box-office disaster: 'the public didn't want anything to do with terror in a Super Bowl', a comment equally applicable to *Black Sunday*.

Neither lone gunmen nor Arab terrorists were appealing figures on home turf. The films touched on a nerve that repelled audiences rather than generating the kind of nervous, semi-wary attraction that later made the film version of *Silence of the Lambs* a smash hit. As with Michael Mann's *Manhunter* a decade later, *Black Sunday* could be cited as an intelligent, finely-crafted work that simply arrived at the wrong time, touching on dark, uncomfortable territory that was literally too close to home for the paying public on its original release. The comparison doesn't really hold up, however, as the earlier film is less an unappreciated gem than a moderately effective, committee-designed suspenser that simply fails to hit its desired marks.

While few would disagree that John Frankenheimer was easily Mann's equal at the peak of his career, the former had been on the slide, both critically and commercially, for nearly a decade before *Black Sunday* came along. Despite his recent success with the return of Popeye Doyle, Frankenheimer remained a 1960s *auteur* fallen on hard times, films like *The Manchurian Candidate* (1962), *Seven Days in May* (1964) and *Seconds* (1966) now ancient history. In accepting the *Black Sunday* assignment, he was merely looking to consolidate his box-office comeback, which rapidly ground to a halt with outright flops such as

Prophecy (1979), a risible eco horror-thriller, and the Japan-set *The Challenge* (1982), a muddled, unattractively brutal culture clash tale. (The film's star, Scott Glenn, later found his own place on the Thomas Harris bandwagon, playing FBI boss Jack Crawford in *The Silence of the Lambs*. In *The Challenge*, he had to settle for being buried up to his neck, eating a passing insect, and vanquishing the Japanese villain with a handy office stapler.)

Frankenheimer was not the only jaded talent working on *Black Sunday*. The screenplay for the film was co-written by Hollywood veteran Ernest Lehman, whose credits include the scripts for such blockbuster musicals as *The King and I* (1956), *West Side Story* (1961) and *The Sound of Music* (1965). Lehman's filmography also featured more dramatic fare, notably *Sweet Smell of Success* (1957), Alfred Hitchcock's *North by Northwest* (1959), for which Lehman received an Academy Award nomination, and *Who's Afraid of Virginia Woolf?* (1966) – which he also produced. A decade on, Lehman was still in demand, with enough clout to produce, direct and write a screen adaptation of Philip Roth's controversial masturbation-themed novel *Portnoy's Complaint*, released by Warner Bros in 1972. Up until the recent success of the gross-out comedies *There's Something About Mary* (1998) and *American Pie* (1999), self abuse has lacked audience appeal and Lehman's inept treatment of the material did nothing to buck the trend. Terrible reviews obliged Lehman to concentrate his energies on the day job, the writer reuniting with Hitchcock for *Family Plot*, a muted, underwhelming effort suggesting that both men were lost in the 1970s 'New Hollywood', out of step with the attitudes and styles of the times. *Black Sunday* proved to be Lehman's last screen credit.

Nor did *Black Sunday* offer the level of star drawing power assumed by the studio. Along with Richard Dreyfuss and Roy Scheider, Robert Shaw had capably headed the cast of Steven Spielberg's shark spectacular *Jaws*, yet all three remained respected character actors rather than transforming into serious box-office attractions. Shaw's post *Jaws* career, oriented entirely towards Hollywood-based commercial success, was a dreary collection of barely remembered items. These included *Swashbuckler* (1976), a charmlessly camp attempt to revive the Errol Flynn pirate movie; *The Deep* (1977), tedious underwater shenanigans sold largely on the strength of Jacqueline Bisset's breasts; *Force 10 from Navarone* (1978), a threadbare sequel to a hit *Boy's Own* war adventure made nearly two decades earlier, and *Avalanche Express* (1979), dull Cold War antics cobbled together after the death of the director, Mark Robson. Always a drinker, Shaw spent much of the *Black Sunday* shoot incapacitated by alcohol. Many of his scenes had to be reworked in order to keep Shaw sitting down, as the actor could concentrate on remembering his lines or standing up but not both. Shaw died from heart failure a year after the release of *Black Sunday*, doomed to be best remembered for being bloodily chewed up by a giant rubber fish.

Whatever the individual failings of the cast and crew, Evans felt that the film hit the wrong note with audiences, being too realistic for its own good. Aiming to show both sides of the Arab-Israeli conflict, *Black Sunday* depicted terrorism as a grey area, rather than simplifying the storyline to a straight, black/white conflict between the forces of good and evil. Giving equal time to the factions involved, the film became overlong – 143 minutes – and overly verbose as various arguments, interesting in themselves, were carefully laid out with more Hollywood dramatics than plausible characterisation. The apparent sympathy for the Palestinian cause went down badly with Jewish groups. According to Evans, the leading Jewish newspaper *The B'nai B'rith Messenger* labelled him a 'Hitlerite', urging a boycott of the movie.

New York Post reviewer Frank Rich offered a less sensational criticism of the film, arguing that the understandable desire to make a fast buck had resulted in an unfortunate political stance: 'Why else would anyone make an ostensibly anti-terrorist film that in actuality could end up promoting terrorism?' After a series of threats, Evans felt obliged to hire 24-hour security for himself and his family. Even allowing for an element of exaggeration, the off-screen furore surrounding *Black Sunday* proved more dramatic than the movie itself. The heralded film event of the year, supposedly 'bigger than *Jaws*', proved just another damp squib. As Evans later put it: 'A blimp ain't no fish – just hot air.'

Prior to the Academy Award-sanctified success of *Silence of the Lambs*, relatively few 'respectable' movies dealt with the theme of serial murder. Filmmakers who did venture into the field tended to opt for a sober, unsensational 'case history' approach, often drawing on real events to legitimise their material. The more notable examples included Fritz Lang's *M* (1930), based on the Peter Kurten case, *The Boston Strangler* (1968) and *10 Rillington Place* (1970), both directed by Richard Fleischer. The less reserved *Dirty Harry* (1971) referenced the elusive Zodiac Killer, while the defiantly uncommercial *Badlands* (1973) retold the story of Charles Starkweather, whose list of victims started with his underage girlfriend's father. Alfred Hitchcock's *Psycho* (1960), which drew from the Ed Gein case, veered into gleeful black comedy, virtually mocking the idea of respectability with its po-faced 'explanation' of Norman Bates in the last scene.

Less concerned than Hollywood with notions of social responsibility and good taste, the Italian film industry contributed the *giallo* serial killer cycle. Writer-director Dario Argento, whose *The Bird With the Crystal Plumage* (1969) popularised the subgenre, devised most of staple ingredients: twisting storylines, stylised visuals, gory set-piece murders, predominantly young female victims, aggressive scoring and black leather gloves. Made in association with an Italian studio boss, cameraman and visual consultant, *Manhunter* is in some ways an American variation on the *giallo* tradition, though the characterisation is more developed and the nastiness of the murders more implied than shown. By the time Michael Mann's film started production in 1985, Hollywood had experienced its own serial killer cycle: the 'teen slasher' shocker. Kicked off by the surprise success of *Halloween* (1978) and *Friday the 13th* (1980), the subgenre had more or less burned out, doomed by its own inherent shoddiness. John Carpenter's film, well-crafted and relatively unbloody, proved too difficult for the rip-off merchants to imitate and most copied the cruder, gorier *Friday the 13th* formula. Only the latter's sequels and the fantasy-tinged *Nightmare on Elm Street* series showed continuing signs of commercial life. Interestingly, recent big-budget excursions into 'slasher' territory, notably William Friedkin's allegedly homophobic *Cruising* (1980), didn't work with audiences. Schlock-horror rollercoaster rides were an accepted, if widely despised, form of entertainment. Anything with more ambition, more ambiguity and more obvious talent had to be suspect.

REMAKES AND ROBOT GORILLAS

The film rights to *Red Dragon* were purchased by Italian movie mogul Dino de Laurentiis, during the period when his reconstituted filmmaking empire was about to crumble spectacularly into ruins for at least the second time. No stranger to high-profile commercial fiascos, de Laurentiis would not have been daunted by *Black Sunday*'s disappointing, yet hardly ruinous box-office showing. A more canny businessman than movies like *Orca - Killer Whale* (1977), *The White Buffalo* (1977) and *King of the Gypsies* (1978) would suggest, de Laurentiis's deal with Thomas Harris also granted the producer first option on all future books by the author, whether or not they featured Hannibal Lecter. Variously derided as Dino de Dum Dum and Dino de Horrendous, de Laurentiis is a real puzzle of a filmmaker. Far better known for his long string of often tacky, horrendously expensive flops – *The Bible* (1966), *Waterloo* (1970), *Dune* (1984) – than his successes, de Laurentiis has nevertheless survived and often thrived on the international film scene for well over 50 years.

Active in the Italian cinema from the 1930s onwards, de Laurentiis enjoyed his first international hit with *Bitter Rice* (1948). This slicker-than-usual slice of neo-realism benefited greatly from the frequently exposed thighs of leading lady Silvana Mangano, a former model who enjoyed a close professional and personal relationship with the producer over several decades. De Laurentiis's eye for the international film market soon led him into Hollywood co-productions, which were popular with American studios who had revenues frozen in European territories. From the start, de Laurentiis often appeared more interested – or at least more successful – in putting together a production deal than making a good film. *Ulysses* (1954), for example, imported the not inconsiderable talents of Kirk Douglas and Anthony Quinn and could have been an exciting, spectacular mythological epic on a par with later Ray Harryhausen efforts such as *Jason and the Argonauts* (1963). Instead, the end result proved static and dull, despite a convincing cyclops, and utterly lacking in drama or tension. The many defects included a clumsy script cobbled together by at least seven writers; flat, television-style direction; poor English-language dubbing and indifferent leading performances. *War and Peace* (1956), largely directed by the respected American King Vidor, marked a slight improvement yet remained hamstrung by its multi-authored, heavily rewritten screenplay and eclectic multinational casting. In between his would-be epics, de Laurentiis found time to finance arthouse fare such as Federico Fellini's *La Strada* (1954), which did a lot more for the producer's reputation, if not his bank balance.

The archetypal de Laurentiis movie, at least in terms of popular appeal, is probably *Barbarella* (1968), a science fiction fantasy starring future militant feminist and Born Again Christian Jane Fonda. Based on commercially proven source material, in this instance a salacious French comic strip, the production followed the standard de Laurentiis blockbuster formula: a many-handed script, American leads, spectacularly lurid sets and costumes, a disjointedly episodic narrative, imaginatively tasteless sadism and coy erotica. The director, Fonda's then husband Roger Vadim, displayed little in the way of cinematic flair, a common failing among the de Laurentiis-appointed *auteurs*. While the producer's credits include successful collaborations with such names as Sidney Lumet, Sydney Pollack, John Milius, David Cronenberg, David Lynch and, of course, Michael Mann, most of his 'big' movies were handled by the likes of Michael Winner, John Guillermin, Michael Anderson and J Lee Thompson. All had good or at least technically accomplished work to their names but were seemingly flattened by the de Laurentiis production machine.

By the late 1960s, not even hits like *Barbarella* could save the de Laurentiis empire from a string of flops and the mounting recession in the Italian film industry. Relocating to America, the producer initially seemed to have found his niche, backing the successful urban thrillers *Serpico* (1973), *Death Wish* (1974) and *Three Days of the Condor* (1975). It says something about de Laurentiis's preferred working method that he initially offered the latter film to *Death Wish* director Michael Winner before hiring Sydney Pollack.

King Kong (1976), generally despised by aficionados of the original 1933 film, made money, thanks largely to a massive marketing campaign. The film arguably did de Laurentiis more harm than good, however, marking the point in his American career when the producer became branded as a cynical rip-off merchant. De Laurentiis sold his *Kong* remake largely on the strength of its supposed technological marvel: a giant, fully functional robotic gorilla built by Italian special effects maestro Carlo Rambaldi. With the exception of one scene, what enraged reviewers and audiences actually saw most of the time was a man in a gorilla suit, romping around miniature sets in the best Godzilla fashion.

De Laurentiis continued to turn out distinguished, financially successful films, notably Milius's *Conan the Barbarian* (1982) and Cronenberg's *The Dead Zone* (1983), yet for many he was forever associated with unrelentingly camp frolics such as *Flash Gordon* (1980). Having dumped original director Nicolas Roeg and sanctioned such special effects miracles as flying hawkmen with blatantly cardboard wings, de Laurentiis looked like a purveyor of gaudy, shoddy goods. During the early 1980s, the producer founded the De Laurentiis Entertainment Group (DEG). Based in Wilmington, North Carolina, some distance from Los Angeles, DEG had its own vast studio complex. Yet it would prove a short-lived enterprise. Undaunted by past mistakes, de Laurentiis hadn't lost his belief that big movies equalled big box office. Among the epic productions in the works were two based on mammoth source novels: Frank Herbert's cult science fiction fantasy *Dune* and James Clavell's colonial saga *Tai-Pan*.

"HE HAS A GOOD EYE... HE'S ALSO WILLING TO TAKE CHANCES"

Quoted in *Manhunter*'s pressbook, a useful if not entirely trustworthy source, Michael Mann described Thomas Harris's *Red Dragon* as 'the best detective story I ever came across... the most exciting and... the most original.' As writer and director of the *Red Dragon* film, Michael Mann enjoyed an unusual level of control for a de Laurentiis employee. But the deal came with at least one major problem clause. If Mann delivered a film that went over the agreed two-hour running time, he would lose his contractual right to final cut.

A native of Chicago, Michael Mann was born in 1943. After studying at the University of Wisconsin, he crossed the Atlantic to train at the London Film School. His filmmaking career began in 1965, as a UK-based director of commercials and documentaries, including coverage of the 1968 student riots in Paris (led by Red Daniel, as opposed to Red Dragon). Mann shot a documentary film in Paris, *Insurrection* (1968), for the American television network NBC. Sixteen years later, director and network reunited for the less reality-bound cop show *Miami Vice*.

Returning to the United States in 1972, Mann established himself as a scriptwriter for television, specialising in fast-paced, violent police series such as *Starsky and Hutch* (1975-80) and the lesser-known *Police Story*. Rapidly working his way up the small screen hierarchy, Mann created *Vega$* (1978), which starred Robert Urich as private investigator Dan Tanna. These shows operated mainly in the realm of escapist fantasy, using authentic urban locations and touching on controversial subjects to add a veneer of realism. David Soul's dedicated cop Ken Hutchinson had a particularly tough time, suffering agonising withdrawal after being forcibly hooked on heroin and falling in love with a prostitute and porn star. Mann's scripts for *Starsky and Hutch* included three of the first half dozen episodes, long before network concerns over the level of violence caused the show to be watered down. A high profile and highly respected figure in the television industry by the late 1970s, Mann was offered a number of acting jobs, making 'guest' appearances in a 1976 episode of *Kojak*, 'By Silence Betrayed', and a 1978 instalment of *M*A*S*H*, 'Major Topper'.

Mann's first film assignment came in the shape of some uncredited script work on the troubled production *Straight Time* (1978). Based on the novel *No Beast So Fierce*, written by ex-armed robber and then convict Eddie Bunker, the movie was a personal project for executive producer, star and first-time director Dustin Hoffman. More of a character study than a thriller, the story focuses on parolee Max Dembo, who emerges from prison genuinely determined to go straight. Finding the odds hopelessly stacked against him, largely in the form of his unsympathetic parole officer, Dembo reverts to his criminal ways, planning the usual big heist that will set him up for life.

Unhappy with his multiple responsibilities, Hoffman soon decided to abandon the director's chair, making way for theatre veteran Ulu

Grosbard. The three credited screenwriters, including Bunker himself, could not come up with the desired result. It probably didn't help that Bunker was still in prison for safe-cracking when he worked on the script (co-writer Alvin Sargent conferred with Bunker during visiting hours). Despite Mann's best efforts, and a fine supporting cast that included Theresa Russell, Gary Busey and Harry Dean Stanton, the movie flopped. Cast in a bit role in *Straight Time*, Eddie Bunker later enjoyed more lasting film success as Mr Blue in Quentin Tarantino's *Reservoir Dogs* (1991).

Mann did benefit from his anonymous film debut in at least one respect. *Straight Time* co-producer Tim Zinnemann subsequently produced Mann's acclaimed television movie *The Jericho Mile* (1979), which starred Peter Strauss as a convict serving a life sentence at Folsom Prison. A gifted track athlete, Larry 'Rain' Murphy aims to earn himself a place on the Olympic team. Scripted by Mann with Patrick J Nolan, the film captures the harsh realities of prison life, with institutional racism and casual brutality, while remaining upbeat in its central quest for sporting glory. Displaying the same judgement, or luck, for casting that later distinguished *Manhunter*, Mann employed leading character actors Brian Dennehy, Billy Green Bush and Ed Lauter. Bit parts were played by genuine prison inmates, a trick Mann repeated for *Manhunter*, casting real SWAT team officers. Mann's work on *The Jericho Mile* earned him an Emmy Award, the television equivalent of an Academy Award, and a Best Director Award from the Director's Guild of America.

Despite his impressive track record with television, Michael Mann's feature film career got off to a commercially shaky start, not gaining real box-office momentum for a decade. Distributed by United Artists, *Thief* (1981) tells the story of a career criminal, played by James Caan, whose unsurpassed professional expertise is countered by a strong desire for a different life. Working from a script loosely based on the novel *The Home Invaders*, by Frank Hohimer, Mann co-produced the film with Jerry Bruckheimer, later famous for his producing partnership with Don Simpson on a series of high concept, low content blockbusters (*Flashdance* in 1983, *Beverly Hills Cop* in 1985, *Top Gun* in 1986 and so on).

While the tale of a high-class, high-tech jewel thief with personal problems might not sound like much of a winner, Mann produced a fine feature debut. Dispensing with dialogue much of the time, he depicts Caan's technically precise work in almost abstract style, with lingering close-ups of lock mechanisms as Caan calmly takes a safe apart. The pulsing synthesizer score by Tangerine Dream adds to the intense, dreamlike atmosphere. Referring to his highly distinctive visual style during the production of *Manhunter*, Mann commented that: 'It helps give a film a certain identity.' Unlike some of Mann's television work, the high style is here matched by content. Having dreamed of a 'normal' family life during a stretch in prison, Caan's character finds this ideal eternally beyond his reach. Discussing his lead characters in *Thief* and *The Jericho Mile*, Mann has commented: 'Both try to get through by dreaming about the impossible.'

For all its undeniable merits, *Thief* never looked like being an easy sell. James Caan, who also served as co-executive producer, was no longer a major star, thanks to a combination of poor career choices, with forgotten flops like *Harry and Walter Go to New York* (1976). Co-stars Tuesday Weld and James Belushi lacked audience appeal and even Country and Western singing star Willie Nelson failed to draw the crowds. Released in the United States on 27 March 1981, *Thief* grossed a disappointing $4.3 million on its home territory. Released in the UK as *Violent Streets*, the film did little business under any title. United Artists, still reeling from the defection of key executives to form Orion Pictures and the commercial disaster of *Heaven's Gate* (1981), was about to be sold to Metro Goldwyn Mayer. *Thief*'s distribution did not figure very highly in the studio's list of priorities, though United Artists did agree to show the film in competition at the Cannes Film Festival.

If nothing else, *Thief* did bring Mann into contact with two gifted collaborators, production designer Mel Bourne and editor Dov Hoenig, both of whom would work on *Manhunter*. Specialising in urban settings, Bourne had been active in films since the late 1950s. A Woody Allen regular during the peak years of the latter's career (working on *Annie Hall*, released in 1977, and *Manhattan*, released in 1979), Bourne's other credits included *The Miracle Worker* (1962) and *The Natural* (1984). Finding Mann to be a demanding filmmaker, Bourne regarded his collaborations with the director as mutually stimulating: 'He has a good eye... He's also willing to take chances.' Dov Hoenig began his career in Israel during the 1960s. He moved into international filmmaking with would-be moguls Menahem Golan and Yoram Globus, editing such negligible items as *Diamonds* (1975), *Lepke* (1975) and *The Magician of Lublin* (1979).

After the box-office disappointment of *Thief*, Mann might have been expected to find a more commercial property for his follow-up film. Instead, he bought the rights to F Paul Wilson's 1981 horror novel *The Keep*, a bizarre tale of World War II German troops encountering vampires in the Carpathian Alps of Romania. Even more bizarrely, to some, Mann decided to drop the vampire element entirely. This radical rewrite of the original story infuriated Wilson, who retaliated with a tale called 'Cuts', where an author puts a voodoo curse on the film-maker who 'butchered' his work.

Financed by Paramount to the tune of $6 million, *The Keep* (1983) is another moody, oppressive, highly stylised piece of filmmaking that makes only the barest narrative sense, yet remains oddly compelling. The cast, which includes Scott Glenn, Ian McKellen and the authentically German Jurgen Prochnow, look understandably bemused at times. Novelist and critic Kim Newman argues that *The Keep* draws on the German expressionist movement of the 1920s, echoing such films as Robert Wiene's *The Cabinet of Dr Caligari* (1919) and FW Murnau's *Nosferatu* (1922). Mann largely drains the screen of colour and replaces the book's conventional undead with a towering, Golem-like creature that tempts wheelchair-bound Jewish scholar McKellen with great powers in order to escape from the confines of the keep.

Commenting on *The Keep*'s resounding commercial failure in America, Mann asserted that 'People didn't understand my message', yet the film's themes are not presented with any real coherency. Unlike *Manhunter*'s coolly chilling examination of psychosis, manipulation and mental disintegration, *The Keep*'s blending of Gothic monsters and Nietzschean ideals with SS stormtrooper atrocities, concentration camps and collective German guilt doesn't really work. Compassionate German Army officer Prochnow talks anguishedly of 'diseased psyches', yet writer-director Mann seems more interested in creating weird imagery, notably blackened monster-charred corpses and the light-show finale, which unreels to an instrumental version of 'The Snowman'. One interesting optical touch, the glowing, 'mirrored' eyes of the monster's victims, would reappear to more effect in *Manhunter*. A resounding flop in America, *The Keep* went straight to video in the UK, subsequently enjoying a limited cinema re-release, presumably on the back of Mann's hit television cop show *Miami Vice*. According to the director, *The Keep*'s disastrous commercial reception made no great difference to Mann's film career, as he'd already been approached by the de Laurentiis organisation to take on the *Red Dragon* project. The week *The Keep* opened in America, Mann was busy writing the screenplay for *Manhunter*.

Prior to *The Last of the Mohicans* (1992), a stirring, unashamedly melodramatic reworking of the classic James Fenimore Cooper novel, Michael Mann's only real popular success was on the small screen. While his early movies all found their admirers, few studios were interested in cult success. Having signed on with DEG in 1983 to write and direct the film version of *Red Dragon*, Mann put the screenplay on hold for a period while he developed a lucrative new television series, initially entitled *Gold Coast*. Supposedly conceived after an NBC executive jotted down two words 'MTV – COPS', *Miami Vice* (1984-89) starred Don Johnson and Philip Michael Thomas as ultra-cool policemen Crockett, a former football star turned vice cop, and Tubbs, a displaced New York lawman. The score was rock heavy, the jackets were pale pinstripe, the sleeves were rolled up. The series featured the usual assortment of guest stars, such as English Rose-for-hire Helena Bonham Carter, raunch-pop starlet Sheena Easton and, more notably, blaxploitation icon Pam Grier.

The show's most pronounced innovation was its self-consciously chic visual style, far more cinematic in approach than most television fodder. Assisted on the pilot episode by Mel Bourne, executive producer Mann apparently took his inspiration from Italian production designer Ferdinando Scarfiotti, who worked on Bernardo Bertolucci's *The Conformist* (1969), Luchino Visconti's *Death in Venice* (1971) and Billy Wilder's *Avanti!* (1973) in his native country, before decamping to Hollywood. In between, Scarfiotti did a tour of duty with Dino de Laurentiis, designing the high-camp, high-tack sets used for *Flash Gordon*. Scarfiotti's American credits included such high profile (and controversial) films as Paul Schrader's *American Gigolo* (1980), produced by Jerry Bruckheimer, and Brian De Palma's *Scarface* (1983).

Schrader characterised Scarfiotti's approach as 'high style', a heavily production-designed look that marked a move back to the 1930s and 1940s after the more realistic approach of the 1950s and 1960s. Scarfiotti proved a big influence on such New Hollywood talents as Schrader, Martin Scorsese and Francis Coppola. Paul Schrader and Brian De Palma both credited Scarfiotti as a 'visual consultant', rather than a mere production designer, on *Gigolo* and *Scarface* – partly because American union problems denied him the standard design credit. Schrader wanted to give Scarfiotti co-directing credit on the ludicrous, sensuous, visually seductive *Cat People* (1982), which was praise of a kind. Schrader, a friend of Michael Mann, claimed that the latter was very impressed by Scarfiotti's work on *Gigolo* and *Scarface* and tried to emulate the same 'high style': '...it's finally reached its conclusion in things like *Miami Vice*. You can trace *Miami Vice* right the way back to *The Conformist*.' Mann's penchant for extreme stylisation, already evident in both *Thief* and *The Keep,* arguably reached its peak in *Manhunter*. For the record, Billy Wilder has an entirely different view of Ferdinando Scarfiotti: '...he was not a designer. He found locations...' Notably, in *Avanti!*, the spectacular morgue on the island of Ischia.

Whatever one's opinion of *Miami Vice*'s stylised lighting, macho posturing, male bonding, pseudo 'gritty' realism, rolled jacket sleeves, designer stubble and fast-cut gunplay – often trimmed for British transmission by a queasy BBC – the show acted as a handy insurance policy for Mann until his film career took off. *Miami Vice* also provided a useful source of employment for some highly diverse talents. Paul Michael Glaser, who'd directed several episodes of *Starsky and Hutch*, was recruited for Mann's new show, helming the second season opener, 'Prodigal Son'. Less expectedly, Mann placed two episodes, 'The Home Invaders' and 'The Dutch Oven', in the scary hands of maverick indie *auteur* Abel Ferrara. Ferrara's career highlights to date did not immediately suggest a filmmaker comfortable with the restraints of American network television. Long notorious in the UK as a hardcore 'video nasty', the infamous *Driller Killer* (1980) demonstrated Ferrara's abiding interest in off-the-wall, off-their-head urban vigilantes, whose warped quests to purge the streets of human vermin show the dark flipside to the Charles Bronson school of 'natural' justice. *Ms.45* aka *Angel of Vengeance* (1981) gave the concept a strong, if still disturbing pseudo-feminist slant, the mute heroine conducting her final cull dressed as a nun. The *Miami Vice*-era *Fear City* (1984), starring Tom Berenger, proved that the director would tone down his approach, relatively speaking, for more mainstream tastes. Even in restrained mode, Ferrara still features a psycho killer who practices karate in the nude before battering strippers to death with his nunchuka chainsticks.

Abel Ferrara subsequently reunited with executive producer Mann for the feature length pilot of *Crime Story* (1986-88), the 1960s-set tale of Chicago police lieutenant Mike Torello. Played by former Chicago policeman Dennis Farina, Torello is both highly cultured and borderline psychotic, taking advice on Major Crime Unit cases from his helpful but dead partner. Farina had acted in *Thief*, his dramatic debut, while still on the police force. His subsequent credits included a couple of *Miami Vice* episodes ('One Eyed Jack' and 'World of Trouble') prior to starring as Michael Mann's most notable small-screen protagonist. For those tired of *Miami Vice*'s relentless Jan Hammer synth-rhythms, *Crime Story* offered the more dynamic, and anguished, strains of the Del Shannon hit 'Runaway' over the opening credits. Given Mann's interest in using offbeat, feel-bad talent on his television shows, it came as little surprise that *Miami Vice* turned increasingly bleak during its five-year run. Ever wary of losing audiences and lucrative advertising revenue, NBC eventually declared this trip into the heart of designer darkness unacceptable. The already bizarre *Crime Story* upped the surrealism element over its two seasons, abandoning the well-worn streets of Chicago for the Nevada desert, then Latin America.

"IT SEEMED LIKE A NATURAL MOVIE."

With *Miami Vice* successfully underway, picking up an impressive 15 Emmy Award nominations, Mann could turn his attentions back to *Red Dragon*. Transforming the book into a workable screenplay required a number of major changes. In line with standard movie practice, minor characters, incidents and story details were rearranged, reduced or deleted altogether. Streamlining the narrative down to feature film length, Mann opted to jettison virtually all the background material on Francis Dolarhyde, rendering the killer a more mysterious, incomprehensible figure. Many fans of the book regard this as a crass error of judgement, yet Dolarhyde, re-spelled 'Dollarhyde', remains both frightening and pitiable. The director also deleted the episode where Dolarhyde devours Blake's 'Great Red Dragon' painting, a sequence difficult to recreate on film without an element of absurdity. In the finished film, the Red Dragon is referred to only in passing, still obviously a source of dark inspiration to a monstrously disturbed mind.

Other changes were less controversial. Retaining only a few of the book's references to Garrett Hobbs, a killer of college girls cornered and shot by Graham before the Lecter case, Mann decided to invest the Doctor with some of Hobbs's characteristics. Stalking teenage girls might seem a bit of a cliché for an original like Hannibal Lecter, but this attribute does serve to cut through the Doctor's charismatic veneer, revealing the banal, nasty reality of the man. Willy Graham, Graham's mildly hostile stepson, became Kevin Graham, his more affable natural son. While *Manhunter*'s father-son scenes are few and relatively brief, they carry a sense of warmth and assurance largely absent from the book.

One of *Red Dragon*'s key story points is Dolarhyde's ready access to eight-millimetre home movie footage of his victims. At the time of the book's original publication 8mm was still the prime format for amateur movie-makers. By the time *Manhunter* started production, videotape had made serious inroads into the market, rendering 8mm largely obsolete. As video doesn't require any specialist outside processing, Mann needed to retain the 8mm format. By way of compromise, he had Will Graham watch the same footage transferred onto videotape, a practise becoming increasingly popular as people switched formats. In *Red Dragon*, Graham goes down into the Leeds's basement to watch their home movies on the family projector. In *Manhunter* he stays in his hotel room, endlessly playing, rewinding and pausing the footage on a video cassette recorder. Seeking to preserve some of Graham's internal monologue as he investigates the crime scenes, Mann came up with the device of a miniature tape recorder, which Graham dictates into during his walk through the Leeds house.

Some of the less palatable elements of Dolarhyde's *modus operandi* were deleted in the interests of audience sensitivities. While the saliva could stay, the semen definitely had to go. Mann changed a number of details to fit his desired visual style for the film, with an emphasis on cool, sharp modernist architecture. Thus Molly's old beach house became a highly chic seafront property, with none of the book's suggestion that the Grahams are struggling financially. Dolarhyde's cobwebbed residence, set in a decaying orchard, was transformed into the epitome of hi-tech modernism, one wall dominated by a vast blow-up photograph of a lunar landscape.

Background information on the victims was kept to a minimum, losing the entries from Mrs Leeds's diary. Other small details had to be sacrificed, notably a brand of police fingerprint powder called 'Dragon's Blood'. The stray dogs collected by Will Graham in the book were discarded in favour of highly symbolic turtles. Graham builds a protective wire enclosure for a batch of turtle eggs on the beach near his house. Dogs, of course, are among the vulnerable creature's many predators, along with crabs. Kevin helps him construct the hatchery, asking his father if the turtles will survive. Graham is positive: 'These are all gonna make it. Guaranteed.'

Satisfied with Mann's finished screenplay, de Laurentiis assigned the *Red Dragon* project, budgeted at mid-range $14 million, to producer Richard Roth. Roth was also overseeing David Lynch's *Blue Velvet* (1986) for DEG. Roth had made his name in the early 1970s with a couple of popular romantic nostalgia pieces, *Summer of '42* (1971) and *The Way We Were* (1973). His later credits were varied: Gene Wilder's misfiring comedy *The Adventure of Sherlock Holmes' Smarter Brother* (1975); Fred Zinnemann's real-life 1930s drama *Julia* (1977) and Peter Hyams's space western *Outland* (1981). Discussing *Red Dragon* for the *Manhunter* pressbook, Roth showed the required enthusiasm for the property: 'I look for three elements when I read material, intensity, power and intelligence. This has all three. I knew it would make an extraordinary film. It seemed like a natural movie.'

PR aside, Roth appeared to pick up on the book's strengths as potential film material. He also sang Michael Mann's praises, rating him as the best possible choice for the film's writer-director. Mann's 131-

page script for *Manhunter* was the finest he'd read since the Academy Award-winning *Julia*.

British executive producer Bernard Williams, de Laurentiis's vice president in charge of production, boasted similarly eclectic credentials. Like Mann, Williams had a background in filmed television, working as production manager on Patrick MacGoohan's hit espionage series *Danger Man* and as co-producer on the star's cult 1967 follow-up, *The Prisoner*. Serving as associate producer on a couple of Stanley Kubrick films, *A Clockwork Orange* (1971) and *Barry Lyndon* (1975), Williams graduated to full-fledged producer on less choice items, such as Michael Winner's remake of *The Big Sleep* (1977). Joining forces with de Laurentiis, Williams had supervised *Flash Gordon*, *Amityville II: The Possession* (1982) and *The Bounty* (1984). The latter, the third cinematic re-telling of the famous mutiny, did minimal business but drew some praise, notably for Anthony Hopkins's non-stereotypical portrayal of Captain Bligh. For *Manhunter*, Williams also took a more hands on role as unit production manager, a return to his old job.

Manhunter's Italian director of photography, Dante Spinotti, appears to have been another de Laurentiis recruit, also working on the 1986 DEG production *Crimes of the Heart*. Mann had no problem with this choice, Spinotti later becoming the director's regular cameraman, photographing *Last of the Mohicans*, *Heat* (1995) and *The Insider* (1999). Mann got his own choices of personnel on at least two counts, recruiting both Dov Hoenig and Mel Bourne for the film.

Composer Michel Rubini had a solid background in pop music, working with pre-fabricated television phenomenon The Monkees during their 1960s heyday. While the jury remains out on The Monkees' lasting contribution to popular culture, all four members of the group rated Rubini highly enough to reunite with him individually after the group split. Rubini's most prominent film credit prior to *Manhunter* was Tony Scott's flop sado-masochistic vampire romance *The Hunger* (1983), a facile mix of pseudo artsy visuals, explicit gore and softcore, soft-focus lesbian fumblings. *The Hunger* kicks off to the accompaniment of Bauhaus's 'Bela Lugosi's Dead', the gothic rock track more memorable than Rubini's own score. On *Manhunter*, Rubini shared incidental music duties with The Reds, who concentrated on the Lecter themes. Rubini is credited with the gentler themes for Will Graham. According to Mann, Rubini composed most of his music for the film before it began shooting, while The Reds' work came later, during post-production. While this could indicate dissatisfaction with Rubini's efforts, *Manhunter* drew on a wide range of musical talents. Mann supplemented the original score with pre-existing music tracks, pop and not so pop, by Kitaro ('Seiun'), Klaus Schulze ('Freeze'), Shriekback ('Evaporation', 'Coelocanth', 'The Big Hush'), The Prime Movers ('Strong As I Am'), and Red 7 ('Heartbeat'). The most famous, and most effective, piece of music in the film is Iron Butterfly's epic 1968 track 'In-A-Gadda-Da-Vida', from the album of the same name, which runs a mighty 17 minutes five seconds in its full version.

Working with regular casting director Bonnie Timmerman, Mann assembled a strong line-up of actors for *Manhunter*. Like *The Keep*, *Manhunter* had a conspicuously star-free cast, many of whom were primarily stage rather than film actors. The lead role of Will Graham went to Chicago-born actor William L Petersen, who had made his film debut as a bartender in *Thief*. An accomplished and respected stage performer, Petersen's theatre credits included a widely-acclaimed performance as a criminal, one Jack Henry Abbott, in the play *In the Belly of the Beast*. Preoccupied with stage work in his native city, Petersen had made little attempt to develop his film career and Mann's appreciation of the actor's talent was not widely shared in Hollywood.

Petersen's only lead film part to date was in William Friedkin's car-chase thriller *To Live and Die in LA* (1985), based on a novel by former secret service man Gerald Petievich. A decade earlier, Friedkin numbered among the hottest, and most commercially successful, of the New Hollywood directors, riding high on the megahits *The French Connection* (1971) and *The Exorcist* (1973). Following a series of spectacular flops, notably *Sorcerer* (1977) and *Cruising*, his stock fell dramatically. Friedkin's most recent film, the Chevy Chase comedy *Deal of the Century* (1983), was a blatant attempt at a box-office renaissance that didn't click with audiences.

Obliged to shoot *To Live and Die in LA* non-union on an extremely modest $8 million budget, Friedkin couldn't afford any star names, though the director rationalised that he didn't want actors with established screen images. Many regarded the film as a calculated return to *French Connection* territory, with its cat-and-mouse games between cop and criminal and an automobile pursuit that took 22 days to shoot. Interestingly, the lead role had some parallels with Will Graham in *Manhunter*. Petersen played US Treasury agent (or T Man) Richard Chance, obsessively pursuing psychotic counterfeiter Willem Dafoe, the man who murdered his partner. The line between lawman and criminal is shown to be perilously thin – much as *Manhunter*'s Hannibal insists that Will Graham could only catch the Doctor because he is just like him. *To Live and Die in LA*'s villain, Eric Masters, is no average homicidal maniac. Like Hannibal himself, he is intelligent, precise and businesslike, a cultured man who paints but destroys all his work. Unwilling to give audiences the expected hero-villain showdown, Friedkin has Chance shot dead by one of Masters's henchmen, his face blown off by a shotgun. By comparison, Will Graham gets off comparatively lightly. Even in Harris's original *Red Dragon*, Dolarhyde's knife was buried in his cheekbone.

Mann had stayed in touch with Petersen since *Thief*, keeping tabs on his impressive theatre work, and named the actor as his first choice for Will Graham. Richard Roth endorsed Mann's selection of leading man one hundred percent, at least in the movie's pressbook. He hailed a new screen icon in the making: 'He has a quality that's a cross between early Steve McQueen and Marlon Brando. He is the character.' Rash pronouncements like this were tempting fate, to say the least, yet Petersen would prove Roth correct in at least one respect.

The part of Molly, Graham's troubled yet supportive wife, went to former model Kim[berly] Greist, who'd previously appeared in a 1984 episode of *Miami Vice*, 'Nobody Lives Forever'. Following an inauspicious film debut in *CHUD* (1984), the everyday story of Cannibalistic Humanoid Underground Dwellers, Griest got her big movie break in Terry Gilliam's dark fantasy *Brazil* (1985). Taken with the idea of using an unknown actress as Jill, dream girl and truck driver, writer-director Gilliam cast Greist on the strength of a 'fantastic' screen test, which displayed a 'feral' quality. Given Greist's relatively low film profile since *Brazil* and *Manhunter*, it is worth noting that she won the part of Jill against competition from Michelle Pfeiffer, Kathleen Turner,

Jamie Lee Curtis, Rosanna Arquette, Ellen Barkin, Kelly McGillis and another unknown called Madonna.

The brief but pivotal role of Hannibal Lecter, spelt 'Lecktor' on the credits, went to Scottish stage actor Brian Cox, who admitted to a childhood fascination with serial killers. Though now a relatively familiar film performer, thanks to appearances in, among others, *Braveheart* (1995), *Rob Roy* (1995) and *Rushmore* (1998), at the time of *Manhunter* Cox's screen credits were sparse. Few paying customers had picked him out from the virtually all-star cast of the downbeat epic *Nicholas and Alexandra* (1971), in which he portrayed an idealistic, if naive Leon Trotsky. Mann's choice of a British actor for the part is interesting, the director perhaps subscribing to the standard Hollywood view that cultured British accents are inherently alien, strange and unsettling. Lecter's nationality is not discussed in either Harris's book or Mann's film. The name 'Hannibal Lecter' doesn't sound distinctively American or British, the Doctor's evil genius transcending mere geographical boundaries. Brian Cox argues that, in *Manhunter* at least, Lecter seems more a product of British imperialist culture, treating the prison guards like humble servants. The spelling change from 'Lecter' to 'Lecktor' is a minor but intriguing puzzle. There seems no great point to it, as only sharp-eyed *Red Dragon* fans who bothered to stay for the film's closing credits were likely to notice. It was certainly deliberate, as a *National Tattler* headline briefly seen in the film uses the same modified spelling.

If rumour, and director William Friedkin, are to be believed, Brain Cox was not Michael Mann's first choice for the role. According to Friedkin's biographer, Nat Segaloff, Mann originally wanted Friedkin himself for the part of Lecktor, at least as Friedkin tells it: 'I don't know what he saw in me...'. Friedkin's carefully nurtured reputation as an on-set tyrant who played sadistic psychological games with his actors could have been a factor. While shooting *The Exorcist*, Friedkin supposedly fired off guns near to the cast just as the cameras were about to roll, claiming that the subject of demonic possession required an especially fraught atmosphere. When a real priest hired to act in the film couldn't give the director what he wanted during a difficult scene, Friedkin asked the man to trust him, then slapped the priest across the face. Whether or not Mann seriously considered William Friedkin for the role of Lecktor, the director's lack of professional acting experience and wavering industry profile made such a casting little more than an amusing pipe dream.

Friedkin aside, Michael Mann found his ideal Lecktor performing on stage in New York. During pre-production on *Manhunter*, the director caught Brian Cox's performance in the hit Irish play *Rat in the Skull*. Cox read through Harris's original *Red Dragon* and conducted a little background research into criminal psychology, developing a clear grasp of the character. With no sense of morality to guide or restrain him, Lecktor perverts the psychiatrist's methods, probing into people's minds and inner fears only to exploit, abuse and destroy them. Uninterested in trivial questions of sanity versus insanity, Lecktor basks in the dark radiance of his unquestioned genius. Cox's professed attitude to the paying public certainly seemed suited to the incarcerated Lecktor: 'Big audiences in Britain are mind-dead. The best British audience I ever played to was in Broadmoor asylum.'

Casting the difficult role of Francis Dolarhyde was similarly challenging, requiring an actor who could generate audience sympathy despite his character's minimal background and appalling crimes. Mann found a perfect Dolarhyde (or 'Dollarhyde') in the imposing form of Tom Noonan. Tall (six foot five), gaunt and sad eyed, Noonan's credits included supporting roles in *Heaven's Gate* (1980) and the intriguing eco-horror film *Wolfen* (1981). In the latter, he played an obsessive, loner zoo employee who empathises with, and is finally killed by, the title creatures while trying to make contact. At one point Noonan shows detective Albert Finney film of wolves being hunted down and shot, making his disgust with the human race very clear. Tom Noonan is sometimes confused with the late comedian and occasional film actor Tommy Noonan, who appeared in *Gentleman Prefer Blondes* (1953) and *A Star is Born* (1954). While Tommy Noonan did co-star with a nude Jayne Mansfield in the softcore sex comedy *Promises, Promises* (1963), he never got to play a character who bit off people's lips.

The part of Dollarhyde's blind colleague, short-term lover, and intended victim went to stage actress Joan Allen. A member of the Chicago-based Steppenwolf Theater Company, Allen had limited film experience, making her debut in the 1985 comedy thriller *Compromising*

Positions. Allen later co-starred opposite Hannibal Lecter Mk II Anthony Hopkins, as Richard and Pat Nixon in Oliver Stone's 1995 presidential biopic, *Nixon*.

Dennis Farina, Mann's *Crime Story* star, signed on for the role of Graham's FBI mentor Jack Crawford. Farina already knew William Petersen from theatre work in Chicago: 'We did a few plays together. I really enjoy working with him. He's a great actor.' Claiming to be a terrible shot in real life, Farina made a convincing screen lawman, giving a little edge to such run-of-mill action movies as the Chuck Norris vehicle *Code of Silence* (1985). Having pursued parallel careers in law enforcement and acting for several years, Farina now decided to quit the police department for good after 18 years of service. He handed in his badge on 1 September 1985, barely a week before *Manhunter* started filming. Stephen Lang, Farina's *Crime Story* co-star, took the part of tabloid reporter Freddie Lounds. Like Joan Allen, Lang had more stage than film experience, including a hit 1984 Broadway production of *Death of a Salesman*, starring Dustin Hoffman.

By the mid-1980s, Dino de Laurentiis badly needed a hit movie, especially after the box-office catastrophe of the $40 million flop *Dune*. *Red Dragon* was a bestseller and the film version would be relatively inexpensive to make, at least by DEG standards. There were no big star egos to contend with and the director, while hot on television, needed to revive his movie career after a serious flop. Interviewed on the *Showtime* television programme at the time of *Manhunter*'s American release, Michael Mann explained his film's theme in the following terms: 'The movie really is about the true violence... What life-taking aggression really is all about.'

Sticking fairly closely to the geography of the book, the locations for *Manhunter* included Atlanta, Georgia; Washington DC; Chicago, Illinois; St Louis, Missouri, and Captiva, Florida. Most of the interior scenes would be shot at the DEG studios in Wilmington. Atlanta's very modernist High Museum of Art doubled as a mental asylum, which had a certain irony given the film's equation of psychosis with art appreciation. Other suitably futurist locations included the Lick Observatory, in Santa Cruz, California, and the National Space Science Data Center, in Greenbelt, Maryland. Mann and production designer Mel Bourne base the look of Hannibal Lecktor's prison-hospital on real places, including the actual Chesapeake County Asylum named in *Red Dragon*.

Having made highly effective use of the 2.35:1 wide-screen ratio for *The Keep*, filmed in Panavision, Mann opted to use the same format for his new film. There seems to be some confusion over which wide-screen process Mann deployed on *Manhunter*, with Panavision, the defunct Todd-AO system and the non-anamorphic Super '35 format variously cited. There is no credit for a wide-screen process on the film itself, which doesn't help matters. Mann appears to have shot *Manhunter* in JDC-Scope, a system DEG favoured at the time, also using it on *Year of the Dragon*, *Blue Velvet* and *Tai-Pan* (1986). Like the 1950s VistaVision system, JDC-Scope is a non-anamorphic format that crops the top and bottom of the 35mm frame, creating a wide-screen effect. Composed for a 2.35:1 cinema ratio, the film could be 'unmasked' for subsequent video and television release, the small-screen viewer gaining rather than losing picture information.

Manhunter commenced filming on 9 September 1985, with a week of interior shooting at the DEG studios. The production then moved to Atlanta for two weeks, the locations used including the newly opened Marriott Hotel. A tall building with distinctive exterior glass elevators, the Marriott perfectly suited Michael Mann's desired visual style for the film. In Washington D.C., Mann and his crew were permitted to film inside the actual FBI headquarters, a movie first, and outside the Customs Building, where the SWAT team sequence was staged. Mann even shot footage for *Manhunter* on the plane from Chicago to Captiva, casting real airline stewardesses. The production finished back at the DEG studios in Wilmington. So far as is known, writer-director Mann and original author Thomas Harris spoke only once during filming, which suggests professional courtesy rather than any fruitful exchange of ideas.

One of the more unusual challenges for the production lay with Dollarhyde's lunar killing cycle. Script supervisor June Randall enlisted the help of a local observatory to ensure that the cycles of the moon and the corresponding dates were accurate in the screenplay. The props man then put together mock newspapers which bore the correct dates.

Manhunter appears to have been a largely harmonious production, no bad thing given the disturbing nature of the subject matter. Judging by his comments in the film's pressbook, William Petersen still found the transition from stage to film a little tricky: 'When I'm acting on stage, I can give a continuous performance,' he said. 'In film, it's a whole different style. An actor can't really continue acting once the scene is over. It's harder to stretch out a performance in a film.'

During the North Carolina-based shoot, Petersen lived in a house on the coast of Wilmington. The building was raised up on stilts and, according to Brian Cox, the area proved to be prime crocodile territory. Taken with the surreal image of the house surrounded by snapping reptilian predators, a fine metaphor for Will Graham's maniac-besieged psyche, Cox liked to drop by when he wasn't required on set. Installed at the Wilmington branch of Holiday Inn during his brief stint on the film, Cox probably needed the change of scenery.

Interviewed by Kate Hardie for the film journal *Projections 7*, Brian Cox discussed in some detail his experiences working on *Manhunter*. Having signed on for the film, he discovered that Michael Mann held at least one prejudice towards British actors, feeling that they didn't properly explore the psychology of their characters, an approach much valued by American performers. This might seem a serious drawback for a movie dealing primarily with the darker workings of the human mind, yet director and actor found they worked well together. Cox, whose theatrical training emphasised a mastery of the written text, felt that the character's evil nature was clearly delineated in the screenplay. Reassured, Mann decided that Lecktor's voice should possess an unusual quality, settling on a slightly high-pitched tone. This both reinforced the character's disturbing otherness and underlined the fact that Lecktor had become unused to speaking, at least in extended conversation, after his years in solitary confinement. Always speaking in polite, reasonable tones, Lecktor appears more civil than both his jailers and visitor Will Graham, though his attitude of complete superiority shows through. Mann wanted Lecktor to treat other people with the amused, patronising contempt of 'a British public-schoolboy'. Lacking the experience of an expensive private education, Cox based this aspect of the character on his own teenage son, though he claims to have been unaware of this at the time.

The first, longest, Lecktor-Graham scene is largely about psychological game playing and manipulation – or plain 'mind-fucking', to use Cox's phrase. Mann rehearsed the scene with Petersen and Cox for ten days, until their multi-level mind-fucking contest met with his approval. The actual shoot lasted around four days, the director filming endless variations of the character interplay. According to Cox, Mann 'absolutely adored' the scene and wanted as many options as possible when it came to cutting the footage together. A line would be shouted out on one take, then played as a near whisper for the next one. Cox initially found the process a little disconcerting, feeling he had no idea how his performance would look in the finished film.

He also felt physically uncomfortable. Wanting to emphasise Lecktor's sinister, unnatural appearance, Mann and cameraman Dante Spinotti opted to put a lot of downlighting on the actor. The bank of glaring white lamps virtually blinded Cox during takes, the actor unable to see William Petersen standing opposite him. Cox believes that most of the footage used in the final edit came from just two consecutive hours of shooting on one particular day. Only the close-ups, which Cox feels show more of Lecktor's 'disgust', were taken from another filming session.

Cox did feel disappointed at Mann's decision to remove some lines the actor particularly liked from the script. Discussing Dr Chilton, Lecktor contemptuously dismisses his keeper's feeble attempts to analyze him: '...He fumbles with your head like a freshman pulling at pantyhose....' Sticking closely to the original book, this vicious, if accurate, observation of Chilton's methods became redundant once Mann decided to reduce the character to a background figure.

One element Cox particularly wanted to bring across in Lecktor was the incarcerated Doctor's sense of utter boredom. Lecktor is like an animal confined in a cage at a public zoo, prodded and gawped at by curious visitors. Cox felt that the Doctor should be virtually falling asleep at some point during his conversation with Graham, even the reported antics of The Tooth Fairy failing to rouse him from his stupor.

"IF ONE DOES AS GOD DOES ENOUGH TIMES..."

Manhunter opens with a brief night-time pre-credit sequence, an unseen intruder working his way to the upper floor of a house. His lack of interest in searching the lower rooms for valuables immediately suggests darker, nastier motives for the break-in. Mann deploys a point-of-view camera throughout the scene, obliging the viewer to both identify with the intruder and share his voyeurism. This is a classic slasher-movie technique, used time and again in the countless *Friday the 13th* sequels and rip-offs. Mann's approach is more subtle, refusing to give his audience the expected gory shock-horror payoff. Accompanied by an ominous synthesizer score, the housebreaker's torch casts the staircase in a blue light. Entering the master bedroom, the intruder shines his torch in a sleeping woman's face. Instead of going in for the attack, he continues to shine the light until the woman wakes up. The screen abruptly turns to black and the title *Manhunter* appears in lurid green lettering. Something horrible has just happened, probably all the worse for being left to the viewer's imagination.

An object lesson in generating suspense, *Manhunter*'s visual style extends far beyond mere audience manipulation. The director's love of extreme detail, well deployed in *Thief*, continues here with lingering close-ups of telephones, cameras, tape recorders, television monitors, firearms and Glazer Safety Slug bullets, all the equipment of an FBI manhunt. Mann's imagery in *Manhunter* verges on the abstract at times, as in the short scene where Will Graham rides in a hotel's exterior elevator. The building, shot from a low angle, resembles the interior of a vast ribcage. A police briefing room is lit so the shutters produce vertical green stripes, for no discernible narrative reason. As Graham studies the home movies in his Atlanta hotel room, Mann places the silhouetted television set in the left foreground, its bulk blacking out nearly half the frame. There is a sense of both extreme focus (Graham's eyes fixed on the television screen), and of confinement (the reluctant FBI star trapped in an anonymous bedroom far from home).

Mann's occasionally self-conscious visual flair is not universally admired. For many, the film resembles nothing more than an extended episode of *Miami Vice*, for which Crockett and Tubbs neglected to show up. At least one paying customer who caught *Manhunter* on its American cinema release complained, as the credits rolled, that he'd just sat through 'a goddamn music video'. British writer-director Alex Cox, probably still best known for *Repo Man* (1984), has accused Mann of being a 'faddy' director, applying the tried and tested styling of *Miami Vice* to Thomas Harris's story simply because it was currently fashionable. Discussing *Last of the Mohicans*, Mann claimed that his shooting style was determined by the content of the story. With *Manhunter*, the heavily stylised lighting and ingenious use of modernist architecture suggest a world viewed through the increasingly distorted perceptions of both Will Graham and Francis Dollarhyde. Beset by his own lingering demons and the need to get inside Dollarhyde's head, Graham's grasp of everyday 'reality' becomes precarious. Interviewed by Alain Charlot and Marc Toullec for the French film magazine *Mad Movies*, Mann explained his approach to *Manhunter*: 'I get bored if I treat the events realistically,' he said. 'I'd rather try to conceptualize them. The torments of the human mind included. I think that I express the fantasies in an expressionist way, which always brings me to the fantastic.'

Time Out critic Gilbert Adair describes Mann's style as 'designer-expressionist', which seems close to the mark. Mann's visual flair certainly impressed his cast, Brian Cox rating the end result as 'superb'. Cameraman Dante Spinotti's work for *Manhunter* is exceptional and it's no surprise that he went on to become one of Hollywood's most respected directors of photography, working on *Nell* (1994), *The Quick and the Dead* (1995) and *LA Confidential* (1997). Brian Cox felt the Italian director of photography was 'just fantastic... very sympathetic to the actor'.

Arguably, Mann's filmmaking is at its peak on *Manhunter*. The sequence where the FBI team work against the clock to analyze a note sent from Dollarhyde to Lecktor retains a strong sense of urgency as the sheet of toilet paper is passed from department to department. Retaining much of Harris's original dialogue, Mann depicts the FBI's technical prowess at work and their professional pride at outwitting the Tooth Fairy: 'You're so sly, but so am I.' There is, however, one minor gap in the narrative. It's never explained why Dollarhyde chooses to write his note to Lecktor on lavatory paper. In the book, the paper is specified as toilet tissue designed for boats and campers, which will dissolve quickly if Lecter has to swallow it.

Aside from copious dried bloodstains and a cop with the back of his head blown off, *Manhunter* is a remarkably gore-free movie. Mann opted to tone down the already minimal explicit violence in post-production, removing footage of Freddie Lounds's charred body from the underground garage scene.

Despite Mann's eye for detail, the film has its share of mistakes, continuity and otherwise. It should be pointed out that some criticism of *Manhunter*'s supposed technical lapses is misplaced. Viewers watching an 'unmasked', fullscreen version of the film on television or video can see the boom microphone at the top of the picture in several scenes. During one FBI conference, the boom is particularly prominent. This may look like shoddy filmmaking, but in the cinema, *Manhunter*'s first and primary medium, the boom mike would be cropped out of the picture. Other lapses cannot be explained away by the mysteries of variable screen ratios. A cigarette suddenly appears in Will Graham's mouth, suggesting an extreme level of intensity. Graham shifts positions during a supermarket scene without appearing to move. During the climactic shootout, the pool of blood surrounding Dollarhyde's prone body seems to abruptly disappear.

While Hannibal Lecktor and Francis Dollarhyde are *Manhunter*'s most colourful characters, the film hangs on the admirably dogged FBI man Will Graham. Graham is first seen in sunny daylight on the beach near his home, with a soothing backdrop of blue sky and sea. His peaceful new existence has been intruded upon by the demands of the FBI, in the person of ex-boss and friend Jack Crawford. The two men sit on opposite sides of a large piece of driftwood, their backs to eachother. The unshaven Graham is dressed in a blue t-shirt and purple shorts, standard beachwear, while Crawford looks out of place in his shirt and tie. The visual distancing of the men is reinforced by the dialogue, as Crawford attempts to draw Will into the investigation. Their conversation is heavy with unspoken thoughts: 'You look alright now'; 'I am. Alright.' Looking at family album photographs of the murder victims, Graham raises his head to look at his own family, Molly and Kevin. The latter serve both as the prime reason for him to refuse the job, staying with them, and a hard reminder that another family like his will die in three weeks time if the Tooth Fairy isn't caught.

Back with the Bureau, Graham re-enters the world of darkness, making a night-time visit to the Leeds house. Literally retracing the killer's steps and thought processes, Graham shines his own torch on the staircase, picking out children's clothes and toys. As Graham enters the master bedroom, Mann deploys one of his trademark overhead shots, scrutinising his lead character at a moment of truth. Confronted with the terrible bloodstained walls, bed and floor, displaying evidence of 'arterial spray', Graham doesn't flinch. He even shows a measure of professional respect for the killer: '...his entry was skilful'. Bathing his face in the bathroom, Graham is disturbed by a ringing telephone, then Mrs Leeds's disembodied voice on the answering machine, a message from the grave. Even the daylight hours become dominated by the Tooth Fairy's presence. Searching the woods that border onto the Jacobi house, Graham realises that the greenery shrouded the killer as he watched the family. Mann's camera circles around Graham as he follows in the Tooth Fairy's footsteps, climbing the same tree from which the latter kept his vigil.

Crawford's faith in his old colleague's ability is soon rewarded with a break. Graham interrupts his study of the home movie footage to make a brief call home, rousing Molly from sleep. The camera slowly zooms in on Molly's peaceful face, followed by a cut to Mrs Leeds's face, a frozen, dead image on a television screen. Looking for a way into the killer's mind, 'What are you dreaming?', Graham finds the answer in front of him: 'God, she's lovely, isn't she...?' Unable to resist this loveliness, the killer removed his gloves to touch her, leaving fingerprints. Raising his voice for the first time, '...sonofabitch...!', Graham scores his first strike against the Tooth Fairy. Meanwhile, lacking Graham's special sensitivity, the regular cops canvass the usual suspects: 'KY cowboys... leather bars.' There is an element of tension between the Atlanta police and the FBI, the former unhappy when their fingerprinting expertise is both challenged and shown to be flawed.

Graham's coolly professional relationship with the local police departments is in marked contrast to his fraught dealings with *National Tattler* reporter Freddie Lounds. In the film, Graham's understandable hostility towards Lounds extends to physical violence, Will throwing the reporter onto the bonnet of a car, shattering the windscreen. Insensitive as always, Lounds appears completely unharmed. Provoking the Tooth Fairy with the kind of lurid tabloid coverage previously aimed at himself, Graham does a fine job of slander. A repressed homosexual, the killer is probably impotent with women and almost certainly engaged in an incestuous relationship with his mother. Graham can also hold his own with Hannibal Lecktor, for a short period of time. Discussing Lecter's 'disadvantages' in *Red Dragon*, Graham comes up with two: 'Passion. And you're insane', the latter appearing almost an afterthought. In *Manhunter*, Graham keeps it even more simple: 'You're insane', which is certainly a punchier comeback.

Graham later discusses the pathology of Hannibal Lecktor with Kevin, as they shop in a supermarket. Framed against countless boxes of reassuringly everyday breakfast cereal – Total, Count Chocula, Fiber One, Grape Nuts, Cheerios – Graham explains how empathising with Lecktor made him ill: 'I still had his thoughts going round in my head... they're the ugliest thoughts in the world.' Mann felt that this scene between Graham and his son made it clear, both to Kevin and the audience, that Will Graham always retains his own sense of humanity: 'I didn't want to play on the ambiguity of Graham's acts,' he said. 'He has to put himself on the level of horror, of the murderer, but only in his mind. It disturbs him a lot.'

In one scene, original to the film, Graham falls asleep during a plane journey, leaving gory crime-scene photographs visible on his lap tray. A small girl sitting next to him sees the pictures and becomes hysterical, causing her mother to summon a stewardess, who hurriedly rouses Graham. Mann based this scene on an exchange between Graham and Crawford in the book's first chapter. When Crawford offers to show his former protege the 'Tooth Fairy' file, Graham tells him not to get out any photographs, as Molly and Willy are both around. Exhaustion is causing Graham to become careless, breaking his own rules of professional procedure.

Attempting to probe Dollarhyde's dreams, Graham has dreams of his own. While sleeping on the plane, he dreams of being back home, at work, hoisting an engine block onto a boat. Molly appears, walking towards Graham, and the camera, in slow motion. Looking radiant, her blonde hair seeming to float around her head, Molly is framed by tall green palm leaves as she walks down a jetty. Graham dreams of himself looking at Molly, Mann using lingering close-ups of his actors, against the bright blue sea and sky. Graham later realises that Dollarhyde dreams of being desired, wanted, and his own dream carries the same yearning. Mann then cuts to the bloody murder scene pictures, Graham looking disoriented and lost as reality rears its ugly head.

The act of voyeurism, whether to a 'normal' or 'abnormal' degree, is at the heart of *Manhunter*. Dollarhyde views 8mm family home movies to select his ideal prey. Graham looks at the same films, as chosen by Dollarhyde, to track down the killer, yet doesn't realise how close he is to the solution. This throws up a series of ironies. In order to understand Dollarhyde, Graham must share the man's voyeuristic obsession. The footage, so prized by Dollarhyde, is the means by which he will be identified. Watching and re-watching the home movie footage of the murder victims on multiple screens, pausing on any apparently significant detail, Graham has inadvertently tapped into the killer's prime source material. His climactic realisation, 'You've seen these films...', is well handled by William Petersen, whose generally low key portrayal of Graham has been unfairly criticised as wooden. Looking for clues in the images, Graham can't initially see that the biggest clue of all is the nature of the images. Dollarhyde's modus operandi exhibits a knowledge of his victims that he could only have gleaned from viewing the 8mm footage.

By the end of filming, Petersen found that his empathy with Will Graham had become too close for comfort, necessitating a radical break from the character: 'After *Manhunter*, I had to actually kill off the character. I cut off most of my hair and dyed it blonde. I changed my whole look just to get rid of him.'

Whatever his difficulties in shaking off the character, William Petersen has yet to find another film role to match *Manhunter*'s Will Graham. Shortly after the Michael Mann film wrapped, William Friedkin offered Petersen the lead in a second de Laurentiis production, *Rampage* (1987). This time out, the actor would play a state prosecutor who must prove that a serial killer is legally sane and therefore fit to stand trial. Wary of being typecast as a troubled law enforcement official, Petersen turned the part down. His subsequent film credits are largely low key, including an appearance as Sheriff Pat Garrett in *Young Guns II* (1990).

While Petersen made for a more impressive Garrett than Patrick Wayne in the original *Young Guns* (1988), inheriting a supporting role from John Wayne's less-than-famous son wasn't going to put the actor on the Hollywood 'A' list.

As Molly Graham, Kim Greist is largely overshadowed by her co-stars, the character mostly a sounding-board for Will Graham. Constrained by the demands of the script, Greist gets little opportunity to shine or even demonstrate her dramatic ability. Having cast the unknown Greist in *Brazil*, Terry Gilliam found that the relatively inexperienced actress couldn't maintain the intensity of her successful screen test during the actual shoot, which lasted a gruelling seven months. This limited the resulting performance to such an extent that the director felt obliged to scale down Greist's role. Taking her cue from 'guest star' Robert De Niro, Greist assumed that Gilliam would permit her endless takes to get the character right, a luxury not possible for the tightly-budgeted production. Interviewed for *Manhunter*'s pressbook, Greist obliged with some rather routine comments about working with Michael Mann, which presumably contained an element of truth: 'It's wonderful working with him. He really knows how to work with actors and he knows exactly what he wants.'

Passive for much of the film, Molly has her moments, upbraiding Crawford for exploiting Will: 'You're supposed to be his friend, Jack. Why don't you leave him alone?' Lying in bed with Will, their room bathed in blue moonlight, Molly seems resigned to losing her husband, at least temporarily. Sharp to Will's thoughts, she brushes aside his attempt at a carefully balanced discussion: 'I think you've already decided and you're not really asking.' The moon is a hard reminder of the killer's lunar cycle. Molly's eyes are drawn to it even as Graham makes love to her, the urgent background music carrying little trace of romantic passion.

It's only fair to note that much of Greist's performance in *Manhunter* ended up on the cutting-room floor. The deleted footage includes an affectionate, yet tense phone call between Will and Molly, which underlines the increasing strain on their relationship during Graham's return to active and potentially dangerous service. A later bedroom scene, where the characters refer to the beginning of their romance, was similarly discarded. As far as can be determined, these cuts were made against Michael Mann's wishes. In the finished film, Molly and Kevin never really seem at risk from Francis Dollarhyde, despite their eminent suitability for his plans. Once Lecktor's message to the Tooth Fairy has been deciphered, they are effectively out of the danger zone. Mann plays with an element of suspense, inserting a new scene where Kevin rouses his mother from sleep when he hears noises downstairs – yet too little time has passed for Dollarhyde to act on Lecktor's information. The beach house turns out to be surrounded by a whole precinct's worth of police. Incidentally, the FBI 'safehouse' where Molly and Kevin are subsequently moved is bordered by woodland, ideal territory for a Tooth Fairy stakeout. Greist's final line in *Manhunter*, 'I thought I wouldn't wait', is touchingly delivered, suggesting a level of conflict and uncertainty in Molly the film otherwise lacks.

Interviewed for *Mad Movies* magazine, Mann expressed a strong interest in the way that dehumanisation can transform an apparently ordinary person into a killer, capable of the most appalling atrocities imaginable. As Mann puts it: '...when people are not human anymore, they become bits... of matter.' First glimpsed as a hand and a pair of legs, Francis Dollarhyde is one of the screen's great psychopaths, casually dangling Freddie Lounds off the ground as he chloroforms the tabloid journalist. A later scene depicting Dollarhyde's 'normal' life, as a production controller for Gateway Film Processing, St Louis, underlines his great height. Abruptly standing up from his desk, he towers over a female colleague, who suddenly seems vastly reduced in size. Thomas Harris gave Dolarhyde a moustache to cover the scar left by his repaired harelip. Michael Mann keeps Tom Noonan cleanshaven, the visible scar rendered insignificant by the actor's prominent forehead, piercing eyes and pale eyebrows.

The scene between Dollarhyde and Freddie Lounds that introduces the killer is expertly played by both actors, the reporter's former cockiness reduced to stumbling, incoherent pleading. His journalistic instincts seem to desert him once the Tooth Fairy is at his side: 'I don't wanna know who you are.' Framed by a sickly green light, Dollarhyde's house is not a comfortable surrounding. Dominated by the vast blow-up lunar photograph, his living room boasts a flickering television set in one corner and a strange, spiked mobile rotating from the ceiling. Tied to a wheelchair, his eyes initially covered by tape, Lounds is returned to consciousness and a vision of hell. The chair used in *Red Dragon* is a tall-backed antique wooden wheelchair, left over from Grandma Dolarhyde's stock of nursing home equipment. Dispensing with this element of dark nostalgia, Mann substitutes a suitably gleaming, high-tech wheelchair. Speaking in soft, urgent tones, Dollarhyde has a stocking pulled over the top half of his head, rolled up just under his nose. Though arguably less alarming than Dollarhyde's fully uncovered visage, this bizarre apparition appears not quite human. The slide show that follows is one of *Manhunter*'s highlights, Tom Noonan investing the line 'Do you see?' with a skin-crawling sense of menace, the phrase repeated like a ritual refrain. Introducing Lounds to William Blake's 'Great Red Dragon', Dollarhyde proceeds with pictures of the Jacobis, the Leeds and a third family, identified in the credits as the Shermans, that he will soon visit. Mrs Sherman (Patricia Charbonneau) sits on the edge of a swimming pool in her bathing suit, holding a baby in her arms, an image of physical beauty and maternal love. While the character of Francis Dollarhyde has been radically reduced from the book, this one moment encapsulates his dark, terrible yearnings.

Mann opted to use a different Blake painting from the one featured in Harris's book. The title is almost exactly the same: 'The Great Red Dragon and the Woman Clothed with the Sun: 'The Devil is Come Down'' (circa 1805). Now housed in the National Gallery of Art, Washington DC, the picture depicts the Devil hovering above the Woman, arms outstretched, as he looks down on her. Drawing on a subsequent passage in The Book of Revelations, this later painting acts as a kind of sequel to the first Great Red Dragon: '...woe to you, O earth and sea, for the devil has come down to you in great wrath, because he knows that his time is short!' Having given birth, the Woman sprouts a pair of holy eagle's wings and escapes the monster. It has been claimed that Mann and his production team simply got the paintings confused and ended up using the wrong one. While Harris identifies the picture clearly enough in *Red Dragon*, this is at least possible. On the other hand, Mann may have used the later picture as a subtle hint that Dollarhyde's next scheduled victim, as personified by the Woman, would escape the coils of his tail.

In the book, Dolarhyde proudly displays his naked, dragon-tail tattooed body to Lounds. Mann settles for a declaration of power: 'Before me, you are a slug in the sun. You are privy to a great... Becoming and you recognise nothing... You owe me awe.' In *Red Dragon*, Dolarhyde puts in his special 'dragon' teeth, places his mouth over Lounds's, and bites off the latter's lips. This ingeniously nasty piece of mutilation is depicted with both more restraint and more ambiguity in the film. Dollarhyde is seen to open a small box and remove something, which he then inserts into his mouth. While it follows that the object is a pair of false teeth, Mann never makes this clear. Leaning over Lounds's trussed, seated body, Dollarhyde delicately touches the man's hair, declaring 'We'll seal your promise with... a kiss'. Cutting to an exterior night shot of the killer's house, Mann lets Lounds's distant, muffled screams tell the real story.

The grotesque death of Freddie Lounds, burned up by the Dragon's wrath, raises an interesting point in both book and film. A professional, highly-committed user and abuser of others, Lounds is scum *par excellence*. Stephen Lang doesn't resemble the 'lumpy and ugly and small' character of the book, but his brash, insensitive, vulgar manner conveys the essentials. While *Red Dragon* devotes more time to Lounds than *Manhunter*, Harris's depiction of the obnoxious, relentless sensation hound borders on caricature: 'He had buck teeth and his rat eyes had the sheen of spit on asphalt.' A fine Chandleresque turn of phrase, perhaps, yet a little too grotesque. Posing as a mysterious 'Mr Pilgrim', Lounds makes a series of sinister phone calls to Graham's FBI office, hoping to trick the latter into giving him information about the Tooth Fairy. This deliberate obstruction of the manhunt for commercial gain, wasting precious FBI time and resources, renders Lounds even less sympathetic. Mann wisely opted not to use this episode, conveying the feeling that the character, however dislikeable, does not deserve his brush with the Tooth Fairy. The 'burning' scene unreels without music, only the noise of the chair wheels and the muffled roar of the flames breaking the silence before Lounds's burning body careers down a ramp into an underground car park (the *National Tattler*'s, though this isn't made very clear). Given Mann's extensive use of mood music in *Manhunter*, the lack of any musical cues during this scene renders what could have been a standard gross-out shock into something more eerie and disquieting.

Lacking most of the book's sense of internal conflict, Dollarhyde's brief liaison with blind co-worker Reba McClane (Joan Allen) can seem abrupt and unmotivated in the movie. Some feel that, in terms of exploring the killer's tormented character, it's too little, too late. This is a valid criticism, yet these scenes work well enough on their own terms. Direct, forward and extremely likeable, Reba compliments Dollarhyde on his excellent enunciation, assuring him that his speech impediment barely shows. Reba's encounter with a symbolic sleeping tiger is especially effective, staged against a clinical white backdrop similar to Lecktor's cell. The camera tracks along the sedated zoo animal, lingering on the huge teeth that rival even the Great Red Dragon's. Presumably, Harris and Mann are drawing on the William Blake connection once more, as the scene has obvious echoes of Blake's poem 'The Tyger', from *Songs of Experience*:

> Tyger, Tyger, burning bright
> In the forests of the night,
> What immortal hand or eye
> Could frame thy fearful symmetry?

Reba lies against the animal, feeling its heartbeat, just as she will shortly lie against Dollarhyde in his bed. Standing back from the operating table, Dollarhyde seems overcome with emotion. In the film, the scene appears to come out of nowhere, which increases its strange, dreamlike quality. The book explains that Dolarhyde has seen the first stage of the tiger's operation on television, and offered the zoo free infrared film in return for the favour. Reba feels the tiger's furry testicles, an action Mann didn't ask Joan Allen to recreate on film.

Back in Dollarhyde's living room, the scene of the Freddie Lounds slide show, the killer projects 8mm film of Mrs Sherman at the swimming pool, his 'homework'. Reba kisses Dollarhyde, his right leg visibly trembling at her touch. In *Red Dragon*, Reba performs oral sex on Dolarhyde as, unknown to her, he watches and rewatches the film of Mrs Sherman. Mann dispenses with the fellatio, settling for Dollarhyde's creepy comparison of the two women's bodies, concentrating on their breasts and legs. At first transfixed by the flickering, light-and-shade images on the screen, he gradually responds to Reba's warm, responsive, living flesh. The ensuing lovemaking, though uneasy to watch, is arguably more persuasive than the earlier, artfully-styled Will-Molly encounter. Reba gently sweet-talks Dollarhyde, who looks both scared and ecstatic, later weeping silently in bed. This scene captures perfectly the tone of Harris's book, Dolarhyde reacting to Reba's advances with a mix of fear, awe, uncertainty, and longing: 'Maybe she liked Francis Dolarhyde. That was a perverted, despicable thing for a woman to do. He understood that he should despise her for it, but Oh God it was good.'

Like Graham, Dollarhyde lives by water, and later stands on the shore with Reba looking at the rising sun, suggesting a clichéd romantic idyll which the Red Dragon can never share. A self-styled creature of the moon, Dollarhyde seems to recognise that he cannot cross the gulf that separates him from Reba, and humanity: 'You look so good in the sun.'

Dollarhyde's taste of normal human emotions is short-lived, the killer hallucinating a passionate kiss between Reba and another male colleague as he watches from his van. As the Prime Movers' track 'Strong as I Am' plays on the soundtrack, the agitated Dollarhyde rips the cover off his dashboard, a taste of the violence to come. In the book, the kiss is real, if entirely chaste, rather than a figment of Dolarhyde's imagination. The end result is the same, the Great Red Dragon triumphant: 'Francis is gone. Francis is gone forever.'

It is notable that Dollarhyde is missing the intricately tattooed dragon's tail on his back that Harris describes in *Red Dragon*. During production, Mann toyed with the idea of the killer having an even more elaborate tattoo, a complete dragon that covered the entire front and most of the back of his torso. Unsure whether or not the design would work onscreen, the director filmed all the scenes where Dollarhyde appears bare chested both with and without the tattoo. Mike Pitt, who runs a website dedicated to *Manhunter*, asked Noonan about Mann's post-production decision not to use the Red Dragon tattoo. According to the actor, Mann worried that the overpowering design could tip Dollarhyde into caricature: 'I remember him saying that it was "too much" and it "diminished" the character.'

Mann also appears to have been concerned about audiences

misinterpreting the tattoo as a deliberate Oriental touch, despite the explicit references to William Blake's 'Red Dragon'. All-over body tattoos, particularly those depicting dragons, are often associated with Japanese Yakuza gangsters. Both book and film use the Oriental angle as a minor red herring, Graham discovering a strange mark carved on a tree trunk by Dollarhyde. It is revealed to be a Chinese character, standing for good luck, that also figures on a Mah Jong piece known as 'The Red Dragon'. *Manhunter* does not explain why Dollarhyde would know this, given that his interest in the Dragon derives from Blake. Then again, the film doesn't even mention the Book of Revelation. On balance, the director's decision to lose Dollarhyde's striking body art seems the right one. Reluctant to follow Mann's lead and discard such an eye-catching image, the DEG publicity department used stills of Noonan with his dragon tattoo in the film's promotion. The pictures are still used to advertise the movie, one such image appearing as the cover art for *Manhunter*'s UK DVD release.

Brian Cox's Hannibal Lecktor has only three scenes in *Manhunter*, yet his well-spoken mass murderer, controlled and ice-cold, pervades the entire movie. Looking to 'recover the mind set', Will Graham goes calling on the Doctor at the mental hospital. The first shot in the scene is from the inside of the stark, all-white cell, the camera pointing through the bars as Graham enters Lecktor's outer chamber. Partly obscured by the lock on his cell door, Lecktor is seen lying on his bunk, face to the wall. Sharp as ever, the Doctor addresses Graham without turning around: 'That's the same atrocious aftershave you wore in court'. Peter Guttmacher describes Brian Cox's Lecktor as possessing 'a brute's face and a predator's sense of smell'. Topped by slicked-back hair, the brutish face houses penetrating eyes and a sharp tongue. Lecktor probes Graham for weaknesses: 'Dream much, Will?'. He takes a sympathetic interest in the activities of the Tooth Fairy, 'This is a very shy boy, Will', treating the killer's *modus operandi* as a moderately stimulating intellectual exercise. Graham is his idiot pupil, indulged out of patient kindness, needing the obvious pointed out to him at every step: 'Have you ever seen blood in the moonlight, Will? It appears quite black.' Tiring of his games, Lecktor coolly taunts Graham, his grip over the latter undiminished by his years behind bars: 'Would you like to leave me your home phone number?'

Cox argues that Lecktor has no respect for anyone, including Will
Graham. His attitude to Graham is comparable to that of a World
War II Japanese soldier confronted with a despised prisoner of war. A
true warrior does not allow himself to be caught, let alone surrender.
Having identified Lecktor as a murderer, Graham permitted the Doctor
to jump him and cut him up, the FBI man only being saved from death
by the arrival of the police. To compound this 'shame', Graham then
proceeded to walk away from his job, citing mental disturbance. Such
weakness is loathsome to Lecktor. The Doctor's contempt for Graham
is compounded by his conviction that the latter refuses to accept his true
nature: a fellow hunter who derives pleasure from the kill. As Graham
flees from Lecktor, moving out of earshot, the Doctor drops his cold,
smooth facade. His last words sound almost bitter: 'You want the scent...
smell yourself.' As Graham exits the hospital, the camera tracks him
down agonisingly long flights of stairs. Mann cuts to a subjective camera
as Graham crashes through the main doors into the daylight. Insert shots
of green grass briefly fill the frame, the first burst of real colour since
the start of the scene. Even this return to wholesome, untainted nature
is undercut, Freddie Lounds snapping away at Graham with his camera
from a car across the street.

Lecktor's second scene in *Manhunter*, where the Doctor obtains Will
Graham's home address, was Brian Cox's personal favourite. Handed a
dial-less, button-less telephone for a call to his lawyer, Lecktor cannily
smooth talks a series of operators, receptionists and secretaries to get the
information he wants. Described as 'a classic acting exercise' by Cox,
the scene makes good use of low-key humour. Pretending not to have
the use of his arms, Lecktor dextrously employs chewing gum foil and a
felt tip pen lid to get at the phone's innards, chomping on the gum as he
works. Mann stages much of the one-sided conversation in a single take,
concentrating on the Doctor's mental and verbal dexterity as he adopts
the personas required to get his way. Regarding the virtual monologue
as 'brilliantly' written, Cox particularly liked the fact that Lecktor
doesn't bother to write down the address he coaxes out of the university
secretary: a man with his mind remembers everything. At the end of the
scene, Lecktor relishes his minor victory, cocky, open-mouthed and thuggish.

Lecktor's last scene in *Manhunter*, a phone conversation between himself and Graham, is the most playful, Lecktor congratulating his nemesis on the Lounds 'job'. Curiously, no mention is made of the Doctor's recent attempt to have the Graham family murdered, though Will does confess to being tired 'of all you crazy sons of bitches'. This third scene is the only occasion in the film when the camera starts inside Lecktor's cell, eliminating the white bars. Kate Hardie compares the staging of the scene to a telephone conversation between two lovers, Graham sitting on his hotel bed. Cox wanted Lecktor to be lying down, relaxed, his shoeless feet clearly visible. Mann and Dante Spinotti allowed Cox to double check the framing of the shot on a monitor. Reclining in his bunk, his sock-clad feet resting against the wall, Lecktor certainly seems in good spirits. As Hardie notes, Graham has bar shapes near him, appearing imprisoned, while Lecktor now looks like a free man. Cox concurs that this is almost certainly a deliberate touch on Mann's part: 'Michael is a stickler for those sorts of points.' Cox wanted Lecktor to sing the Stevie Wonder hit single 'I Just Called to Say I Love You' down the line to Graham ('quite sweet'). While the treacly, if Oscar-winning theme tune to Gene Wilder's hit comedy *The Woman in Red* (1984) was ripe for a subversive send-up, legal considerations prevailed. Mann liked the idea but had to pass on it for copyright reasons. *Woman in Red* was produced by Orion Pictures, who would resurrect Dr Lecter in *Silence of the Lambs* five years later. In philosophical mood, Lecktor articulates his morality-free take on the human condition: 'We don't invent our natures. They're issued to us along with our livers and pancreas and everything else.' Will should relax and be at peace with himself. Cox's reasoned delivery of the lines is almost persuasive enough to make the argument seem plausible. Critic and broadcaster Mark Cousins, onetime director of the Edinburgh Film Festival, rates Cox's performance in *Manhunter* as 'great cinema acting'. Michael Mann described his Hannibal Lektor as simply 'phenomenal'.

Watching his special collection of other people's home movies, Francis Dollarhyde is mainly interested in one particular feature. The women in the films, all wives and mothers, have what Will Graham describes as 'a bloom', a term not found in the book. In Graham's dream, Molly has a similar 'bloom'. Having followed in Dollarhyde's tracks throughout the film, exploring the same houses, watching the same films over and again, Graham momentarily breaks into the Tooth Fairy's mindset. Staring into the Leeds bedroom, Graham has a waking vision of Mrs Leeds as Dollarhyde sees her. Her mirrored, glowing eyes and mouth reflect back at Graham the sensation of being accepted, wanted and desired that Dollarhyde craves. Hannibal Lecktor's theory, original to the film, provides Graham with the key to Dollarhyde: 'If one does as God does enough times, one will become as God is.' Dollarhyde's grotesque parody of being desired, repeated with enough families, will make him truly desirable.

The finale of *Manhunter* is set up when Will Graham offers Jack Crawford his thoughts the killer's background: 'My heart bleeds for him as a child. Someone took a kid and manufactured a monster.' This is the film's only reference to Dollarhyde's past, a neat summation of *Red Dragon*'s extended flashbacks. Concerned that Graham's empathy is sliding into outright sympathy, Crawford is soon reassured. Will Graham's solution to the 'irredeemable' adult Dollarhyde is brutally simple: 'Someone should blow the sick fuck out of his socks.'

A lot of Thomas Harris fans are critical of Mann's rewriting of the book's ending, yet *Manhunter*'s climactic night-time shootout is both visually – and aurally – spectacular and dramatically satisfying. The sequence's background music, 'In-A-Gadda-Da-Vida', was written by Iron Butterfly frontman Doug Ingle, whose musically gifted father served as a church organist. Much influenced by the austere, classical sound of religious music, Ingle incorporated this quality into his own compositions. Regarded by many as the ultimate psychedelic, acid-rock anthem, 'In-a-Gadda...' is played on tape by Dollarhyde as he prepares to ritually sacrifice Reba McClane (the track subsequently made a memorable church appearance in a 1995 episode of *The Simpsons*, 'Bart Sells His Soul'.) According to rock folklore, the song's intended title was 'In the Garden of Eden', but the band were so stoned during the recording session they could neither recall nor pronounce the correct name of the track. Nor could they remember how to get to the end of it, hence the elongated length. Francis Dollarhyde's copy of the song is on multi-track cartridge, an outmoded music format even in the mid-1980s.

Smashing a bathroom mirror, Dollarhyde selects fragments to use on Reba. A dagger shaped piece will end her life, while the smaller

ABOVE: Thomas Harris, author and creator of Dr Hannibal Lecter.

ABOVE: In April 1994, Thomas Harris attended the trial of
Pietro Pacciardi, the so-called 'Monster of Florence'.

ABOVE: Producer Dino de Laurentiis in 1980.

ABOVE: Brian Cox as the screen's original Hannibal 'Lecktor' in *Manhunter* (1986).

ABOVE: Will Graham (William Petersen) in *Manhunter* (1986).

RIGHT: Will advises *National Tattler* reporter Freddie Lounds (Stephen Lang) to back off. *Manhunter* (1986).

ABOVE: Will and Molly Graham in *Manhunter* (1986).

ABOVE: Molly Graham (Kim Greist) in *Manhunter* (1986).

ABOVE: Reba McClane (Joan Allen) embraces the sleeping tiger in *Manhunter* (1986).

ABOVE: Serial killer Francis Dolarhyde (Tom Noonan) gives tabloid reporter
Freddie Lounds (Stephen Lang) the Red Dragon slideshow in *Manhunter* (1986)

ABOVE: 'Do you see?'

RIGHT: Anthony Hopkins - perfectly normal.

ABOVE: Anthony Hopkins as convicted child murderer Bruno Haptmann in the based-on-fact television drama *The Lindbergh Kidnapping Case* (1976). Awaiting execution in the electric chair, Hopkins's Hauptmann bears a striking resemblance to his subsequent portrayal of Hannibal Lecter.

shards will be placed in her eyes and mouth, reflecting the 'desired' Dollarhyde's image back at him (ironic, given Reba's lack of sight). In a neat reversal of the opening sequence, Graham sneaks through the dark woods towards Dollarhyde's house, gun in hand. Seeing Dollarhyde struggle with Reba in a window, Graham calls out: 'Stop it! Stop it!', the words directed as much at himself as Dollarhyde. With Reba pinned to a table, the pointed glass at her throat, Graham takes an impressive, if reckless slow motion leap through the plate glass window, only to be grabbed, cut and knocked senseless to the floor by Dollarhyde. As helpless before the killer as he is in *Red Dragon*, Will Graham is saved this time by police gunfire, Dollarhyde distracted as he takes on the sharpshooters. Making almost surreal use of jump cuts, slow motion, and the Iron Butterfly track, Mann gives Graham back the hero role denied him by Harris. Graham recovers to blow the 'sick fuck' Dollarhyde to hell with a gun full of Glazer Safety Slugs. Lying on his kitchen floor, arms outstretched, framed against a spreading pool of his own dark blood, Dollarhyde is as close to resembling the Great Red Dragon as he will ever get. These dragon wings aren't going to take him anywhere. Mann stresses that Graham finds the killing of Dollarhyde a painful act, the FBI manhunter taking hold of Reba and exiting the house as the police move in. As the symbolic dawn breaks on the new day, a tearful Reba asks her rescuer's name. His response, 'Graham. I'm Will Graham', is as much a reaffirmation of his identity as a courteous reply.

Manhunter's coda, which unwinds to the questionable strains of Red 7's 'Heartbeat', sees Graham back home, back on the beach, back with Molly and Kevin. While Dollarhyde's glass dagger has left a long cut on his face, this time the injuries are only physical. Graham saved Reba, family number three and the baby turtles: 'Most of them made it.' Together again, the Graham family strolls down the beach to the sea as the credits roll, Mann ending on a freeze-frame of sunny domestic bliss. It's the kind of image Francis Dollarhyde would covet, but he's dead.

"IF DOSTOYEVSKY HAD BEEN HIRED TO SCRIPT AN EPISODE OF MIAMI VICE..."

Having successfully completed filming and editing, *Manhunter* began its awkward, all-too brief journey to the cinema screens. Throughout its production, the film retained the original Thomas Harris title, *Red Dragon*, which had always been Mann's preferred choice. The last-minute change can have done little for the film's public profile or potential box-office, with many of the book's fans utterly unaware that there was a screen version doing the rounds. The reason for the title switch now seems absurd, yet demonstrates very well Dino de Laurentiis's capacity for blinkered short-term thinking, showing an apparent lack of faith in both Mann's film and Harris's book.

Another DEG production, Michael Cimino's *Year of the Dragon* (1985), had recently been released to very disappointing domestic box-office, grossing $7.3 million on a $24 million budget. The former wonderboy *auteur* of *The Deerhunter* (1977) had been attempting a much-needed comeback after the $45 million fiasco of *Heaven's Gate* (1980), the film which sunk United Artists. Cimino's new movie centred on a Vietnam veteran turned New York cop, obsessively pursuing a Chinatown heroin dealer. Far from rehabilitating Cimino, *Year of the Dragon* proved only that audiences didn't care for racist, foulmouthed, humourless characters played by Mickey Rourke with dyed white hair. Convinced either that having 'Dragon' in a film's title was a box-office turn-off, or that filmgoers would confuse *Red Dragon* with the Cimino film and stay away once again, de Laurentiis insisted on a new name. In itself, *Manhunter* is a perfectly adequate title, taken from a *National Tattler* headline in the film, shifting the emphasis from Dollarhyde to Graham in much the same way as Michael Mann's script. The new title didn't come with a bestselling novel attached, however. Mann has his own explanations for the title change, odd though they seem. Interviewed for *Mad Movies* at the time of the film's French release in 1987, the director argued that *Red Dragon* was the book's title and should remain exclusive to the Harris novel. This aside, '...above all, we changed it so that the audience wouldn't mistake it with a kung-fu film.' Given the dearth of high-profile martial arts movies in America during the mid-

1980s, a decade after the death of Bruce Lee and long before Jackie Chan broke into Hollywood, this seems a thin rationalisation.

DEG's enforced changes to *Manhunter* didn't stop with the title. Mann's preferred cut of the film was re-edited by de Laurentiis, getting *Manhunter*'s length down to just under the contracted two hours (119 minutes). As Mann presumably realised, de Laurentiis had a reputation for re-cutting his director's films. John Milius called the producer's working methods 'unsound' after *Conan the Barbarian* was substantially re-edited, especially for the American market. Removing a key character from the final sequence of Milius's film, de Laurentiis changed the pace and tone of the climax considerably. In the case of *Manhunter*, de Laurentiis dropped at least six scenes, totalling around eight minutes of footage. Graham's conversation with an estate agent at the Jacobi house, now cleaned up and on the market, was deleted. The character of Dr Chilton, already reduced from the novel, diminished even further, de Laurentiis removing a short scene prior to the first Lecktor encounter, where Chilton attempts to probe Graham's own fragile psychological state. In the standard print, Chilton doesn't appear until the sequence where various FBI experts analyze the note sent from Dollarhyde to Lecktor. Far from the arrogant and scheming figure later seen in *Silence of the Lambs*, *Manhunter*'s Chilton seems a consummate professional: calm, efficient and helpful. Shots of Hannibal Lecktor being videotaped in his cell, presumably by Dr Chilton, were also removed, though stills of this footage were subsequently used as promotional material. Dollarhyde's date with Reba McClane lost a scene after the visit to the zoo, their subsequent dinner together reduced to a throwaway remark. Most crucially, de Laurentiis tampered with the final section of the movie, removing a scene with the Sherman family, Dollarhyde's intended third mass killing. The Shermans appeared in Mann's cut at the very end of the film, with Mrs Sherman played by the suitably 'blooming' Patricia Charbonneau. Probably still best known for her performance in the cult lesbian romance *Desert Hearts* (1985), Charbonneau later appeared as a recurring character in the first season of *Crime Story* (1986-87). Having gunned down 'The Tooth Fairy', a battered-looking Will Graham visits the Sherman house, presumably to see for himself what had compelled Dollarhyde to select the family. It is likely that de Laurentiis simply wanted to speed up the film's conclusion, concentrating on the 'In-A-Gadda-Da-Vida' climax rather than spend time on extra characters he considered superfluous.

In defence of the producer, it has been suggested that *Manhunter* works better without the Sherman family scene. Previously seen only in briefly glimpsed slides and home movie footage that barely identifies the characters, the Shermans do not make the same impression on the viewer as the Jacobis and the Leeds. Mr Sherman does not appear at all until the end of the film. The scene seems too abrupt, the family thinly sketched, to serve as a suitable finale. Questioned in 1987 by *Mad Movies*, Mann appeared not only sanguine about the cuts made to his film but virtually in denial: 'Nothing was cut... only scenes that seemed not very fruitful to us.'

Manhunter was released in the United States on 15 August 1986, supported by a promotional campaign that didn't really convey the film's true character, or make the obvious, and commercially helpful link with the Thomas Harris book. Bearing the ambiguous tagline: 'It's just you and me now sport', the American poster depicted two images of Will Graham, divided by a diagonal, blood-red line. Brooding in moody close-up at the top of the picture, Graham was seen in action underneath, entering a crime scene, flashlight in hand. Neither Dollarhyde nor Lecktor made an appearance. Publicity lines for the film included: 'Enter the mind of a serial killer... you may never come back.' Most audiences declined the less-than-appealing offer and the film grossed only $8.62 million in its home territory ($1 million more than *Year of the Dragon*). Given *Manhunter*'s bleak, unsentimental, un-Hollywood tone, the best de Laurentiis could have probably hoped for was a cult hit on the lines of David Lynch's *Blue Velvet*, released the same year. Lacking Lynch's unstinting surreal quirkiness and Dennis Hopper's show-off star performance, *Manhunter* couldn't grab enough media attention to become a hot title. *Rolling Stone* magazine had recently profiled William Petersen, in its 22 May edition, lauding the actor as the hottest upcoming Hollywood leading man (which must have seemed a bad joke when the box-office grosses came in). A personal endorsement from Thomas Harris might have helped the film, yet the author declined to make any public comment on Mann's reworking of *Red Dragon*. In any case, it is rumoured that Harris dislikes *Manhunter*, presumably because of the radical changes to the story, a common author's grievance in the face of Hollywood 'tampering'. The film's American cinema release came and went so quietly that some current fans, introduced to *Manhunter* on television and video, assume that it never received theatrical distribution.

Manhunter's poor domestic box-office, coupled with the De Laurentiis Entertainment Group's inexorable slide into bankruptcy, caused problems with the film's overseas distribution. *Manhunter* was picked up for British cinema release by the small-scale outfit Recorded Releasing, who submitted the film to the British Board of Film Classification in late 1986. If it mattered to Michael Mann at this point, his handling of the potentially repellent subject matter earned the approval of the BBFC. Probably the strictest censorship board in the western world, the BBFC was extremely sensitive towards films that dealt with torture, murder and mutilation in a realistic, familiar context. On 2 December 1986, the Board granted *Manhunter* an adults only '18' certificate, with no cuts. Armed with the BBFC's seal of approval, the film then proceeded to sit on the shelf for over two years, Recorded Releasing unable to get bookings for a flop release from a bankrupt production company.

Screened at the London Film Festival in November 1987, *Manhunter* remained unreleased in Britain until late February 1989. By way of compensation, the film's long-delayed UK distribution did attract attention from the major league reviewers. *Time Out* critic Gilbert Adair hailed Mann's film as a 'splendidly stylish and oppressive thriller... the film functions both as a disturbing examination of voyeurism, and as an often almost unbearably grim suspenser.' Adair went on to rate *Manhunter* as: 'One of the most impressive American thrillers of the late '80s.' Given that the film had begun pre-production in 1983 and was completed by the end of 1985, this tribute carried a certain irony. The *Financial Times* critic drew a favourable, if offbeat parallel with the director's best known television success: 'If Dostoevsky had been hired to script an episode of *Miami Vice*, he might have come up with the screenplay for Michael Mann's *Manhunter*.' The film's pacing, criticised as both plodding and frenetic by American reviewers, was hailed as a major asset: 'It moves so fast that its thrilling blur becomes one with the eerie disorientations of [the] plot.' Writing in the *Evening Standard*, Alexander Walker rated *Manhunter* as 'a serial-killer thriller of quite unusual mood, intelligence and surprise.' *Observer* film reviewer Philip French went even further: 'One of the most stylish and compelling crime pictures of the past decade.'

Elsewhere, *Manhunter* received a slightly less belated release. In France, the film hit the screens on 22 April 1987, under a new title, *Le sixieme sens* ('The Sixth Sense'). Presumably this was intended as a reference to Graham's ability to probe and empathise with disturbed minds. In Germany, the distributors reverted to Harris's original title, the film going out as *Roter Drache*. The Greek poster for *Manhunter* abandoned any pretence at subtlety, depicting a dynamic, comic book version of Will Graham standing over Dollarhyde's prone body, his gun held firmly in both hands in finest *Dirty Harry* style. Interviewed for *Empire* magazine, Michael Mann discussed the film's relatively favourable critical reception outside America: '*Manhunter* did get big play in Europe. I was doing a lot of interviews for England for a long while after release. Which doesn't mean zip in terms of box office.'

In financial terms, 1986 was not a good film year for Michael Mann. His name appeared, as executive producer only, on another of the year's releases, the forgettable – and largely forgotten – *Band of the Hand*. Directed by Paul Michael Glaser, the film starred *Manhunter* actor Stephen Lang as Joe Tiger, a Vietnam veteran turned unorthodox social worker. Located in *Vice*-trendy Miami and the Florida Everglades, the story has Joe turn five teen delinquents into both model citizens and budding urban vigilantes during a jungle survival course. Back home in Miami, the transformed gang decide they've had enough of the crime-fuelled violence and corruption and take on the local drug gangs. Even Crockett and Tubbs might have frowned at this simplistic, reactionary, wipe-em-all-out solution to the narcotics epidemic. Scored by Michael Rubini, *Band of the Hand* featured a title song by, of all people, Bob Dylan. Despite the blatant failings of Glaser's feature directing debut, he was subsequently hired to direct the hit Arnold Schwarzenegger vehicle *Running Man* (1987), which happened to be co-produced by Tim Zinnemann. Why Mann agreed to lend his name to this cinematic junk meal is something of a mystery, though loyalty to old colleagues probably played a part.

If Michael Mann felt that his film career had yet to gain the momentum it needed for long-term success, Dino de Laurentiis had problems on a much larger scale. The commercial failure of *Manhunter* amounted to the merest drop in the ocean compared to the huge losses racked up by *Dune*, *Tai-Pan* and too many more. In 1988, de Laurentiis was forced to resign as DEG's chairman. The production company went bankrupt mere months afterwards. In August 1988, DEG filed for Chapter 11 bankruptcy. The company's assets, including the Wilmington studios, amounted to $163 million, as opposed to a reported $200 million in liabilities.

A commercial bust, *Manhunter* earned a fair level of acclaim from crime thriller devotees. In 1987, the film was nominated for an Edgar Allan Poe Award for Best Motion Picture. The same year, Michael Mann won the Critics Award at the Cognac Festival du Film Policier. Over the years, *Manhunter* gradually picked up a devoted, ever-increasing group of admirers as it did the rounds of video, laserdisc, cable and network television. *Interview* magazine editor Graham Fuller, who profiled Mann at the time of *Last of the Mohicans*, lauded *Manhunter* as 'a movie that edges into hyperspace... a small, but visionary masterpiece.'

De Laurentiis's post-production tampering did not mark the end of the film's adventures in the editing suite. In the United States, the cable, syndicated television and video versions of the film were all different from the theatrical print. In at least some instances, this proved to be a good thing. While famously mangled films such as *Spartacus* (1960) and *Pat Garrett and Billy the Kid* (1973) had to wait for decades before being restored to their original versions, approximations of Mann's cut of *Manhunter* were soon available, albeit briefly, to a select viewing public. In 1988, a mere two years after the film's theatrical release, the American cable network ShowTime screened an extended edition of *Manhunter* as part of its 'Director's Cut' series. Prefaced by a ten-minute interview with Mann, the ShowTime version restored the Sherman family scene to the end of the film, deleting a brief post-shootout scene with Will Graham and Jack Crawford. A second ShowTime re-edit restored the estate agent scene and the two deleted scenes featuring Will and Molly Graham. NBC then got in on the act, screening a censored-for-language version of ShowTime's Mk II print, which also toned down Graham's examination of the gory crime scene photographs. ShowTime subsequently broadcast a third version of *Manhunter*, restoring footage to the Atlanta briefing room scene, the Dr Chilton scene, a fourth Lecktor scene, and an exchange between Graham and Crawford which explains Molly's appearance in the former's hotel room. Unfortunately, ShowTime appeared to share Dino de Laurentiis' concern about 'excessive' running time and cut or re-edited other sections of the film. After *Silence of the Lambs* hit the screens, NBC gave their version of the film a blatantly misleading new title: *Red Dragon: The Pursuit of Hannibal Lector*, and re-cut it to fit a two hour time slot.

In the UK, the film enjoyed a major video re-release on the back of *Silence of the Lambs'* box office success. It was the same murky, full-screen version as before, but the shops piled copies high on the shelves, next to paperback editions of Harris's sequel. A sticker on the video box proclaimed 'The prequel to *The Silence of the Lambs'*.

In 1988, two years after *Manhunter*'s unsuccessful release, Thomas Harris published his sequel to *Red Dragon*, *The Silence of the Lambs*. Readers who had ignored the Michael Mann movie snapped up the literary return of Hannibal Lecter. Dino de Laurentiis, who still had first refusal on the film rights, passed on *Lambs* and has probably been kicking himself ever since.

PART TWO
STARLING, LECTER AND GUMB

*Problem-solving is hunting; it is savage
pleasure and we are born to it.*
THOMAS HARRIS, *The Silence of the Lambs*

Dr Lecter likes his fun.
JACK CRAWFORD, FBI, *The Silence of the Lambs*

All credit to Orion Pictures, their poster campaign for the film version of *The Silence of the Lambs* proved one of the most effective in movie history. Two faces stare out at the passer-by: Jodie Foster, pale and intense, Anthony Hopkins, red and devilish. Both their mouths are covered by a Death's Head moth, wings spread to reveal the skull-like markings. Anyone familiar with the Thomas Harris source novel would know the basic plot, involving two serial killers and a trainee FBI agent with demons of her own. This was a no-holds-barred splatter shocker, with ghoulish face-biting, skin flaying and two highly-respected big name actors, one cast as an unrepentant cannibal. Surely such a thing could not be.

It has long been a Hollywood maxim that big stars do not appear in horror movies. Only unknowns in need of rent money or has-beens short of offers reluctantly agree to dip their toes in this most disreputable of genres. Take Demi Moore's early appearance in the 3-D shocker *Parasite* (1982), or Veronica Lake's best-forgotten movie swansong, *Flesh Feast* (1970). When Ida Lupino found herself attacked by a giant worm in *Food of the Gods* (1976), her co-starring role opposite Humphrey Bogart in *High Sierra* (1941) must have seemed a very long time ago.

Like most sweeping generalisations, this bold assertion isn't really true, though there have been periods throughout film history when horror did appear to be both a literal and figurative graveyard for talent. Lon Chaney, one of the biggest silent era stars, made his name with grotesque characters, often deformed in both mind and body. The majority of Chaney's films were weird melodramas rather than outright horror, yet his most famous roles were *The Hunchback of Notre Dame* (1923) and *The Phantom of the Opera* (1925). John Barrymore, probably the most acclaimed actor of his generation, starred in a 1920 screen version of *Dr Jekyll and Mr Hyde*, a cunning double act that enhanced rather than diminished his reputation. When Universal Studios embarked on its famous 1930s horror cycle, the company had little trouble attracting respected theatre and film actors. While Boris Karloff and Bela Lugosi remained largely trapped in the scary movies that made them famous, other stars treated horror as just another movie genre. Claude Rains, who made his starring debut in *The Invisible Man* (1933), returned to shock territory in *The Wolf Man* (1941) and a disappointingly genteel remake of *The Phantom of the Opera* (1943). Charles Laughton cracked a mean whip in *Island of Lost Souls* (1932), then suffered the agonies of deformity and unrequited love as *The Hunchback of Notre Dame* (1939). Fredric March picked up a Best Actor Academy Award for his performance in *Dr Jekyll and Mr Hyde* (1932). Even Spencer Tracy tried the Jekyll and Hyde role, though his appearance in the 1941 film version of the story suggested a star eager to be elsewhere.

"NOBODY WANTS TO SEE A MOVIE ABOUT SKINNING WOMEN..."

Once horror became the sole provenance of 'B' picture merchants, the genre declining in the late 1940s, the bigger name actors were out of the picture, both for career and economic reasons. Stars would not appear in second features, even if the producers could afford to pay their salaries. Hammer Film Productions' late-1950s British revival of the Gothic horror movie made deserved genre stars out of Peter Cushing and Christopher Lee, whose talents had not been permitted to flourish in more mainstream films. Respected stage and film actor Vincent Price experienced a career revival as the star of the 1960s Roger Corman-AIP Edgar Allan Poe films. Never an understated performer, Price's flamboyant, borderline camp acting style found a natural home in *House of Usher* (1960) and its successors.

Produced on low budgets and short production schedules, the Hammer and AIP films filled a niche the major studios had no apparent wish to touch. That said, Hammer's films were distributed by Warner, Universal-International, Columbia, Paramount and Twentieth Century Fox, all of them happy to cash in on the new horror cycle. There is the suspicion of a double standard at work here. When Cary Grant, still a big box-office name in the early 1960s, expressed a desire to star in Hammer's remake of *The Phantom of the Opera* (1962), his agent talked him out of it. Grant's contemporaries Joan Crawford and Bette Davis had committed the unforgivable Hollywood crime – for a leading lady – of growing older, their careers declining accordingly. Co-starring in Robert Aldrich's scary psychological drama *Whatever Happened to Baby Jane?* (1962), both Crawford and Davis enjoyed a new lease of box-office life on the back of the film's success. Davis appeared in two films for Hammer, *The Nanny* (1965) and *The Anniversary* (1968), subtly malevolent in the first, then in full blown bitch-queen mode for the second.

From the late 1960s onwards, the big Hollywood studios were ready to play a more direct role in the horror genre. Produced by Paramount, *Rosemary's Baby* (1968) derived from a bestselling novel which transcended the standard horror elements in its contemporary New York story of diabolical pregnancy. The film's writer-director, Roman Polanski, had the acclaimed psychological thriller *Repulsion* (1965) to his name, plus the American-financed Hammer pastiche *Dance of the Vampires* (1967). If stars Mia Farrow and John Cassavetes were not quite Hollywood 'A' list, they did at least offer names familiar to mainstream audiences. William Friedkin's *The Exorcist* (1973), a similarly expensive Warner production, also cast familiar and undeniably talented character actors, led by Ellen Burstyn, Max Von Sydow and Lee J Cobb. Followed by a slew of low grade, high vomit rip-offs, *The Exorcist* paved the way for one of the 1970s' least-expected sub-genres: the ageing big name horror movie. Gregory Peck starred in *The Omen*, reviving his stagnant career. William Holden took over for *Damien – Omen II* (1978), getting stabbed to death on screen for his pains. Burt Lancaster played a largely subdued mad scientist in *The Island of Dr Moreau* (1977). In *The Manitou* (1977), Tony Curtis discovers a 400-year-old Native American medicine man reincarnated on the back of Susan Strasberg's neck. Kirk Douglas appeared in both *The Fury* (1978) and *Holocaust 2000* (1978), movies he does not mention in his autobiography. Rod Steiger (over)played a troubled priest in *The Amityville Horror* (1979), though Steiger and just about everyone else wished he hadn't. Laurence Olivier turned in an energetic, if overwrought performance as Van Helsing in a new screen version of *Dracula* (1979). Even Charlton Heston, who passed on *The Omen*, agreed to star in *The Awakening* (1980). A botched reworking of Bram Stoker's novel *The Jewel of Seven Stars*, the film proved most notable for Susannah York being impaled through the neck by a shard of broken glass.

By the time *The Awakening* crawled into the cinemas, the horror genre had been taken over by the slasher movie (see Part One). The only star names to be found here were the ones just at the start of their careers. Kevin Bacon took an arrow through the neck in *Friday the Thirteenth*, Holly Hunter dodged the Cropsy Maniac in *The Burning* (1980) and Tom Hanks did nothing much in *He Knows You're Alone* (1981). The nearest the slasher genre got to a legitimate star was Robert Englund, who played child molester turned wisecracking supernatural avenger Freddie Kreuger in the *Nightmare on Elm Street* films (1984-94). Michael Caine turned up as a razor-wielding transvestite in Brian De Palma's more lavish slasher movie *Dressed to Kill* (1981). Jobbing screen crazyman Dennis Hopper made a belated stab at the genre in Tobe Hooper's grisly satire *The Texas Chain Saw Massacre Part 2* (1986). Cast as an ex-Texas Ranger who can wield a chainsaw with the best of them, Hopper made America's First Cannibal Family wish they'd never gone into the human barbecue business.

If there was any kind of recent precedent for the film version of *Silence of the Lambs*, it was probably Stanley Kubrick's *The Shining* (1980), starring Jack Nicholson as everyone's favourite axe-wielding maniac. Based on the bestselling shocker by Stephen King, this film adaptation screamed quality even to those who regarded the source novel as gory trash. Despite a mixed box-office track record, Nicholson had undoubted current star status, not to mention a recent Best Actor Academy Award win for *One Flew Over the Cuckoo's Nest*. Writer-director Kubrick, whose deal with Warner Bros gave him *carte blanche* in his choice of projects, was a proclaimed *auteur* rather than a mere genre filmmaker. Kubrick's previous film, the three-hour eighteenth-century morality tale *Barry Lyndon*, scorned accepted notions of popular entertainment. With *The Exorcist* still one of the all-time top grossers, Warner probably felt a little relief when Kubrick chose King's highly commercial scare story for his next project. The director's admirers assured themselves that Kubrick's intense personal vision would transcend the schlock elements in the source material. For all the ghosts, axe murders, rotting corpses, shrill screams and gallons of blood, *The Shining* had to be more than a mere horror movie.

A decade after *The Shining*'s mixed critical and commercial reception, *Silence of the Lambs* came along to give the paying public a 'class' horror movie they could really endorse. The reviews were favourable too, Peter Guttmacher hailing the film as 'a mirror held to manage the tabloid monsters of real life'. While none of the people connected to *Lambs* had Kubrick and Nicholson's platinum star status, they weren't exactly movie deadbeats. Lead actors Jodie Foster and Anthony Hopkins were both highly respected performers, with distinguished, if erratic film careers behind them. Foster had recently won a Best Actress Academy Award for her performance as a rape victim in *The Accused* (1988). Director Jonathan Demme, though hardly a household name, had come a long way since his brief stint as a producer of exploitation movies.

First published in 1988, the year Jodie Foster gave her Oscar-calibre performance in *The Accused*, Thomas Harris's *Red Dragon* sequel proved as big a literary sensation as its predecessor seven years earlier. Harris had spent five years planning and writing *Silence of the Lambs*, conducting in-depth research at the FBI's Department of Behavioral Science. This time around, the celebrity endorsement came from Stephen King's fellow bestselling horror writer Clive Barker: 'Thrillers don't come any better than this... It takes us to places in the mind where few writers have the talent or sheer nerve to venture.'

For all the minutiae of investigative procedure, technical detail and psychological profiling, *Silence of the Lambs* is a classic fairy tale of escape and rescue. Chained 'monster' Hannibal Lecter, longtime inmate of a maximum security hospital, breaks free after an ill-advised move to a Memphis cell. Catherine Martin, innocent if not exactly chaste daughter of a powerful Republican senator, is imprisoned by another monster, only to be rescued at the last minute by a lone knight short of body armour. These characters, who never meet, are linked by the figure of FBI student Clarice Starling, Lecter's confidante and Catherine's saviour. The *Lambs* storyline is a reworking of *Red Dragon*, where a male veteran FBI investigator is brought out of retirement to track down a serial killer, consulting with convicted mass murderer Hannibal Lecter to gain more insight in his quarry. This time around, a female trainee FBI agent is taken out of school to hunt a serial killer, though her initial brush with Lecter is supposedly on an unrelated matter.

Retaining his fondness for classical allusions, Harris prefaces *Silence of the Lambs* with a couple of quotes, one from the New Testament (1 Corinthians) and another from metaphysical poet John Donne. The Donne quote comes from *Devotions*: 'Need I look upon a death's head in a ring, that have one in my face?' By the same logic, need the reader look upon the foul crimes of fictional serial killers, that have the real thing in the newspapers at regular intervals?

Much of *Lambs* centres on the FBI's Quantico academy, where star student Clarice Starling is plucked from training by Jack Crawford to consult with celebrity mass murderer Hannibal Lecter. Crawford's Behavioral Science department, which deals with all suspected serial murder cases, is symbolically situated on the bottom floor, 'half-buried in the earth'.

Starling herself has dark memories to deal with, notably the violent death of her father when she was a young girl. A deputy marshall, or glorified nightwatchman, Mr Starling disturbed armed robbers while on patrol and got shot, his murder reducing the family to poverty. Sent to live with a cousin after her father's death, Starling found herself on a farm that raised lambs for the dinner table and slaughtered horses at the end of their working lives. Haunted by the screams of the lambs as their throats were cut at daybreak, Starling fled the farm on the back of a blind slaughter horse. Both child and animal found refuge at a Lutheran-run children's home. Ever since, Clarice Starling has found stability and success, if not much happiness, in institutional surroundings, prospering at college and the FBI academy.

Given Thomas Harris's liking for symbolism, it is tempting to read some kind of significance into Clarice Starling's name. According to the *Concise Oxford Dictionary*, a starling is a 'small gregarious partly migratory bird with blackish-brown speckled plumage inhabiting chiefly cultivated areas, a good mimic.' Highly conscious of her small town, poor family background, Starling probably fears accusations of mimicking the 'better' classes with her academic scholarships, carefully chosen wardrobe and suppressed regional accent. Cautious in her dealings with people, Starling is initially wary of Jack Crawford's motives for giving her the Lecter assignment, regarding the FBI man as 'a two-faced recruiting sergeant son of a bitch'. For all its declarations of equal opportunities, the Federal Bureau of Investigation can be as deeply chauvinistic as any other male-dominated institution. Doctor Chilton suggests that Crawford has sent Starling to Hannibal Lecter on the off-chance that the normally aloof Lecter will respond to an attractive young woman, an insinuation Starling rejects without much conviction.

Starling's attitude to the grimmer aspects of her work is both pragmatic and idealistic: 'She felt she could look at anything, if she had something positive to do about it.' Harris adds a cynical coda: 'Starling was young.' Still enmeshed in her demanding training school routine, Starling finds that the 'Buffalo Bill' hunt requires her to grow up at speed. Confronted with one of the serial killer's victims, their corpse recently retrieved from a river, Starling is faced with the reality of human evil: 'The knowledge would lie against her skin forever, and she knew she had to form a callus or it would wear her through.'

"DON'T EVER FORGET WHAT HE IS!"

When Crawford first mentions Hannibal Lecter to Starling, Harris drives home his prize character's all-pervasive menace: 'A brief silence follows the name, always, in any civilized gathering.' Cautioning Starling to be on her guard at all times against Lecter, Crawford resorts to bold pronouncements:

CRAWFORD
...don't ever forget what he is.
STARLING
And what's that? Do you know?
CRAWFORD
I know he's a monster.

Starling is sent to Lecter clutching a questionnaire devised for the Bureau's new Violent Criminal Apprehension Program (VI-CAP). His answers, if any, will supposedly be added to a database for psychological profiling. Dismissing the psychology practised by Behavioral Science as 'on a level with phrenology', Lecter will not be a willing subject.

Lecter is first encountered lying on his bunk, looking at an Italian edition of *Vogue* magazine. This Italian theme extends to the cell's back wall, which is covered by the Doctor's sketches of Florence. Drawn from memory, the historic views depicted include the Palazzo Vecchio and the Duomo. A useful piece of cultural background this time around, Florence would assume a more crucial role in Harris's next book. Lecter has retained his interest in acts of God, still collecting pictures of churches brought down on their faithful congregations. Lecter's distinctive features now include six fingers on his left hand, a rare form of polydactyly – two perfectly formed middle fingers – not mentioned in *Red Dragon*.

Prior to Starling's first question and answer ordeal with Lecter, Crawford emphasises the latter's predatory nature: 'It's the kind of curiosity that makes a snake look in a bird's nest.' Lecter initially subjects the FBI student to the same kind of 'mind-fucking' he practised on Will Graham. Then things change, thanks to a grossly unpleasant incident. The normally ice-cool Lecter becomes unusually agitated after fellow inmate 'Multiple' Miggs throws sperm at Starling: 'The sparks in his eyes flew into his darkness like fireflies down a cave.' Even locked up securely in his cell, Miggs doesn't last the night.

Lecter's leisure pursuits include a bizarre watch-face that he wants to patent. In the tradition of the Mickey Mouse wristwatch, Lecter's design is a crucified Christ, his moving outstretched arms serving as the hour and minute hands. Lecter's sketch for the figure has Starling's face perched on Christ's shoulders. The Lamb of God meets the lambs that scream in the darkness.

Looking to be moved into a new cell with a view, Lecter's price for his thoughts on Buffalo Bill is almost touching in its modesty: 'I want a window where I can see a tree or even water.' Lecter's typically astute summary of Bill's quest is unusually crude: 'He wants a vest with tits on it.' In the film of *Silence of the Lambs*, Clarice Starling puts it a little more delicately. Realising that the strange mutilations on a corpse are dressmaking patterns, she excitedly tells Crawford: 'He's making himself a woman suit... out of real women.'

Lecter is pulling a fast one on the forces of law and order, as he already knows all about Jame Gumb through ex-patient and murder victim Benjamin Raspail, a professional flautist with a dangerous taste for unhinged male lovers. Jack Crawford claims that Lecter has at least one weakness: '...he has to look smart, smarter than anybody.' By the end of *Lambs*, Lecter has comprehensively proved himself smarter than anyone else. For the time being.

Lacking Hannibal Lecter's cultured tastes and verbal dexterity, Jame Gumb, aka 'Buffalo Bill', is a decidedly lowlife psychopath. Gumb murdered both his grandparents at the tender age of 12, for no apparent reason. No-one called him 'cunt face'. No-one threatened to castrate him with a pair of false teeth. Thomas Harris supposedly based Jame Gumb on three real-life serial killers, Ed Gein, Ted Bundy and Gary Heidnick, all of whom preyed on women. Gein skinned and dismembered his victims, wearing the 'hides' and using the other body parts as house decorations. Bundy put a fake cast on one arm, in which he concealed a crow bar to bludgeon his victims. Like Gumb in *Silence of the Lambs*, Bundy would approach a prospective victim for some kind of help, his apparent disability drawing sympathetic interest. Heidnick imprisoned his victims in a basement pit, a modern day version of the medieval *oubliette*, a hidden dungeon accessible only by a trap door. Thomas Harris also drew freely on one of his own fictional serial murderers, *Red Dragon*'s Francis Dolarhyde. Gumb treats his killings with the same sense of ritual, a taste of the great metamorphosis to come: 'he always finished a harvest naked and bloody as a newborn.'

When Catherine Martin offers to help the supposedly disabled

Gumb shift an armchair into the back of his van, she notices the
odd smell of his 'chamois' shirt. The garment still has hairs sticking
from it, 'curly ones across the shoulders and beneath the arms'. By
implication at least, this hand-crafted shirt is made from human skin.
As with Francis Dolarhyde in *Red Dragon*, Jame Gumb's occupation
reflects the demands of his dark fantasies. A professional dressmaker
and dress designer, Gumb turns out cheap Armani knockoffs during the
day, devoting his leisure to the 'Special Things'. Gumb's other hobbies
include the armed pursuit and slaughter of his terrified victims through
the pitch black basement rooms of his cavernous house. Gumb's nightvision goggles are Israeli military surplus, a strange reference to Thomas
Harris's first novel, *Black Sunday*, which features the country's Mossad
secret service.

Like Francis Dolarhyde, Gumb is a keen movie watcher, though his
format of choice is VHS videotape rather than 8mm film. Gumb's special
tape, viewed when his work is about to climax, features two short films.
The first is Movietone News coverage of the 1948 Miss Sacramento
quarter finals. The contestants in the beauty contest heat include Gumb's
own mother, 'Mom', decked out in a white swimsuit and high heels.
The specially copied tape automatically reverses and freezes her image
over and again. The second film is cheesy 1950s sexploitation footage,
featuring a swimming pool, a water slide and a woman Gumb believes to
be his mother.

Like *Psycho*'s Norman Bates, Gumb has a twisted, lethal fixation on
his idealised dead mother. He longs to become her, believing that his
lovingly tailored garment of young woman's skin will transform him
into the figure in the films. As Gumb explains to his pampered pet dog:
'Oh, Precious... Mommy's gonna be *so* beautiful.' Even more than the
cross-dressing, grave-robbing Bates, Gumb is drawn from Wisconsin
necrophile Ed Gein. Obsessed with his dead mother, Gein murdered
women who resembled her and attempted to take on their identity,
gender and otherwise. Gein wore the women's skinned faces over his
own and covered his despised male genitalia with their severed vaginas.
Jame Gumb shares Francis Dolarhyde's conviction that his miraculous
transformation, symbolised by the Death's Head moth chrysalis, will
feed his desire to be attractive, wanted.

While Francis Dolarhyde's appalling background is dwelt on at length in *Red Dragon*, Harris doesn't get to the hard facts on Jame Gumb until Chapter 59 of *Lambs*, when the killer is dead and his prisoner safe. Having lost the 's' in James thanks to a clerical error on his birth certificate, Gumb's childhood didn't get much better. One month pregnant with her son at the time of the Miss Sacramento quarter final, Mrs Gumb turned to booze when the expected film career failed to materialise. Stuck in a foster home from the age of two, Gumb went to live with his grandparents when he turned ten, killing them both a couple of years later. In *Red Dragon*, Harris carefully charts how a deformed yet perfectly good-natured child was turned into a 'monster' by the cruelty, abuse and callousness of others. Gumb, on the other hand, appears to be a classic case of 'Born Bad', right down to the bone.

The supporting characters in *Lambs* are effectively sketched in. Doctor Frederick Chilton, Lecter's self-important keeper, is even less likeable than he was in *Red Dragon*. A sexist pig of the lowest order, he hits on Starling in the first minutes of their meeting, visibly sulking when she fails to respond. Left with an inmate who only wants to discuss defecation, Starling concludes that the latter is preferable company. Chilton repeats the Lecter nurse-biting story as he takes Starling down to the Doctor's cell, even showing her a photograph of the unfortunate woman. In *Red Dragon*, Chilton explains that Lecter tore out the nurse's tongue with his teeth. This time around, we learn that the Doctor swallowed it as well. Chilton is an extreme example of the casual chauvinism Starling must face every day of her life, as she deals with institutions and cliques even less enlightened than the FBI. Even 'normal' men, Harris seems to be hinting, are capable of treating women as mere objects. Chilton's passion for Clarice Starling is expressed in surprisingly eloquent terms, the lust-struck jailer implausibly sharing his thoughts with fellow Starling enthusiast Hannibal Lecter: 'She's glorious, isn't she? Remote and glorious. A winter sunset of a girl, that's the way I think of her.'

There are a number of flaws in *Silence of the Lambs*, the narrative both implausible and overwritten at times. It seems highly unlikely that Jack Crawford, an experienced senior FBI man, would send an untested trainee, however bright or attractive, to extract information from

Hannibal Lecter, a man he describes as 'a monster'. Crawford, above all people, knows that Lecter is the most dangerous and insidious creature alive, both mentally and physically. Harris does occasionally overdo the striking prose, notably: 'Down where it is never dark the tormented sense beginning day as oysters in a barrel open to their lost tide.' At one point, Clarice Starling likens Lecter to 'a cemetery mink', who 'lives down in a ribcage in the dry leaves of a heart'. Lutheran upbringing or not, this seems an odd turn of phrase for an educated, scientifically trained woman in her early twenties. Referring to the tabloid press's fascination with Lecter, the *National Tattler* still leading the pack, Jack Crawford claims that 'They love Lecter even better than Prince Andrew.' A strange, and now rather dated, comparison.

There are a number of references in *Silence of the Lambs* to Will Graham, *Red Dragon*'s ill-fated near hero. Warning Starling about Lecter, Jack Crawford recounts the Doctor's attack on the former FBI man: 'He gutted Will with a linoleum knife.' Crawford's loathing for Hannibal Lecter is made clear when he mentions Graham's appearance after being stabbed through the cheekbone by Francis Dolarhyde: 'Will's face looks like damn Picasso drew him, thanks to Lecter.' The Doctor gave Dolarhyde Graham's home address, the self-styled Red Dragon paying a surprise visit after the FBI closed in on him. Doctor Chilton explains to his celebrity captive during a gloating session: 'I don't think you know how much Crawford hates you for cutting up his protege.' Meeting Starling for the first time, Lecter asks after his old nemesis, particularly Graham's face: 'How is Will Graham? How does he look?' Presumably abandoned by his wife and stepson, the down and out Graham does not offer a promising example to budding FBI manhunters: 'a drunk in Florida... with a face that was hard to look at...'.

In contrast to *Red Dragon*, *Silence of the Lambs* concludes with a sense of positive resolution. Lecter may be on the loose but Gumb is dead, Catherine saved, and Clarice Starling has both proved her FBI credentials and come to terms with herself. Jack Crawford offers Clarice the finest tribute she could hear: 'Starling, your father sees you.' Having carefully distanced herself from the men who sniff around her, Starling decides to take a chance on moth expert Noble Pilcher. Unlike Will Graham, Clarice Starling has at least the possibility of companionship and peace, the screaming lambs of her nightmares quieted, for the time being. Harris ends the book on an optimistic note: '...she sleeps deeply, sweetly, in the silence of the lambs.'

After the bestseller came the bids for the film rights. Director William Friedkin, the self-proclaimed original choice to play Lecter on the screen, saw *Lambs* in manuscript form in late 1987 and fell in love with it: 'This is terrific. Dr Lektor [sic] escapes. He's in a straitjacket and he bites a nurse's eye out.' Friedkin badly wanted the rights to Harris's book, probably the best chance he would ever get to revive his ailing film career. While the *auteur* of *The Exorcist* could have named his own terms to make *Silence of the Lambs*, the director-for-hire of the television movie *CAT Squad: Python Wolf* (1988) never looked like a serious contender.

Lambs' bestseller status and potent leading characters drew a lot of interest from filmmakers, yet for a period the book appeared just too dark for many to stomach as movie material. Gene Hackman, an Academy Award winner for his performance in William Friedkin's *The French Connection*, optioned the screen rights in association with Orion Pictures. Intending to make the *Lambs* movie his directing debut, Hackman had mixed feelings about also starring in the film as Hannibal Lecter. There were rumours that he would take the less showy supporting role of FBI boss Jack Crawford and hire *Manhunter* co-star Brian Cox to reprise his role as Lecter/Lecktor. As Cox explained to *Daily Mail* reporter Rebecca Hardy: 'there was a great deal of interest in my doing the part.' Playwright and fledgling screenwriter Ted Tally, who knew Thomas Harris socially, heard about the Orion-Hackman deal and offered his scripting services to the studio, which commissioned a first draft.

After starring in the Orion release *Mississippi Burning* (1988), a based-on-fact 1960s story of racial murder, Gene Hackman reconsidered the *Silence of the Lambs* project. Academy Award nominated for his performance in Alan Parker's film, where he played a veteran FBI agent taking on the Ku Klux Klan, Hackman felt he'd seen enough of the dark side of human nature for the time being. The actor also worried that he'd become typecast as a screen psychopath, dishing out the sadism in *Bonnie and Clyde* (1967), as bank robber Buck Darrow, *The Hunting Party* (1971), as a wife-beating rancher, *Prime Cut* (1972), where he turned his enemies into sausage meat, and *Superman* (1978), as arch villain Lex Luthor, who plans to knock Los Angeles into the ocean by detonating the San Andreas faultline. Even Popeye Doyle, nominal hero of *The French Connection*, acted like a borderline psycho, shooting an unarmed suspect in the back and showing no remorse when he kills an FBI man by mistake. Not always the best judge of material, as movies like *Lucky Lady* (1975) clearly demonstrated, Hackman quickly got cold feet and dropped the *Lambs* project before he'd even read Ted Tally's first draft screenplay. Across the Atlantic, Anthony Hopkins, acting on the London stage in an acclaimed production of David Henry Hwang's play *M. Butterfly*, went to an afternoon showing of *Mississippi Burning*. A big fan of Hackman, Hopkins enjoyed the film, wishing he could land another high profile Hollywood movie for himself.

At one point, pre-publication, the *Lambs* film rights were held by noted director John Badham, a television graduate whose big screen career had taken off with his second feature, the John Travolta disco smash *Saturday Night Fever* (1977). A decade on, Badham had successfully maintained his industry profile with big-budget, high-concept movies such as *War Games* (1983), *Blue Thunder* (1983), *Short Circuit* (1985), and *Stakeout* (1987), which offered surface gloss and visual dynamism rather than any great depth of feeling. His box-office flops were rather more interesting, including a darkly romantic, if uneven remake of *Dracula* (1979), starring Frank Langella as the undead, yet devilishly handsome Count.

Badham's television credits included a 1973 episode of the hugely popular series *Kung Fu* (1972-74), entitled 'Alethea', where wandering Chinese-American monk Caine (David Carradine) encountered a 12-year-old girl, played by Jodie Foster. Highly impressed by Foster's performance as the tough, prematurely adult Alethea, Badham remembered her 15 years later and put Foster's name forward as his first choice for the part of Clarice Starling. Despite Badham's relatively strong commercial track record, every studio he approached turned him down flat, citing the unsavoury subject matter. As one studio executive put it: 'Nobody wants to see a movie about skinning women... I have no intention of making *Silence of the Lambs*.' Reluctantly admitting defeat, Badham sold his option on the film rights.

One studio production head didn't balk at the idea of skinning women onscreen. Far from shunning *Silence of the Lambs*, Orion boss Mike Medavoy had eagerly taken on the project when Gene Hackman expressed a strong interest. Given his studio's precarious financial position at the time, Medavoy may have been on the lookout for a suitably high profile property that would either make or break Orion as a serious Hollywood contender. He gave the *Lambs* project to Jonathan Demme, a respected, if not widely known director who'd made two previous films for Orion, including the recent hit *Married to the Mob* (1988). In Medavoy's opinion, the star of the latter film, Michelle Pfeiffer, would make an ideal Clarice Starling.

"...EMINENTLY GIFTED PEOPLE..."

A graduate of the famed Roger Corman school of filmmaking, Demme had first broken into movies as a publicist for independent producer-distributor Joseph E. Levine. An unrepentant hustler, Levine's career nevertheless offered a fair balance of commerce and art, the profits from exploitation movies like *Hercules Unchained* (1959) financing such esoteric fare as Federico Fellini's *8 1/2* (1963). Like Michael Mann, Demme began his filmmaking career in London, working as a producer in the television commercial industry. Demme's first job for Roger Corman was as publicist for the United Artists release *Von Richtofen and Brown* (1971), the cut-price *auteur*'s last directorial credit until *Frankenstein Unbound* nearly 20 years later. Interviewed by David Thompson in 1989, Demme praised his former boss as 'one of my favourite people'.

In truth, Jonathan Demme's early stint with Corman's New World production company did not seem especially promising. His feature debut was as producer and co-writer on *Angels Hard as They Come* (1971), a relatively late entry in the biker movie cycle (so to speak), initiated by the success of Corman's own *The Wild Angels* five years earlier. According to Demme, the film started out as a biker version of *Rashomon* (1950), Akira Kurosawa's celebrated meditation on the fallacy of absolute truth. If so, Demme failed to communicate this to co-writer and director Joe Viola. Budgeted at $120,000, *Angels Hard As They Come* could hardly fail to make a profit.

Demme took the same producer-writer roles for *The Hot Box* (1972), a Women in Prison (WIP) saga, and co-wrote the original story for *Black Mama, White Mama* (1972), another WIP epic. Shot on location in the Philippines, these drive-in specials weren't as salacious, or tasteless, as the titles suggested. There were even hints of social comment and vague pro-feminist attitudes between the bouts of sex and violence. When bad weather forced the *Hot Box* production behind schedule, Demme turned second-unit director to get the film back on track, shooting footage on the island of Negros.

Still waiting to get his official directing break with New World, Demme returned to England, where he'd been offered the chance to direct *Secrets of a Door-to-Door Salesman* (1973), a soft-core sex farce starring comic actor Graham Stark. Creative differences prevailed, however, and Demme received his marching orders. Demme finally made his directorial debut at New World with what sounded like yet another WIP potboiler, *Caged Heat* (1974), filmed on a budget of $180,000. While the publicity followed the usual angles: 'White Hot Desires Melting Cold Prison Steel!', the film itself boasted a few unusual touches. The prison's wheelchair-bound warden was played by former Rank starlet turned Italian horror icon Barbara Steele. Demme had written the part with Steele in mind, the latter's distinctive English accent lending her already bizarre character a mildly surreal air (the warden dreams of dancing with a top hat and cane). Cheaply made, overstretched at 84 minutes and often tasteless, *Caged Heat* earned some favourable reviews in the mainstream press. The film's mostly dubious characters include a demented male prison doctor who, aside from the expected shock treatments and lobotomies, drugs and molests the inmates in his infirmary, taking pictures of their prone naked bodies. Demme has pointed out that his film depicted the institutional abuse of psychosurgery a good year before Milos Forman's *One Flew Over the Cuckoo's Nest* (1975), yet somehow the latter drew the greater acclaim.

Demme remained with Corman and New World to consolidate his new directing career, working on a script for what eventually became *Fighting Mad* (1976). With around one hour's notice, Corman gave

Demme the directing job on *Crazy Mama* (1975), which he took over from underground filmmaker Shirley Clarke. Designed to cash in on the success of Corman's AIP hit *Bloody Mama* (1970) and New World's very own box-office winner *Big Bad Mama* (1974), the film proved a flop, a rare thing for a Roger Corman production. Saddled with zero preparation time, a three-week schedule and a lousy script he rewrote between set-ups, Demme felt he'd been landed with a no-win situation. Unhappy with the movie, which didn't feature the required climactic bloody shootout, Corman threatened to cancel the production of *Fighting Mad*, relenting when he realised that Demme had done his best under the circumstances.

Like most Corman 'graduates', Demme felt the latter gave his fledgling filmmakers a generous break, once the ground rules were established. As Demme explained to David Thompson: 'Having made sure that you accepted the rules of how to make a Corman movie, Roger then gave you an enormous amount of freedom to go ahead and do it.' In the event, the most interesting thing about *Fighting Mad* is its genesis as a made-to-measure audience pleaser. According to Corman biographer Beverly Gray, Demme examined three recent low-budget action hits, *Billy Jack* (1971), *Walking Tall* (1973) and *Dirty Mary, Crazy Larry* (1974), picking out the elements that seemed to make them work. He concluded that the ideal drive-in storyline required a rural setting and a two-fisted hero with an unusual vehicle, weapon and sidekick. Even with *...Crazy Larry* star Peter Fonda in the lead, the formula just didn't click in this instance.

Parting company from both Corman and crass commercialism, Demme began the next phase of his career with *Citizens Band* (1977) aka *Handle With Care*, a script rejected by most established directors. Distributed by Paramount, this quirky character-based drama proved ideal material for Demme, the director no longer constrained by the need for frequent gunfire and regular flashes of bare flesh. Good reviews were not matched by hot box-office, however, the film proving to be one of the biggest flops of the year. Like Michael Mann, Demme experienced a decade of minimal commercial success before his first hit. Short of both film offers and money after *Citizens Band*, Demme found temporary refuge in network television. Peter Falk, a fan of *Citizens Band*, invited the director to work on an episode of *Columbo*, 'Murder under Glass' (1978).

Following the failed Hitchcock homage *Last Embrace* (1979), Demme achieved critical recognition with the Academy Award-winning comedy *Melvin and Howard* (1980). Several light years away from the tone and style of *Silence of the Lambs*, the film starred Jason Robards as eccentric multi-billionaire Howard Hughes and *Citizens Band* actor Paul Le Mat as the milkman who encounters Hughes on a desert road.

Demme got his break into big-time filmmaking with the Warner production *Swing Shift* (1984). A World War II romantic comedy, the film should have confirmed Demme's place in the Hollywood 'A' list. Instead, it proved the worst experience of his career. Controlled by producer-star Goldie Hawn, *Swing Shift* underwent intensive rewrites and reshoots, the original script largely discarded. Reduced to little more than a hired hand, Demme had no real say on set and fell out with Hawn. Released with a pseudonymous screenplay credit and a half-hour of footage supposedly shot by another (anonymous) director, the film flopped.

Demme spent the next few years away from feature-film work, directing the hit Talking Heads concert movie *Stop Making Sense* (1984) and a film record of actor-writer Spalding Gray's acclaimed monologue *Swimming to Cambodia* (1987). The director's Hollywood career took an upturn after he joined forces with Orion Pictures to make the 'Yuppie Nightmare' comedy drama *Something Wild* (1987), starring Jeff Daniels and Melanie Griffith, with a title song by Talking Heads frontman David Byrne. A somewhat overrated excursion into Strangeville, USA, the film is remembered chiefly for Griffith's Louise Brooks wig and taste in light bondage. Veering towards arch kookiness, *Something Wild* benefits greatly from the threatening presence of Ray Liotta as Griffith's violent ex-con husband. Though by no means on the Hannibal Lecter level of psycho-menace, Liotta's climactic attack on Griffith is genuinely unsettling. Handcuffed to a kitchen sink, the previously conservative, straitlaced Daniels breaks free and in the ensuing struggle plunges a knife into his girlfriend's assailant. Clutching his punctured abdomen, the mortally wounded Liotta seems almost impressed by this show of nerve.

Founded in 1978 by a group of disgruntled former United Artists executives, Orion Pictures Corporation had quickly established itself in the marketplace. Affiliated with industry giant Warner, which handled the distribution of Orion's product, the company enjoyed a huge box office hit with the lowbrow Dudley Moore farce *Arthur* (1981). At the same time, Orion successfully promoted itself as the studio of first choice for more serious filmmakers. Staying loyal to the people rather than the logo, UA mainstay Woody Allen moved to Orion to make *A Midsummer Night's Sex Comedy* (1982), which also initiated his long-term screen partnership with Mia Farrow. Orion also produced John Boorman's striking near-masterpiece *Excalibur* (1981), Milos Forman's lavish Mozart biopic *Amadeus* (1984) and Oliver Stone's anguished Vietnam catharsis *Platoon* (1986). Both *Amadeus* and *Platoon* picked up Best Picture Academy Awards. Also active on the small screen, Orion scored a sleeper hit with the female-oriented police series *Cagney and Lacy* (1982-88). Despite the termination of the Warner deal, Orion seemed in extremely good shape, both in terms of talent and finance.

Boosted by the success of *Something Wild*, Jonathan Demme stayed with the company to make another offbeat romantic comedy, *Married to the Mob* (1988). Starring Michelle Pfeiffer and Matthew Modine, the film successfully mixed Mafia widows, lustful crime bosses, FBI agents, hair salons, adultery, murder and a character nicknamed 'the cucumber'. Demme already knew Pfeiffer from the production of *Into the Night* (1985), a John Landis comedy in which he had a cameo role along with fellow directors Don Siegel, David Cronenberg, Jack Arnold, Lawrence Kasdan, Paul Bartel and Amy Heckerling, among others. A friend of Landis, Demme shared his liking for putting non-actor friends in front of the camera. Demme describes *Married to the Mob* as 'a blatant attempt at a full-tilt, crassly commercial entertainment', which nevertheless has a subtle, pro-tolerance, anti-racism subtext. Roger Corman would be proud. As Demme explained to David Thompson: 'I hope that *Married to the Mob* has a lot of the elements and feeling of a Corman movie, because that means our aggressive attempt to entertain is coming across.'

Discussing his career with Thompson in 1989, Demme explained one reason for his diverse choice of projects: '...I hate the idea of doing films that are similar. I think it's important, creatively, to do something as different as possible from what you did the last time.' Moving from a relatively light-hearted comedy to the unrelentingly grim drama of *Silence of the Lambs* certainly made for a change of pace. In some ways, Thomas Harris's story offered all that Demme most disliked in the exploitation movie genre where his career began. During his time with New World, the director had made several films, notably *The Hot Box* and *Caged Heat*, which highlighted graphic acts of violence, particularly against women. Tailored to the more dubious appetites of male filmgoers, the Women in Prison genre exhibited a misogynist streak that even a director of Demme's promise couldn't eliminate. Tiring of this element, Demme changed the ending of *Crazy Mama* so that the criminal female leads escaped, rather than bloodily expiring in a hail of police gunfire. *Silence of the Lambs* featured a male character who kidnapped, imprisoned, starved, murdered and skinned his female victims, dumping their mutilated bodies in rivers. Even Roger Corman, who'd given the world rapacious aquatic reptiles in *Humanoids from the Deep* (1980), would probably draw the line here. Harris, however, didn't dwell on Jame Gumb's incredibly gruesome activities, nor did he make Gumb in any way sympathetic. The grisly aftermath of the abductions and the build-up to Catherine Martin's encounter with Buffalo Bill formed the backdrop to the FBI investigation. Demme felt that *Silence of the Lambs* was first and foremost the story of Clarice Starling, a woman fiercely committed to saving the lives of other women. Both novel and screenplay took the emphasis away from the actual serial murder. As Ted Tally explained: 'In terms of Hollywood, serial killers are really a tacky, overdone crutch, dramatically.' According to Tally, Orion boss Mike Medavoy had no doubts that director and project were ideally suited: 'I think this picture needs him and I think he needs it.' In the event, Demme agreed to direct *Lambs* before he'd even read Ted Tally's script.

With the slasher movie cycle mercifully burned out, serial killers weren't exactly a hot film subject in the late 1980s. *Manhunter* aside, the only recent example of note was John McNaughton's low-key, unflinchingly horrible *Henry: Portrait of a Serial Killer* (1987), which wasn't widely seen until 1990. Orion Pictures had another reason to treat their *Silence of the Lambs* project with caution: Thomas Harris's earlier novels *Black Sunday* and *Red Dragon* had both been international bestsellers, yet the film versions flopped. The budget for *Lambs* was set at a realistic and relatively modest $22 million.

The producers on *Silence of the Lambs* were Edward Saxon, the late

Kenneth Utt and Ron Bozman, with Gary Goetzman serving as executive producer. All four were director Jonathan Demme's choices. Utt and Saxon had both worked with Demme and Orion on *Something Wild* and *Married to the Mob*. Utt's film career dated back to the late sixties, when he'd served as an associate producer on *Midnight Cowboy* (1969), a downbeat urban 'buddy' drama that won three major Academy Awards despite its controversial 'X' rating. Working on *The French Connection* and Bob Fosse's *All That Jazz* (1979) during the 1970s, Utt had turned producer by the time he reunited with Fosse for *Star 80* (1983), the director-choreographer's last film. Utt's association with Demme extended beyond producing, Utt playing bit roles in both *Something Wild* and *Married to the Mob*, in which he appeared as one of Matthew Modine's FBI colleagues. Utt would act again in *Silence of the Lambs,* as the doctor in the Elk River autopsy sequence, the producer's strikingly lined face conveying a weary disgust at the sight of Jame Gumb's mutilated victim.

Like Kenneth Utt, Edward Saxon had worked in front of the camera with Demme, playing a bit role in *Something Wild*. Ron Bozman, associate producer and assistant director on *Something Wild*, continued with the latter job for *Lambs*. Former actor Gary Goetzman, a producer on *Stop Making Sense*, had played bit roles in Demme's films from *Caged Heat* onwards, even appearing in the director's episode of *Columbo*.

Unlike *Manhunter* director Michael Mann, Demme did not write his own screenplays anymore, abandoning the practise after the failure of *Fighting Mad*. The job of adapting *Silence of the Lambs* remained with Ted Tally, who stayed more or less faithful to the source material. Tally's only big-screen credit prior to *Lambs* was *White Palace* (1990), co-scripted with *Straight Time* writer Alvin Sargent. Starring Susan Sarandon as a forty-something waitress and James Spader as her younger executive lover, this role reversal age-gap, wrong-side-of-the-tracks romance owed more to its leading performances than the script. Nevertheless, Demme expressed total confidence in Tally: 'I knew he was going to nail it.' Demme claimed that 85 percent of the writer's first-draft screenplay ended up in the completed film.

Tally aside, most of the *Lambs* production team were hardened Demme veterans. Cameraman Tak Fujimoto had been Demme's regular director of photography from *Caged Heat* onwards, missing out only on *Fighting Mad* and *Citizens Band*. For *Crazy Mama*, Fujimoto agreed to work on the second unit, an apparent 'demotion' which suggests a strong regard for his director. Interviewed by David Thompson, Demme explained his preference for retaining long term collaborators: 'For me, that's the key to good directing: hire eminently gifted people and let them pursue what they do.'

Educated like Michael Mann at the London Film School, Fujimoto's first major film credit was Terrence Malick's *Badlands*, a rural tale of alienation and casual slaughter. Martin Sheen's denim-clad juvenile murderer would probably not impress Hannibal Lecter, accepting his date in the electric chair without a flicker of concern. Like Demme, Fujimoto had done his time with Roger Corman and New World, photographing the satirical car-crash movies *Death Race 2000* (1975) and *Cannonball* (1976). Serving as a second-unit cameraman on *Star Wars* (1977), Fujimoto established himself in mainstream Hollywood independently of Demme, working on the teen comedy hit *Ferris Bueller's Day Off* (1986). Demme claims to never discuss a film's lighting with Fujimoto: '...his ideas would be far richer than mine.' Editor Craig McKay's association with Demme dated back to *Melvin and Howard*, while production designer and second unit director Kristi Zea had recently collaborated with the director on *Married to the Mob*. Composer Howard Shore, working with Demme for the first time, offered both impeccable horror film credentials and an interesting background. Born in Toronto, Canada, Shore's first professional engagement was as saxophone player with the 1960s rock group Lighthouse, supporting big name acts such as Jimi Hendrix and The Grateful Dead. Shore went on to become the first music director on the popular television comedy show *Saturday Night Live*. Shore's best-known film work was for Canadian nightmare maestro David Cronenberg. Even those who shunned works such as *Scanners* (1980) and *Videodrome* (1982) had to admit that Shore knew how to write effective background music for an exploding head. Cronenberg's move to bigger budget, slightly more respectable fare such as *The Fly* (1986) and *Dead Ringers* (1988) raised Shore's Hollywood profile. His non-Cronenberg credits included the body-swap comedy *Big* (1988).

"I WOULD HAVE CRAWLED OVER BROKEN GLASS FOR THE ROLE..."

When it came to Orion casting the star role of Clarice Starling, no-one rated the chances of Jodie Foster, despite her recent Academy Award win for *The Accused*. A professional child actor from the age of three, Foster had quickly become a Walt Disney mainstay on both television and film. Movies such as *One Little Indian* (1973), *Candleshoe* (1977) and *Freaky Friday* (1977) were bland, if pleasant live action Disney fare, yet most critics noticed Foster's assured, gutsy performances. While still a Disney star, Foster pursued a parallel film career in more weighty, adult dramas. Having cast Foster as a streetwise juvenile shoplifter in *Alice Doesn't Live Here Anymore* (1974), director Martin Scorsese gave her a leading role in the much darker *Taxi Driver* (1976). Her casting as a twelve-year-old prostitute stirred up a lot of controversy, not least for the scene where she unzips paying customer Robert De Niro's trousers and offers to perform assorted sex acts on him. By comparison, *The Little Girl Who Lives Down the Lane* (1976) attracted little attention. Here, Foster's character is actively homicidal, poisoning child molester Martin Sheen with arsenic in his tea.

As a young adult, Foster's film career lost momentum and direction. She gravitated towards offbeat roles that tended to involve an element of victimisation. Surviving a gang rape in Tony Richardson's extremely black comedy *The Hotel New Hampshire* (1984), Foster was stalked by a penguin-slaying psychopath in Tony Bill's *Five Corners* (1987). In terms of Hollywood recognition, Foster's biggest film between *Taxi Driver* and *The Silence of the Lambs* was *The Accused* (1988). Playing another rape victim, Foster invested her flirtatious, dope-smoking, foulmouthed 'trailer-trash' character with both dignity and determination. Sharing Clarice Starling's deprived background, Sarah Tobias refuses to be ignored by the legal system, reduced to just another crime statistic on the tacit assumption that she 'provoked' her attackers. Foster's performance in the film is both admirable and courageous, though the extended flashback to the rape borders on unsavoury exploitation. Whatever *The Accused*'s failings, Foster deserved her Academy Award for Best Actress, though the trophy didn't seem to make any immediate difference to her patchy career. *Catchfire* (aka *Backtrack*) (1989) marked an ill-advised return to offbeat melodrama, the film chiefly notable for being disowned by director-star Dennis Hopper after studio re-editing. Jonathan Demme charitably described Foster's pre-*Lambs* resume as 'all over the chart'. Though widely respected within the industry for work such as *Taxi Driver*, she had never starred in a major commercial success.

Jodie Foster had read the Thomas Harris book and immediately recognised Clarice Starling as an ideal role. Here was a heroine who relied on her brains and courage to track down and apprehend a psychotic murderer: 'it's about the capacity of intelligence to combat the enemy.' In Foster's opinion, this would be a Hollywood first. The recent science fiction hits *Terminator* (1984) and *Aliens* (1986) had offered strong, self-sufficient female leads in Sarah Connor (Linda Hamilton) and Ellen Ripley (Sigourney Weaver). Both exhibited strong feminine qualities, notably a powerful maternal instinct, yet writer-director James Cameron arguably invested the gun-toting characters with traditionally masculine traits in their fight against hostile life-forms.

Inspired by Clarice Starling, Jodie Foster attempted to buy the screen rights to *The Silence of the Lambs* herself, only to discover that her recent Academy Award win counted for little in the hard-dealing movie marketplace. Had director John Badham still been associated with the project, Foster would probably have made the front running for the part, if not the guaranteed number one choice. Without Badham's support, Foster had to fight for the role. Once the film version of *Lambs* became a 'go' project, she approached screenwriter Ted Tally and expressed her strong interest in the part. Subsequent meetings with Orion and Jonathan Demme made it clear to Foster that she wasn't the first or even second choice for the film.

Studio boss Mike Medavoy and Demme wanted Michelle Pfeiffer, star of the director's *Married to the Mob*, for the part of Starling. Director and actor had got on very well during production on the latter film, Demme rating Pfeiffer as 'a very intelligent, nice person'. Still at the peak of her career, Pfeiffer's post-*Mob* work included a couple of Academy Award-nominated performances in *Dangerous Liaisons* (1988) and *The Fabulous Baker Boys* (1989), undeniably classy acts that also did respectable box office.

Pfeiffer agreed to read Tally's script, only to express a strong dislike for the 'too bleak' subject matter. As Demme put it: 'she was unable to come to terms with the overpowering darkness of the piece.' Pfeiffer had serious problems with what she considered *Lambs'* 'glorification' of evil. Jame Gumb, the serial killer hunted down by Starling, did not present a problem, as the character was presented as a warped, disturbing figure throughout the film and finally vanquished. In this instance, good won out over evil. Hannibal Lecter, on the other hand, represented the apparent triumph of darkness. A charismatic, witty scene-stealer, the Doctor cunningly escaped from his jailers and remained at liberty as the closing credits rolled. Cannibalistic serial killers who slice off and wear other people's faces should not be depicted as glamorous anti-heroes. It has been claimed that Pfeiffer also shunned the *Lambs* project on the less idealistic grounds of money, Orion unable to meet her asking price. Despite her principled refusal to appear in *Silence of the Lambs*, Pfeiffer admired Anthony Hopkins's performance in the finished film. Meeting the actor after *Lambs'* huge success, Pfeiffer briefly regretted her decision not to reunite with Demme.

Realistic about her chances, Jodie Foster had offered herself to Jonathan Demme as a possible substitute if Michelle Pfeiffer passed on the film. Even with Pfeiffer out of the picture, Foster found she was still behind in the running. Though a declared fan of the star's work, Demme felt she lacked the necessary versatility for Starling: 'At the end of the day, all of her characters were Jodie Foster.' The director's next choice was Meg Ryan, largely on the strength of her performance in *When Harry Me Sally* (1989). Though Ryan had yet to achieve Pfeiffer's level of star power, her career looked healthier than Foster's from a commercial point of view and her screen persona more immediately engaging. But Ryan had yet to prove herself in a heavyweight, dramatic role, and both Demme and Mike Medavoy began to favour Foster. The director felt that the star's non-Disney work was 'never terribly far from the edge', Foster's commitment to her often-troubled characters showing through whatever the quality of the overall film. He also liked her approach to the role of Starling: 'Her identification was with a character who felt deeply for victims.'

Meeting with Demme in New York, Foster convinced the director that she both understood and appreciated the dark, disturbing tone of the material, which she connected with on a 'serious personal' level. As the star later admitted: 'I would have crawled over broken glass for the role – wearing shorts.' Given Meg Ryan's cringe-making performance as an alcoholic in the 'serious' drama *When a Man Loves a Woman* (1994), Demme probably made the right decision.

"I UNDERSTAND MONSTERS"

While Thomas Harris's *The Silence of the Lambs* was widely publicised as the sequel to *Red Dragon*, the film version of *Lambs* had a rather different relationship to its cinematic predecessor, *Manhunter*. Had the earlier film been more successful, it is possible that Dino de Laurentiis would have held on to the Harris/Lecter franchise, despite his serious commercial problems. In the event, the *Lambs* producers could more or less ignore the Michael Mann film, which had barely registered with the fickle paying public. They had a new hero, a new active serial killer, not to mention an entirely different production team. The only significant link between the two movies was a handful of recurring characters, notably Doctor Chilton, Jack Crawford and Doctor Hannibal Lecter. While neither Dennis Farina nor the less well-known Benjamin Hendrickson seem to have been considered for the *Lambs* film, the producers were definitely interested in Brian Cox. Though still relatively unknown to filmgoers, Cox had brought the Doctor to sinister life onscreen, offering a ready-made piece of ideal casting. The role of Lecter presented a considerable challenge to even the most accomplished actor, not to mention a temptation to slide into camp pantomime villainy. According to Brian Cox, Thomas Harris had been 'very complimentary' about his performance in *Manhunter* and sent the actor an advance copy of *Silence of the Lambs*. This seal of approval from the notoriously close-mouthed Harris should have made Cox the natural choice for any film sequel. The actor certainly appreciated that *Lambs* promoted Hannibal Lecter from supporting player to co-star: 'When I read it, I knew it would be a success because of Lecter.'

It has been claimed that Brian Cox declined to reprise his portrayal on the straightforward grounds that he didn't do sequels. If this sounds a little glib, the actor appears also to have had more personal reasons. As Cox explained to Kate Hardie: 'Hannibal Lecter is not a part you want to be sitting around with a lot.' Following *Manhunter*'s release, Cox received a succession of scripts featuring well-spoken psychopaths, a career path he had no great wish to follow. Cox seems also to have been dubious about the script for *Silence of the Lambs*, which gave Lecter a near anti-hero status he'd lacked in *Manhunter*. Interviewed by *Entertainment Weekly* following *Silence of the Lambs*' huge box-office success, Cox declared himself a little perturbed by Lecter's almost glamorous new image: 'I was interested in that kind of childlike immorality that Lecter had, and while a lot of people get off on him, I never imagined him as the heroic figure that he became. I still have a problem with that.'

For the record, it has also been claimed that Cox simply had a prior stage commitment that prevented him from appearing in *Lambs*. Jonathan Demme's involvement with the *Silence of the Lambs* film appears to have finally ruled Brian Cox out of the sequel. According to Cox: 'He wanted to make his own film and he didn't want anyone who had been in the original, which is understandable.' In the event, two of *Manhunter*'s supporting cast would appear in *Lambs*, though not in their original roles. Whatever the case, Cox has rarely expressed regret at declining the role that earned Anthony Hopkins an Academy Award: '...I wasn't too unhappy that I didn't go on with the part, that I didn't do *The Silence of the Lambs*.'

A highly respected theatre actor since the early 1960s, Anthony Hopkins's Hollywood status three decades on could best be described as negligible. Trained at the Royal Academy of Dramatic Art, Hopkins first came to prominence as a sensational new star of the National Theatre, the heir to Laurence Olivier's throne. A film career commenced soon afterwards, Hopkins making his feature debut as Richard the Lionheart in *The Lion in Winter* (1968). Unlike the actor's classical theatre work, which continued to draw accolades, Hopkins's film appearances were sometimes less assured. Miscast as a Bond-style agent in *When Eight Bells Toll* (1971), Hopkins subsequently teamed up with actor-turned-director Richard Attenborough for *Young Winston* (1972). Playing fellow Welshman David Lloyd George, Hopkins made his mark in the big-name cast, which included *Black Sunday* star Robert Shaw as Randolph Churchill.

Moving to New York in 1974 to star in the Broadway production of Peter Schaffer's acclaimed play *Equus*, Hopkins stayed on in America for ten years. The actor's first big Hollywood movie was also his first excursion into horror-tinged material. Based on a best-selling novel by Frank DeFelitta, *Audrey Rose* (1977) dealt with the theme of reincarnation. Hopkins's character is convinced that his dead daughter, Audrey, has been reborn as a wealthy New York couple's twelve-year-old girl. Directed by Robert Wise from co-producer DeFelitta's own screenplay, the movie showcased Hopkins's skill at depicting understated neurosis, yet seemed uncomfortable with its own quasi-supernatural theme. Wise's earlier ghost story, *The Haunting* (1963), demonstrated the director's flair for atmospheric excursions into the spirit world, where the dead never rest easily. *Audrey Rose* goes for a more low-key approach, as if a sober, unsensational treatment would lend the reincarnation theme some validity. Initially dismissed as a crank by the child's parents, Hopkins's story gradually becomes more credible to the mother, leading to a bizarre court case over the girl. The scenes where the child apparently relives Audrey Rose's terrible death, burned alive in a car wreck, are disturbing in an exploitative way.

Hopkins returned to borderline fantasy with *Magic* (1978), directed by Richard Attenborough, who originally wanted Jack Nicholson for the lead. Cast as a schizophrenic ventriloquist who invests his dummy with the cruder, nastier aspects of his personality, Hopkins looked uneasy throughout, overdoing the subdued hysteria. Scripted by William Goldman, from his bestselling novel, *Magic* seemed a derivative, uninspired retread of an episode from the British compendium film *Dead of Night* (1945), where Michael Redgrave's equally troubled ventriloquist is mocked, taunted, threatened and finally 'taken over' by his dummy. Whatever the merits of Goldman's book, the film version of *Magic* proved only that beating someone to death with a ventriloquist's doll in inherently undignified. *Magic* was produced by Joseph E Levine, Jonathan Demme's former employer.

Arguably, Anthony Hopkins didn't really find a strong starring role in films until *The Elephant Man* (1980), directed by future *Blue Velvet auteur* David Lynch. Hopkins played eminent Victorian surgeon Frederick Treves, a pioneer of medical science whose professional zeal is tempered by a strong sense of humanity. Discovering the horribly deformed John Merrick (John Hurt) as the star attraction at a freakshow, Treves 'borrows' the man to serve as a sensational living specimen for a lecture given to his medical peers. Realising, with a certain amount of self-disgust, that Merrick has only ever known abuse and exploitation, Treves decides to help him, discovering an intelligent, articulate and sensitive man beneath the grotesquely twisted body. While Treves borders on near saintliness at times, just as Hannibal Lecter appears to have climbed up from hell, Hopkins invests him with just enough flawed humanity to make the character touchingly plausible.

Hopkins's deserved success with *The Elephant Man* was followed by a return to Hollywood and a starring role opposite Shirley MacLaine in the Columbia-financed 'adult' comedy *A Change of Seasons* (1980). The production proved extremely fraught, Hopkins often clashing with the notoriously opinionated MacLaine, and the film flopped. For all Hopkins's undeniable talent and screen presence, Hollywood stardom looked increasingly unlikely. It says something about the precarious state of Hopkins's screen career that he spent much of the 1975-85 period in American-financed made-for-television films. His performance as *The Hunchback of Notre Dame* (1982) offered a fair stab at the noble, self-sacrificing 'monster' role made famous by Lon Chaney and Charles Laughton. Hopkins screened the 1939 Laughton version before starting on the tv film, happy to steal some tips from an actor he admired. *Hollywood Wives* (1985), an Aaron Spelling production based on a Jackie Collins novel, was nothing more than a fat paycheque. Hopkins made light of his appearance in it, yet the cast line-up of Angie Dickinson, Rod Steiger, Stefanie Powers and Candice Bergen suggested that he'd already joined the ranks of Hollywood has-beens.

Busy with lucrative television work during the early 1980s, Hopkins found time for the occasional feature film. *The Bounty* (1984) was a Dino de Laurentiis production originally intended for director David Lean. Like most other de Laurentiis productions of the time, the film did poor box-office business, many reviewers feeling that it lacked the epic scope promised by the subject matter. Hopkins's repressed Captain Bligh is a sympathetic, if deeply flawed man rather than the sadist portrayed by Charles Laughton and Trevor Howard in earlier film versions. Lacking a clear hero and villain, *The Bounty* ultimately seemed unsure of what it wanted to achieve.

While *The Silence of the Lambs* marked the first and, to date, only film collaboration between Jodie Foster and Anthony Hopkins, their paths had lightly brushed on a previous occasion. Nearly a decade earlier, Hopkins and Foster had been contracted to co-star in Ken Russell's aborted biopic-cum-detective-story *The Beethoven Secret*, to be filmed on location in Austria. Focusing on the composer's previously mysterious love life, the script attracted a cast that also included Russell veteran Glenda Jackson and fellow sixties icon Charlotte Rampling. A portrait of anguished musical genius along the lines of the director's earlier *The Music Lovers* (1970) and *Mahler* (1974), the project collapsed only days before the start of shooting when the German financiers withdrew.

Interviewed by Saskia Baron for the BBC's *Late Show* arts programme in May 1991, Demme explained the choice of Hopkins for the part of Lecter: 'Anthony Hopkins appears to be exceptionally intelligent; there's something about his face, something about his eyes, something about the way he expresses himself.'

Demme wanted Lecter to possess both intelligence and humanity, rendering the character more than 'a brilliant icicle'. This could be taken as a criticism of Brian Cox's decidedly cool interpretation of the Doctor. Hopkins certainly appears to have been Demme's number one choice for the part. A longtime fan of the actor, Demme felt that Hannibal Lecter represented the inverse of Hopkins's compassionate Doctor Frederick Treves in *The Elephant Man*. Treves, though ambitious, is decent, moral and humane.

Demme sent Hopkins a copy of Ted Tally's 120-page script, which the actor skimmed through, not wanting to get too drawn by the material in case the role fell through. Nevertheless, Hopkins felt from the start that the *Silence of the Lambs* film would 'touch the pulse of people'. According to Hopkins biographer Michael Feeney Callan, Demme's partners at Orion Pictures were initially unconvinced by his choice of

Lecter. The part needed someone with a real hint of darkness to them, a 1990s equivalent to Boris Karloff or the original *Psycho* himself, Anthony Perkins. Moreover, Mike Medavoy did not want a British actor for the role. Presumably not a fan, or simply unaware, of Brian Cox's performance in *Manhunter*, the Orion boss felt that Lecter was written for an American. Medavoy favoured Robert Duvall for the part, feeling that the latter had the instant sinister quality he wanted for the character. A highly respected actor in the same league as Gene Hackman, Duvall's career boasted its share of villainous roles. In *True Grit* (1969), as 'Lucky' Ned Pepper, he'd gone head-to-head with Big John Wayne, ending up shot to pieces. His interpretation of outlaw Jesse James in Philip Kaufman's *The Great Northfield Minnesota Raid* (1972) suggested extreme psychosis. Duvall's greatest screen madman was probably Colonel Kilgore in Francis Coppola's hallucinogenic Vietnam trip *Apocalypse Now* (1979). Though not a serial killer in the eyes of the law, Kilgore leads his boys into battle with an almost sexual thrill, Wagner's 'Ride of the Valkyries' blaring from loudspeakers as his helicopters strike against a Vietcong stronghold. Distributing 'death cards' to the fallen enemy soldiers, Kilgore proclaims: 'I love the smell of Napalm in the morning', a Wild West-style cavalry hat perched incongruously on his head.

Undeterred by Medavoy's scepticism, Demme travelled to London, where Anthony Hopkins was finishing his run in *M. Butterfly*. Over dinner, the director reiterated his desire for Hopkins to play Lecter in *Lambs*, the actor still half-convinced that the part would go to someone with a bigger Hollywood profile. Against Hopkins's expectations, Orion and Demme subsequently summoned him to New York, where he read for the part with Jodie Foster, his rich, commanding voice silencing all doubts.

For Hopkins, *Silence of the Lambs* did not represent an absolutely certain break back into big-time American movies. While Jonathan Demme had directed nine feature films to date, he remained on the fringes of the Hollywood 'A' list. Even *Married to the Mob* had scored a modest rather than runaway box-office success. Two weeks before the trip to New York, Hopkins spoke on the telephone with Ed Lauter, an American actor he had befriended during the production of *Magic* back in 1978. A specialist in tough, often brutal characters, Lauter had appeared in *The Longest Yard* (1974), *French Connection II* and Dino de Laurentiis's *King Kong* remake before Richard Attenborough cast him in *Magic*. True to type, Lauter played the boorish, disagreeable and doomed husband of Ann-Margret, Hopkins's sort-of love interest. According to Michael Feeney Callan, Lauter urged the still-sceptical Hopkins to pursue the role of Lecter, claiming that it could be an Academy Award winner for him. Just before the New York audition at Orion's office on Fifth Avenue, Hopkins spoke with Lauter again and demonstrated the voice he intended to use for the character. The portrayal that would win Hopkins his Oscar was already fully developed before he'd even been offered the part. As Lauter explained to Callan: 'He had every nuance. He knew what he wanted to do with Lecter.'

The producers now wanted Hopkins badly enough to reschedule his start date on *Lambs*, as the actor was committed to co-starring in Michael Cimino's suspense drama *The Desperate Hours* (1990), an ill-advised remake of the 1955 film starring Humphrey Bogart and Fredric March. Executive produced for Fox by Dino de Laurentiis, whose DEG company was now ancient history, the film proved conclusively that Mickey Rourke made a poor substitute for Bogart. Cimino, whose career had continued in violent freefall since the relative failure of *Year of the Dragon*, seemed an apt companion-in-misfortune for the beleaguered *Manhunter* producer. By all accounts, Hopkins didn't get on with Rourke any better than he had with Shirley MacLaine. This aside, he enjoyed working on the film, even telling Cimino that *Desperate Hours* was the first time he had really been directed in a movie.

Like the Scottish Brian Cox, the Welsh Hopkins was British but not English, his cultivated tones carrying no hint of public school clichés. Michael Feeney Callan compares Hopkins's Lecter to Lambert Le Roux, the character he played in the hit 1985 National Theatre production *Pravda*, by David Hare and Howard Brenton. A South African press baron (or tyrant), based on Robert Maxwell and Rupert Murdoch, Le Roux is a less literal devourer of humanity than Lecter, if just as deadly. For Lecter's voice, Hopkins wanted something suitably 'detached', settling on the disembodied tones of HAL, the murderous, yet impeccably spoken computer in Stanley Kubrick's *2001: A Space Odyssey* (1968): '...cold, mechanical, exact. Terrifying'.

Other influences were less conscious. Shortly after settling in the
United States, Hopkins signed on for a co-starring role in NBC's true-
life drama *The Lindbergh Kidnapping Case* (1976), an above-average
television mini-series directed by Buzz Kulik. Cast as Bruno Hauptmann,
the man convicted of kidnapping and murdering the celebrity aviator's
young son, Hopkins gave a strong performance that netted him an Emmy
Award. Little remembered 25 years on, the tv series proved significant
for the actor's career in at least one respect. Hopkins's Hauptmann bore
more than a passing resemblance to Hannibal Lecter, especially in the
climactic scene where he goes to the electric chair.

Unlike Brian Cox, Hopkins didn't bother with in-depth research
into serial killers, feeling that Ted Tally's script gave him all he needed.
As the actor explained to reporters after his Oscar win for Lecter:
'...the character becomes like a photographic plate. The image begins to
show itself to me, and from inside my head I begin to see what he looks
like.' Hopkins certainly felt comfortable with the new role: 'I am able to
play monsters well. I understand monsters. I understand madmen. I can
understand what makes people tick in these darker levels.'

Despite the rescheduling of his start date on *Lambs*, Hopkins had very
little turnaround time between the *Desperate Hours* shoot and the new
film. Finishing work on the Cimino production in early December 1989,
Hopkins had to report for his Lecter make-up tests in Pittsburgh barely
two weeks later.

"RESPONSIBILITY FOR THEIR CHARACTER..."

The supporting roles for *Silence of the Lambs* were cast with relative
ease. Looking for a new Jack Crawford, Jonathan Demme settled on
Scott Glenn, whose characterisations tended to be more laid back than
Dennis Farina's brusque, fiercely driven men of authority. Demme's
association with Glenn dated back two decades to *Angels Hard As
They Come*, in which the actor had a small role. As a budding New
World writer-director, Demme recast Glenn in *Fighting Mad*, their last
film together until *Lambs*. A forceful screen presence, Glenn made for
a natural leading man, yet remained primarily a character actor. His

occasional starring roles tended to be in offbeat films that didn't click with audiences. Aside from Michael Mann's *The Keep*, Glenn had appeared in Philip Kaufman's epic pioneer astronaut saga *The Right Stuff* (1983) and Lawrence Kasdan's semi-serious western *Silverado* (1985), both of which flopped at the box-office.

Cast as one 'Glaeken Trismegestus' in *The Keep*, Glenn rode a motorbike with more restraint than he had in *Angels Hard As They Come*. Turning up in the Carpathian mountains to do battle with the keep's monster, Trismegestus turns out to be another supernatural creature, though not before Glenn and leading lady Alberta Watson have enjoyed a bedroom encounter. Sucked back into the symbolic castle along with the vanquished monster during the film's climax, the Nazi-bashing, green-blooded character makes about as much sense as the rest of *The Keep*. Thanks to Glenn's low-key playing, Trismegestus at least has a measure of dignity.

By the time of *Silence of the Lambs*, Scott Glenn's name tended to be found slightly further down the cast list, adding a little weight to movies like *The Hunt for Red October* (1990). Determined to do his character justice, Glenn went back to Thomas Harris's original inspiration for Jack Crawford, John Douglas, now head of the FBI's Investigative Support Unit. Serving as the Bureau's senior official consultant on the film, Supervisory Special Agent Douglas agreed to spend time with actor, coaching him in the role. Though most of the attention generated by *Silence of the Lambs* focused on Jodie Foster and Anthony Hopkins, Glenn featured prominently in the publicity stills, staring over Hopkins's shoulder while the latter appeared to sniff Jodie Foster's hair. On the film itself, Glenn received above-the-title billing, just below Foster and Hopkins.

Casting the extremely unattractive role of serial killer Jame Gumb presented a few problems. Lacking the screentime, witty lines and show-stopping escape accorded to Hannibal Lecter, Gumb seemed relatively anonymous. In *Manhunter*, Francis Dolarhyde emerged as a person, albeit a highly disturbed one, rather than just a slaughtering monster. Glimpsed only in full psychotic mode prior to the final sequence, Gumb didn't even show his face properly until *Lambs'* closing stages. What the part did require was an actor willing to dance naked, with his penis tucked between his thighs. Demme found his ideal Gumb in the form of Ted Levine, who'd recently appeared in the Orion production *Love at Large* (1990), directed by Alan Rudolph. Though not as physically distinctive as *Manhunter*'s Tom Noonan, Levine's broad, hard face and muscular physique suggested a high level of brute strength on top of Gumb's ingrained psychosis. Curiously, Levine's hairstyle in *Lambs* resembles Michael Mann's at the time of *Manhunter*. Prior to *Lambs*, the actor had appeared in two episodes of Mann's television series *Crime Story* (both 1986). Levine later featured in the director's hit crime thriller *Heat*, alongside Al Pacino, Robert De Niro and Tom Noonan. The Tooth Fairy and Buffalo Bill, together at last.

Prior to *Silence of the Lambs*, Ted Levine's most high profile film credit was the Costa-Gavras political thriller *Betrayed* (1988). An ambitious examination of grass-roots racism in the Midwest, the film centres on a female FBI agent, Debra Winger, sent to infiltrate a white supremacist group. The investigation becomes extremely complicated when she falls for the group's leader, redneck farmer Tom Berenger, who is suspected of murdering an outspoken radio talk show host. Unfortunately, neither Costa-Gavras nor producer-writer Joe Eszterhas developed this premise into anything very effective. Despite strong performances, Levine's included, the film ends up as just another variation on the standard Eszterhas plotline, also used in *Jagged Edge* (1985), *Basic Instinct* (1991) and *Jade* (1995), where cop and murder suspect become emotionally entwined. Though undeniably fascinated by Hannibal Lecter in *Lambs*, FBI agent Clarice Starling knows where to draw the line. On this occasion, anyway.

Auditioning for *Silence of the Lambs*, Levine worked hard to scare Jonathan Demme. Suitably shaken, the director also felt that Levine possessed 'a really vivid imagination' and, fortunately, 'a complete absence of inhibitions'. Demme's praise of Levine neatly encapsulates the director's attitude to casting: 'this is the kind of actor who takes full responsibility for their character.'

Lacking Gumb and Lecter's long criminal records, Doctor Chilton is in many ways as distasteful as the psychopaths he claims to study. Determined to turn himself into a media celebrity, Chilton's reckless decision to move Lecter out of his cell results in at least five deaths.

Manhunter diminished the character of Dr Chilton, the pompous, ineffectual schemer of *Red Dragon*, to a virtual walk-on. If anything, Ted Tally's *Silence of the Lambs* screenplay built up the part of Hannibal Lecter's keeper. Demme gave the role to Anthony Heald, a character actor previously seen in the Meryl Streep films *Silkwood* (1983) and *Postcards from the Edge* (1990).

Many of the supporting roles in *Silence of the Lambs* were taken by regular Demme actors. Tracey Walter, best remembered as the car-despising, John Wayne-slandering philosopher of *Repo Man*, had acted in *Something Wild*. Demme recast him in *Lambs* as an eccentric yet graceful funeral home manager. The somewhat larger Charles Napier was a particular favourite of the director's: 'I think he's one of America's finest actors.' Napier had first come to notice, of a kind, in the films of sexploitation *auteur* Russ Meyer, featuring in *Beyond the Valley of the Dolls* (1970) and *Supervixens* (1975), among others. Rising above the overall tackiness, misogyny and camp absurdity of the movies, the actor had undeniable screen presence. While shooting *The Hot Box* on the island of Negros, Demme watched the earlier Meyer effort *Cherry, Harry and Raquel* (1969) at a local cinema, his first encounter with the director's *oeuvre*. Cast as Harry, Napier made a lasting impression on Demme: 'This guy is an incredible actor.'

Reasoning that any actor who appeared in Russ Meyer films could not be too expensive, Demme gave Napier a call. Cast by the director in *Caged Heat*, Napier became one of Demme's most frequent collaborators. Tall and rugged, the square-jawed actor offered a fair dramatic range, appearing as a surprisingly likeable bigamous trucker in *Citizens Band* and a ruthless, if not entirely competent assassin in *Last Embrace*. Napier's non-Demme mainstream credits included *The Blues Brothers* (1980), as a Good Ol' Southern Boy, and *Rambo: First Blood Part II* (1985), as a US Army officer who foolishly betrays Vietnam veteran Sylvester Stallone. For *Silence of the Lambs*, Napier took the brief, if memorably grisly role of one of Doctor Lecter's police guards. Shortly before *Lambs* started production, Napier acted in the Orion crime thriller *Miami Blues* (1990). Co-produced by Jonathan Demme, Kenneth Utt and Edward Saxon, the film used a number of the director's regular cast and crew, notably Napier, Tak Fujimoto and Craig McKay.

While Brian Cox had passed on the chance to reprise his Lecter role, a couple of *Manhunter*'s supporting cast got to appear in *Silence of the Lambs*. Both were given new roles, their original characters not featuring in *Lambs*. Dan Butler is now best known as the male chauvinist sports pundit Bulldog in the television sit-com *Frasier*. Prior to this big break, he'd featured in three scenes of *Manhunter* as fingerprinting expert Jimmy Price. Though the role is more than a mere walk-on, Butler is only easily recognisable in a couple of brief shots during the FBI conference scene. In *Lambs*, Butler appears as eccentric moth expert Roden, introduced playing beetle draughts with fellow insect enthusiast Pilcher (Paul Lazar). Black actor Frankie Faison had appeared as Police Lieutenant Fisk in the climactic sequence of the Michael Mann film. Prior to *Manhunter*, Faison played another cop in Paul Schrader's *Cat People*, which marked a step up from his brief part as a gang member in Milos Forman's *Ragtime* (1981). By the late 1980s, Faison had put rent-paying roles in trash movies like *Exterminator 2* (1984) and *CHUD* behind him, appearing in Alan Parker's *Mississippi Burning* (1988) and Spike Lee's *Do the Right Thing* (1989), both race-themed movies that attracted controversy. Faison joined the *Lambs* cast in the fairly prominent role of Barney, Doctor Lecter's favourite hospital orderly.

For the supporting, and supportive, role of Ardelia Mapp, Starling's fellow FBI trainee and confidante, Demme chose black actress Kasi Lemmons. Now a successful writer-director of films like *Eve's Bayou* (1997), a well-received period drama, Lemmons found a niche in the early 1990s as the white heroine's gutsy, intuitive best friend. Shortly after *Lambs*, Lemmons appeared in Bernard Rose's offbeat horror-thriller *Candyman* (1992), based on the Clive Barker story 'The Forbidden'. This time around, Lemmons provided back-up to bold academic Virginia Madsen as she researched the legend of an immortal hook-handed killer in a rundown Chicago housing project.

The brief, though pivotal, role of Senator Ruth Martin went to Diane Baker, the actress returning to film work after a decade's absence. Probably best remembered as Sean Connery's devious sister-in-law in Hitchcock's *Marnie* (1964), Baker's movie career had peaked around the mid 1960s, with co-starring roles opposite Paul Newman in *The Prize* (1963) and Gregory Peck in *Mirage* (1965). No stranger to cinematic butchery, Baker had played an axe-wielding homicidal maniac in William Castle's typically outlandish *Strait Jacket* (1964). If the script's psychological insight didn't quite reach the Thomas Harris level, its explanation for Baker's behaviour made a kind of sense. As a small, impressionable child, she'd witnessed screen mother Joan Crawford slaughter her unfaithful husband and his lover with the family chopper. The film's climax, where Baker appears disguised as her mother, complete with a *Scooby Doo*-style mask, is quite surreal.

Jonathan Demme cast his old boss Roger Corman as FBI director Hayden Burke, one of several bit parts the latter had taken in films directed by former 'proteges'. Corman had previously acted in Francis Coppola's *The Godfather Part II* (1974), Paul Bartel's *Cannonball*, Joe Dante's *The Howling* (1980) and Demme's own *Swing Shift*. Interviewed by David Thompson in 1989, shortly before he began work on *Lambs*, Demme revealed a piece of prime Corman film advice: 'your villain has to be the most fascinating, if not likeable, person in the piece.' In the case of *Silence of the Lambs*, Doctor Hannibal Lecter came made-to-measure. The director's more novel casting also included singer Chris Isaak, a friend of Demme's, and horror-satire film director George Romero. Isaak, who'd previously acted in Demme's *Married to the Mob*, would play a SWAT team leader who tries to prevent Lecter's Memphis breakout. Cast as a demented clown hitman in *Mob*, Isaak saw most of his scenes end up on the cutting room floor, Demme obliged to trim radically his original three-hour cut of the film. This time out, Isaak stayed on the screen. Romero, who occasionally appeared in his own films, had a split-second non-speaking part as an FBI man assigned to keep an eye on Lecter in his Memphis cage. Sharing Michael Mann's liking for authentic background figures, Demme also cast a couple of real FBI agents, Lawrence A Bonney and Lawrence T Wrentz, both of whom appear in the Quantico sequences.

Ted Tally's screenplay for *Silence of the Lambs*, which ran to four drafts, did an efficient job of reducing and streamlining the Thomas Harris novel. Tally dispensed with non-essential story details, such as the episode where Starling tangles with a WPIK-TV reporter and her crew, subsequently appearing in an unfavourable light on the television news. Tally also decided not to feature Hannibal Lecter's six-fingered hand, perhaps recalling William Hurt's less-than-believable extra toes in *Altered States* (1980). Focusing firmly on Clarice Starling, the screenplay lost a poignant subplot involving Jack Crawford's terminally ill wife, Bella. Lecter sends Crawford a letter of sympathy, written on his usual mauve notepaper. Lacking any kind of personal life in the film, Crawford is very much the driven, single-minded lawman. All references to Will Graham were dropped, as the character assumed prior knowledge of either *Red Dragon* or *Manhunter*.

Sharing Michael Mann's queasiness about Thomas Harris's more perverse details, Tally did a little toning-down in his script. The hardwood dildo fitted to a dummy sitting in Benjamin Raspail's vintage car is nowhere to be seen. Jame Gumb's abduction of Catherine Martin now ends with him cutting the dress off her unconscious body. Harris has the killer prod his prone victim's breasts with his fingers, to check 'their weight and resilience'. Harris also offers a very detailed account of the skinning, curing and working of human hides, not to mention Gumb's intricate 'dress pattern', for which Catherine is intended to provide some of the raw material.

Tally also reworked the character of Catherine Martin, removing elements that could render her less sympathetic to audiences. In the book, Starling discovers explicit photographs of Catherine, carefully hidden underneath her jewel box, depicting her having sex with an unidentified boyfriend. In the movie, there are polaroid photographs of another Buffalo Bill victim, Frederica Bimmel, looking mildly sheepish in her white underwear. It is implied that these pictures were taken by Jame Gumb himself, the latter a friend of Frederica before he became her murderer. Already dead, Bimmel has little need for viewer empathy. Searching Catherine Martin's room in the book, Starling also finds an old sheet of blotter acid, a largely obsolete form of LSD. Presumably, sexually active and exhibitionist drug users were not felt to be sufficiently deserving of Starling's or filmgoers' compassion. In the film, Catherine is introduced at the wheel of her car, singing along to 'American Girl' by Tom Petty and the Heartbreakers. As regular as Apple Pie.

Tally's clean-up job on Catherine Martin also removed the novel's only scene where Starling and Senator Martin meet. Reluctant to show the Senator her daughter's amateur pornography, Starling is firmly requested to hand it over. Starling leaves Catherine's bedroom resentful of the wealthy and powerful Senator Martin's tacit assumption that the FBI trainee from the humble background was trying to steal something.

Along with the explicit sexual activity, the *Lambs* screenplay also dropped some of the book's more scatological detail. Trussed up for his plane trip to Memphis, Lecter is obliged to relieve his bladder into a portable urinal, in full view of the waiting security men. Doctor Chilton is doubtless delighted, given his earlier assessment of Lecter: 'It's *indignity* you can't stand, Hannibal...' Tally also changed the bogus name that Lecter hands out to Senator Martin and her law enforcement cronies. In the book, the fake killer's name is 'Billy Rubin', which derives from bilirubin, the pigment in human bile that is also the main colouring agent in excrement. Presumably, Tally felt this pseudonym was both too gross and too tricksy for most audiences. The screenplay uses the joke name 'Louis Friend', an anagram of 'iron sulfide' or fool's gold. For whatever reason, the *National Tattler* of the book has become *The National Inquisitor*. The front page pinned to Jack Crawford's notice board bears the typically sensational headline: 'BILL SKINS FIFTH'.

The more striking sets built for *Silence of the Lambs* included Hannibal Lecter's glass-fronted cell, an unusual design that came about by chance. Demme originally intended to stick with the book's description of Lecter's prison, putting the Doctor behind white bars, just as he'd been in *Manhunter*. This presented the director with a major problem. During the extended Starling-Lecter dialogues, Demme wanted both characters' eyes to be visible at all times. Having experimented with various colours and thicknesses of bars, spaced at different distances, the production team could not arrive at a satisfactory result. Horizontal bars highlighted the eyes, as required, but obscured the rest of the features. Demme also felt that the standard cell bars would carry associations of a prison movie, with all its accompanying clichés, not the effect he wanted. As he explained to Saskia Baron: 'it would deprive these encounters of the unique, special nature that they were entitled to by virtue of how intense the characters in the scenes were.' According to the director, during yet another unsuccessful bar test, one of the production crew suggested putting Lecter behind a wall of reinforced glass, like a laboratory rat. If nothing else, this would ensure total visibility.

Having fought for the part of Clarice Starling, Jodie Foster spent two weeks at the FBI training academy in Quantico, Virginia, where co-stars Scott Glenn and Ted Levine also did background research. Jonathan Demme declined to join his actors, feeling that he saw quite enough horror in the daily news bulletins. Foster partly based the role of Starling on one of their guides, FBI special agent Mary Ann Kraus. Foster's determination to make her character as authentic as possible led her into harrowing territory, looking at grisly crime scene photographs and attending the autopsy of a female murder victim. It was reported that she declined to join Scott Glenn when John Douglas played him the taped screams of two young women as they were tortured to death. Douglas only played the tape for a minute.

Neither Foster nor Jonathan Demme wanted to make a film that could be accused of sanitising or glamorising murder. Foster also worried that *Lambs* might depict the regular FBI personnel in a negative light, bumbling and foolish. Though not uncritical of the FBI's operations in the service of the establishment, both Foster and Demme felt that the individual agents deserved to be shown as courageous, honourable professionals regularly faced with appalling, often dangerous situations.

Two weeks before the start of filming, Foster took a four-hour night-time tour of the Los Angeles morgue. 'You can't make a movie like *The Silence of the Lambs* which ultimately deals with the pain and horror of death and not have death in front of your eyes.' Foster was particularly interested in what happened to the human body after death, the way the hair and fingernails continue to grow for a short time while the rest of the body starts to shrivel and decay. For her own appearance in the film, Foster dyed her hair dark brown, subtly altering the established screen image that Jonathan Demme had wanted to avoid.

By most accounts, *Silence of the Lambs* proved to be a smooth, crisis-free shoot. Production commenced on 15 November 1989, while Anthony Hopkins was still busy filming *The Desperate Hours* with Michael Cimino in Utah. Hopkins's prior work commitment did not stop him from contributing to *Lambs* while still working for Cimino. Requiring Hopkins's voice for the final scene where Lecter phones Starling, Demme arranged for the actor to be linked to the *Lambs* set to record the dialogue.

The locations for *Silence of the Lambs* included Bellaire, Ohio; Perryopolis, Pennsylvania, and Pittsburgh, Pennsylvania, home of zombie movie maestro and *Lambs* bit player George Romero. The final scene, where successful escapee Hannibal Lecter calls Clarice, was shot at Bimini Airport on North Bimini Island, in the Bahamas. The winter shoot often meant dawn starts in freezing January weather. The less picturesque locations included the Westinghouse factory complex in Turtle Creek, just outside Pittsburgh. An abandoned turbine factory, the building was basically a huge steel shed.

"IT MATTERS, MR CRAWFORD"

According to Buddy Foster, Jodie Foster's older brother and unauthorised biographer, the star didn't initially rate her director very highly. Shooting Foster's first dialogue scene, where Crawford informs Starling that Lecter has driven a fellow inmate to suicide, Demme criticised his star's accent, which sounded more Los Angeles than West Virginia. Foster responded that Starling would exhibit only a trace of accent, having strived for years to get rid of it. This didn't satisfy Demme, who felt that Foster was just speaking in her standard voice. According to the director, Foster got it right on take two, yet this initial difference seems to have stirred resentment in the star. Part way through the shoot, Foster supposedly made public her feeling that Jonathan Demme had mishandled the film. She listed scenes which needed to be re-shot and production personnel who needed to be replaced. Reportedly, Demme didn't take kindly to this open criticism and informed Foster in no uncertain terms that she wouldn't take over his film. There does appear to have been some form of heated exchange between director and star, stemming from Foster's inability to trust Demme for the first few weeks of filming. Having encountered more than one film director she utterly loathed, the star felt convinced that Demme's relaxed, affable manner concealed a hard, manipulative tyrant just waiting to pounce.

Whatever their initial differences, Foster's personal commitment to the role of Starling and her weeks of gruelling background research proved invaluable to the director: 'She helped me understand the character better... she connected me with some of the scenes I became preoccupied with in the movie.' Anthony Hopkins also impressed Demme, the actor one hundred percent in character before his first scene was shot: 'Tony was uncanny. He just turned up as Lecter.' According to Michael Feeney Callan, Hopkins had copious notes on how Lecter looked, acted and moved. The slick hair and boiler suit already existed as drawings in the margins of his script.

Supposedly, Foster didn't get to meet her co-star on set until they were preparing to shoot the cellblock scenes, Hopkins behind the glass barrier in his Lecter costume. Departing from the script, Hopkins began to ad-lib, mocking Foster's accent. This real-life version of the famed Lecter mind games did not initially go down well with Foster: 'I wanted to cry or smack him. I was so upset.' Hopkins/Lecter sneering at Foster/Starling as the cameras rolled could easily be taken as a sly personal attack, as Foster later explained: 'It was a moment where the boundary got very fuzzy between me and Clarice.' Despite this unnerving start, both Demme and Foster soon realised that Hopkins's apparently mean-spirited improvisation was ideal for his character: 'It was the perfect thing for Lecter to do, because Clarice has been hiding her rural accent, trying to... escape her origins.' Foster compared Lecter's intimate interrogation of Starling to 'psychological therapy'. Many of the production team, Foster included, found Hopkins as Lecter a disquieting presence, glad that the actor remained behind reinforced glass most of the time.

Hopkins rated his co-star as 'very cool, calm and collected and very accessible', entirely free from the eccentricities and tantrums displayed by Shirley MacLaine and Mickey Rourke. He especially liked her close-up reactions to Lecter: 'it just shows on her face, she doesn't have to act it.' Hopkins recognised in Foster something he valued very highly, a committed fellow professional: 'She learns her lines, does her job and goes home.'

Another of Hopkins's improvisations during the first prison scene caused less upset. As Lecter smells Starling's perfume, Hopkins stood up on his toes to sniff her through the ventilation holes in his glass-fronted cell. This might seem a logical course of action, yet neither Ted Tally nor Demme had thought of it. The director later expressed his appreciation that Hopkins's ad-lib had 'turned that into a far more special moment than it would otherwise have been.'

The Silence of the Lambs wrapped on 1 March 1990, the cast and crew well satisfied with their efforts. Orion's relationship with Demme was sound enough for the studio to take a hands-off approach throughout the filming and post-production. Foster was particularly impressed: 'Orion didn't interfere at all, where there are a lot of people that would have liked to make... something which would have been less risky and much less interesting.'

Unlike *Manhunter*, *The Silence of the Lambs* did not undergo any major post-production tampering. Demme delivered a director's cut that ran 118 minutes, just within the agreed two-hour running time. While Michael Mann had to make at least one key change to his film, Demme lost nothing of significance to the cutting room floor. The lock-up garage scene where Starling finds a severed head pickled in a jar underwent a little tightening up. Some dialogue, mostly lifted from the original book, was cut, along with Starling tucking her trousers into her socks to prevent 'rodent intrusion'. Demme also removed shots of Starling breaking into a locked car with a piece of wire, perhaps wary of copycat behaviour.

Other cuts included Starling checking out a handgun from the Quantico armoury, prior to the Elk River trip with Jack Crawford. The FBI instructor who issues the weapon rather needlessly points out that 'A floater's no day at the beach, Starling.' On the drive back from Elk River, Starling discusses with Crawford the possibility of 'Buffalo Bill' having placed moth cocoons in the throats of other victims. Starling also argues that Lecter must know the identity of the killer. Demme dropped this expository dialogue in favour of Starling chiding Crawford for putting on a sexist front when dealing with the local cops: 'It matters, Mr Crawford'. As Doctor Chilton eavesdrops on Lecter and Starling's subsequent discussion of Jame Gumb, Demme originally had Lecter give out more information on the killer, while the camera prowled through Gumb's old dark house, ending at the edge of the pit.

One scene cut from *Lambs* in its entirety featured Roger Corman's big moment as FBI Director Hayden Burke. Following Lecter's Memphis break-out, Starling and Crawford are summoned to Burke's office. Held responsible for the bloody fiasco (which seems a little unreasonable), Crawford is placed on leave, losing command of the case, while Starling is suspended from the Quantico Academy, pending an official enquiry. The dialogue plays up the tension between Crawford and self-serving Department of Justice official Paul Krendler (Ron Vawter), who barely appears in the release print. Efficiently staged and acted, this episode plays like the cliché hand-in-your-badge scene of a thousand cop dramas, complete with a firm-but-sympathetic-boss ('I can promise you'll get a fair hearing'), and a sniping subordinate.

If nothing else, *The Silence of the Lambs* must be one of the few mainstream Hollywood films where the leading lady has sperm thrown in her face by a gibbering lunatic. Jonathan Demme has described this semen-chucking moment as 'One of the most distasteful shots I've ever been involved with,' a mainstream version of the porn industry's ever-popular 'cum shot'. This unsavoury close encounter aside, Clarice Starling is treated with sympathy and respect throughout the film. While Starling does not appear in every scene of *Lambs*, Demme wanted to tell the film's story from her point of view. Audiences might be drawn to Lecter's dark wit, but they would identify with the nervous yet determined young woman he both taunts and enlightens. Aiming to stage Starling's scenes from her viewpoint wherever possible, Demme and director of photography Tak Fujimoto employed a subjective camera, to 'force identification with the character... show exactly what she sees in every single scene.' Demme claims that *Lambs* made the most extensive use of the subjective camera since the Raymond Chandler screen adaptation *The Lady in the Lake* (1946). Here, director-star Robert Montgomery chose to stage the entire film from Philip Marlowe's point of view, the character only seen as a reflection in a mirror. Montgomery's use of the technique was generally dismissed as a pointless gimmick that distracted and alienated audiences. Aware of this danger, Demme and his crew decided to stick with their less intensive approach, 'because the potential was there to up the emotional ante quite a bit.' The director found the subjective camera shots relatively easy to stage, Tak Fujimoto simply duplicating Jodie Foster's viewpoint as observed during the rehearsals. Editing in the point-of-view shots during post-production also proved fairly straightforward, each one preceded by a close-up that clearly identified the person doing the looking. Preparing to film the first Hannibal Lecter scene, Demme asked Anthony Hopkins how he thought the character should be introduced to audiences. The actor endorsed his director's preferred visual style, suggesting that Starling, and the subjective camera, should just approach the cell in a naturalistic fashion.

The brief flashback scenes in *Lambs* are perhaps less successful. Demme wanted to include pivotal moments from Starling's childhood, so that 'Her past would be a certain part of the movie.' Following the first Lecter encounter, we see the young Clarice greet her Deputy father on his return from work, her bond with him unusually strong after the death of her mother (alive, if not particularly well, in the Thomas Harris novel). During the Elk River autopsy sequence, the adult Clarice imagines being back at her father's funeral service, the latter gunned down by two robbers while out on night patrol. Demme originally intended to show a third, more surreal flashback, where Starling flees the farm with a lamb. Entering the barn where the screaming lambs are being slaughtered, Starling encounters a farmhand. The man turns around to look at her, revealing Hannibal Lecter's face.

Like the camera, the music used for *The Silence of the Lambs* focuses firmly on Clarice Starling. Looking to underline the strong emotional depth of the character, composer Howard Shore used electronic ambiences and slowed-down whale calls to complement the standard orchestral scoring. For the scenes down in Lecter's cell block, Demme and his sound editor added submarine noises to emphasise the feeling of Starling being isolated in the murky, hostile depths. Having read through Ted Tally's script, Shore watched Demme's early edits of the film to get the feel of Starling's long journey through the darkness. The composer took it as a compliment when female musicians who'd seen *Lambs* told him the score affected them emotionally. The identification with Starling was total. Film director Sidney Lumet praised Howard Shore's score for *The Silence of the Lambs* on the grounds that he could 'feel' it. Appreciative of Shore's contribution to *Lambs*' overall success, Jonathan Demme used the composer on his next film, *Philadelphia* (1993).

For all the grimness of its theme, *The Silence of the Lambs* is a slick, highly commercial piece of filmmaking. Jonathan Demme employs a fluid visual style, making regular use of the gliding steadicam. By contrast, the predominantly grey and brown tones lend the film a sombre quality light years away from *Manhunter*'s often acid-bright colour schemes. Compared to the director's earlier works, such as *Citizens Band* or *Melvin and Howard*, there is, arguably, something impersonal about the movie. A big fan of the Thomas Harris book, Demme didn't want to impose an *auteur* 'signature' on the film version, as Michael Mann had done with *Manhunter*, feeling that a 'slavish loyalty to the text' would produce the best results. This is debatable, and *Lambs* does have the air of a movie carefully calculated and assembled for multi-level appeal to the Thomas Harris fans, the horror-thriller crowd and the wider cinema audience. For all its minor flaws, notably the studio-imposed re-edit, *Manhunter* plays like a movie devised and controlled by one filmmaker, rather than a taste-and-trend conscious committee. The screen credit 'A Michael Mann Film' seems accurate. *Silence of the Lambs* does not feel like a Jonathan Demme film in the same way. Discussing his approach to 'high-concept' filmmaking in a 1998 television interview, Demme quoted Roger Corman: 'As a director, you're 40, 45 per cent artist and 60, 55 per cent businessman. Never forget that.'

The Corman factor surfaced in Demme's earlier conversation with David Thompson. 'I feel that all films are exploitation films. To one degree or another, almost all films finally adhere to the Corman policy.' Demme cites Francis Coppola's *Godfather* saga as the classic example: 'the most expensive Roger Corman films ever made'. *The Silence of the Lambs* certainly offers the action and muted social statement central to the Roger Corman formula. The humour, mostly provided by Hannibal Lecter, veers towards the jet black. The sex is non-existent, at least in any conventional fashion. Aside from Jame Gumb's creepy disco diva turn, the only nudity in the film is that of the carefully framed corpses, horribly mutilated young women undergoing the first stages of bodily decay.

Finding the right approach to the depiction of graphic gore in *Lambs* was one of Jonathan Demme's main concerns during pre-production. The director had been impressed by Tobe Hooper's rural cannibal horror hit *The Texas Chain Saw Massacre* (1974), which generated relentless terror and tension with almost no onscreen blood. Demme felt *Lambs* should strive for a similar atmosphere, the horror lying largely in what the viewer didn't get to see. Along with Ted Tally, Tak Fujimoto and designer Kristi Zea, the director tried to arrive at an approach that was faithful to Harris's book without sickening the audience. Accepting that much of the novel's power derived from the horrific, clinically described detail, Demme didn't want to be accused of watering down the material in the name of good taste. Following Ted Tally's approach in the script, the director opted to show some extremely graphic material in brief, almost split-second shots. There would be no lingering close-ups of flayed faces or bitten flesh. A close shot of Gumb carefully sewing human skin is gone before the audience really registers what has been shown. In the climactic scene where Starling corners Gumb, a highly detailed rotted corpse can be glimpsed in a bathtub for barely a second before the lights suddenly go off. Demme did not want to pander to the appetites of sado-voyeurs. 'We felt that this definitely had the potential for being revolting, and we didn't want to go that far.'

To keep his options open during post-production, the director shot more gory footage than he felt he would need, which turned out to be a good thing. When *The Silence of the Lambs* previewed, Demme realised that he'd underestimated the audience's appetite for graphic carnage. Scenes intended to make the viewer cringe didn't have the desired impact. Demme and editor Craig McKay returned to the cutting room and restored some of the discarded gore, 'until finally we felt we'd achieved that delicate balance.' During the garage scene, there was now a lingering close-up of Benjamin Raspail's severed head, modelled on that of co-producer Edward Saxon. Despite the quantities of blood and flayed human flesh, Demme did not find this material the toughest to shoot. The director hated filming the disturbing scenes where Catherine Martin is trapped, begging and screaming, in Gumb's basement dungeon. While *Caged Heat* had dwelt on forced confinement and torment 17 years earlier, *The Silence of the Lambs* took this idea to new extremes.

While *Lambs* sold itself mainly on the serial killer and cannibal elements, the film gains a surprising amount of potency from what the British Board of Film Classification refers to as 'sexual swear words'. If 'fuck' is now commonplace in mainstream cinema, the word 'cunt' is still relatively rare. Repeating 'Multiple' Miggs's abuse, 'I can smell your cunt', for Lecter's benefit, Starling pronounces the word clearly, but quietly. Just to hear Jodie Foster say this seems oddly unsettling. Barely acceptable in the cinema, this kind of language was not going to make it to American network television. The specially prepared American 'tv version' of *Lambs*, screened once in the UK by ITV, redubbed the more extreme lines to typically incoherent effect. The line became 'I can smell your scent'. The tv version also used a different take of Miggs's sperm-throwing, the fluid no longer visible. For all his loathing of discourtesy, Lecter further tests both Starling's and the audience's sensitivities. Starling tells Lecter the story of her brief two-month stay at the Montana ranch, from which she tried to flee with a single lamb ('he was so heavy'). Lecter asks Starling if the owner sexually abused her: 'Did the rancher make you perform fellatio? Did he sodomise you?' Lecter subsequently sketches Clarice holding a happy lamb, prior to ordering a lamb chop dinner.

For all its in-depth research and technical skill, *The Silence of the Lambs* does contain a few mistakes, minor and otherwise. During the showdown between Starling and Gumb, a shadow is briefly visible in the supposedly pitch dark room. A small flaw, yet one which apparently troubled Jodie Foster at the 1992 Academy Awards ceremony as she awaited the announcement of the winner for Best Actress. There are also blatant breaches of standard FBI procedure. John Douglas singled out the garage scene as one glaring example, where Starling crawls underneath a jammed door to explore a dark storage room with no back-up. The fingerprinting techniques used during the Elk River autopsy are also incorrect and could lead to a real FBI agent being dismissed and possibly prosecuted.

Jonathan Demme had hoped that Thomas Harris would agree to view the finished film and offer his comments. Harris declined, ostensibly on the grounds that he didn't want to see his characters 'stolen' from him by the actors. The author cited the example of bestselling espionage novelist John Le Carré and his most famous character, retired spymaster George Smiley. Having seen Alec Guinness make the character his own in the BBC adaptations of *Tinker, Tailor, Soldier, Spy* (1979) and *Smiley's People* (1982), Le Carré felt unable to write about Smiley anymore. That said, Thomas Harris does appear to have seen *Manhunter* and, according to Brian Cox, appreciated the actor's performance as Hannibal Lecktor. More to the point, this film adaptation didn't prevent Harris from writing two more books featuring Lecter.

"THAT WAS GOOD"

Disregarding the later Academy Award hype, the stars of *Silence of the Lambs* are undeniably forceful on screen. Modesty aside, Jodie Foster rates her performance as Clarice Starling as '...one of the most true and progressive portrayals of a female hero ever.' Ted Tally's first draft script introduced Starling in the midst of a mock hostage rescue exercise at Quantico, a sequence now seen much later in the film. Jonathan Demme chose to show Starling on her own, completing an FBI assault course, also the first scene to be shot. Running through misty woodland, prime slasher movie territory, Starling pulls herself up a steep bank with a rope. Demme cuts to close-ups of Starling's determined, alert face as she jogs along, her strength of character established before she utters a word. There is a series of signs on a tree behind Starling, reading: 'HURT', 'AGONY', 'PAIN', 'LOVE IT'. This 'encouragement' to FBI students is quite genuine, Demme shooting the opening sequence in the grounds of the Quantico Academy.

Inside the Quantico building complex, Demme provides a neat visual summation of Starling's struggle to succeed in a male-dominated institution. Walking into an elevator still wearing her grey running sweatshirt, the out-of-breath Starling is surrounded by much taller male students, all dressed in the same bright red t-shirts. Staring at the elevator ceiling, Starling looks quite capable of holding her own. During the later scene at the Grieg Funeral Home, in Elk River, West Virginia, Starling is encircled and stared at by the local police officers. Starling subsequently orders these same men out of the autopsy room, cannily employing her strongest Virginia accent for the only time in the film.

Starling's relationship with Jack Crawford is tentative, nervous and apparently respectful. That said, Jodie Foster attributes Crawford with less-than-honourable motives for sending Starling to Lecter. The FBI veteran knows full well that Lecter will get inside Starling's head. He gives her the mission because he doesn't dare confront the 'mind-fucking' Doctor himself. This undermines the theory that Crawford represents the Good Father vying with Hannibal Lecter's Bad Father to take the place of Clarice's deceased real father and steer her down the correct path.

Though rightfully concerned for her safety at times, Starling rarely looks vulnerable prior to the Jame Gumb showdown. During Starling's second visit to Lecter, Demme employs an effective overhead shot of the rain-drenched agent looking warily into the cell's sliding tray, only to discover that it contains a bath towel. Starling doesn't take too many chances.

Starling's approach to the 'Buffalo Bill' investigation is hardly detached and clinical, as Foster explained: '...the more my character gets into the work, she experiences a kind of exhilaration. She's excited. She wants to get inside the skull of the man who did this.' Starling's professional elation is always tempered by a sensitive appreciation of the appalling acts committed. She compares the crime scene pictures of Frederica Bimmel's flayed corpse with her high school graduation photograph, a standard touch that nevertheless conveys a sense of loss and waste. Starling seems to identify with Bimmel, whose rural neighbourhood reminds the FBI trainee of her own childhood home. One of Bimmel's friends, stuck in a dead-end job, expresses heartfelt envy at Starling's 'brilliant' career. During the Elk River autopsy, Starling is obviously disturbed, and moved, by the sight of the woman's corpse. The scene's grimmest moment comes when male FBI Agent Terry (Chuck Aber) inserts a special camera into the mouth of the corpse to photograph the teeth. There is no dignity in 'wrongful death'.

The autopsy scene climaxes with the discovery of a moth cocoon in the victim's throat. Starling's subsequent encounter with two insect specialists provides one of the film's few light moments. The good-natured, if eccentric Pilcher (Paul Lazar) asks Starling if she'd be interested in a date. Amused by this direct approach, Starling replies with an affable, if non-committal 'Are you hitting on me, Doc?' Demme also throws in a striking low angle composition, Roden (Dan Butler) flanked by Starling and Pilcher as he examines the Death's Head moth, the trio surrounded by darkness. Pilcher is later glimpsed at Starling's graduation ceremony, presumably at her invitation.

During the endless round of media interviews that accompanied *Lambs*' release, Jodie Foster offered the following assessment of Starling: 'She's such a complex character – somebody who's all about what she's not admitting.' Treating Jack Crawford with near reverence during their first meeting, Starling is soon offering her bluntly honest

opinion of his behaviour. Foster particularly liked the scene where
Starling chides Crawford for putting on a sexist front to win the
confidence of a small-town sheriff.

Foster suggests that Starling recognises a common bond between
herself and Lecter: 'She is compelled the same way that Hannibal Lecter
is compelled.' Foster also feels that Starling and Lecter end up with 'a
quite beautiful, quite intimate, respectful relationship.' If so, the first
encounter does not start very well. Taking Starling in with a casual
glance, Lecter offers a fairly damning verdict, dismissing Clarice as 'a
well-scrubbed hustling rube. With a little taste.' Tired of the back-seat
fumblings with small-town boys, Starling dreamed only of escape and, in
Lecter's phrase, 'advancement', leading to a career at the FBI. Lecter's
attitude to Starling seems dismissive at first, the Doctor turning his back
on her with the amused contempt: 'You fly back to school now, little
Starling.' Lecter appears to do a complete turnaround when Starling
is pelted with sperm by Multiple Miggs: 'discourtesy is unspeakably
ugly to me'. As opposed to biting out eyeballs and devouring livers.
Incidentally, it's arguable that Lecter gives Starling the most vital clue to
catching Gumb on their first meeting. His sketches of Florence are from
the vantage point of the Belvedere Hotel. Belvedere is also the name of
Jame Gumb's home town.

While Ted Tally wanted the Starling-Lecter scenes to play as
seductions, the underlying sense of uneasiness is always there. During
the third Starling-Lecter exchange, Demme places Starling's intent face
in medium close-up at the centre of the frame. Lecter's blurred reflection
lingers on the left of the screen, haunting Starling like a mocking ghost.
As with Will Graham, there is a teacher-pupil aspect to the relationship,
Lecter looking for signs of intelligent reasoning. He seems impressed
by Starling's part in Jack Crawford's attempt to fool him with a phoney
offer: 'That was *good*'. At the end of their last encounter, in Memphis,
Lecter brushes Clarice's finger with his own, the Doctor's only contact
with human flesh prior to sinking his teeth into a guard's face.

There is nothing remotely intimate or respectful about Clarice
Starling's brief relationship with Jame Gumb, who lacks even a shred
of Francis Dollarhyde's pathos. As Gumb, Ted Levine speaks with
a deep, nasal, slightly strangled voice that underlines his disturbed

mentality. It is easy to see why *Silence of the Lamb*'s depiction of Gumb drew accusations of blatant homophobia. Gumb tends towards camp mannerisms, pursing his lips as he pets his clipped poodle, Precious. Gumb also boasts a fine selection of necklaces and a nipple ring, giving the latter a sharp tug during his make-up routine (Ted Levine was fitted with a prosthetic nipple for the scene). As Gumb puts on the lipstick, Demme cuts to a *Rocky Horror*-style close-up of his mouth, which utters such musings as 'Would you fuck me? I'd fuck me.' Gumb likes to work naked at his sewing. Dancing and singing along to pop music in his favourite female scalp, Gumb looks like a nightmare drag queen on karaoke night, complete with a disco glitterball in the background. Draped in red material, the otherwise naked Gumb stretches out his arms like another *Red Dragon* wannabe, penis pushed between his legs to simulate a female pudenda. Getting in touch with the supposedly feminine side of himself does not appear to make Gumb a better person. As Catherine Martin screams from the bottom of the well, Gumb jeeringly mocks her cries, just as the cannibal family in *Texas Chain Saw Massacre* taunts unwilling dinner guest Sally Hardesty. Both women are regarded as mere 'things', sources of clothing and nourishment.

Hannibal Lecter's assessment of Jame Gumb is essentially a rehash of Will Graham's take on Francis Dollarhyde in *Manhunter*: 'Our Billy wasn't born a criminal, Clarice. He was made one through years of systematic abuse. Billy hates his own identity, you see.' It's interesting that Jonathan Demme regarded the lack of background explanation for Gumb's behaviour as a flaw in the film, and by implication the book: 'My one disappointment with the movie is that I failed to accentuate child abuse enough.' *Lambs* offers hints that the adult Gumb is both an ultra patriot and a neo Nazi, swastikas and American flags decorating his house. There is another American flag draping the vintage car in the lock-up garage, perhaps placed there by Gumb along with Benjamin Raspail's severed head. Demme attributes the latter touch to production designer Kristi Zea, along with the *Psycho*-style stuffed owl that looms out of the darkness at Starling ('little Starling').

The Starling-Gumb encounter came on Jodie Foster's last shooting day for *Lambs*, the cast and crew working a gruelling 22-hour shift. Jonathan Demme initially wrong foots the audience by crosscutting between Jack Crawford's FBI strike team ringing the suspect's doorbell and Gumb being interrupted by a specially rigged door alarm. Unfortunately, the FBI and SWAT officers find themselves storming an empty house, while Gumb answers his front door to be greeted by Clarice Starling. This technically accomplished sleight of hand would work better if the film didn't clearly signpost a Starling-Gumb stand-off.

Questioning Gumb about Frederica Bimmel, Starling quickly spots a telltale moth on a reel of thread. In Jodie Foster's opinion, Gumb has already given himself away with the line: 'Was she a great big fat person?' In this instance, size does matter. Starling's solo pursuit of Gumb is another flagrant breach of FBI procedure, Demme claiming that the character is led by 'humanistic impulses'. In the Thomas Harris book, Clarice plausibly reasons that Gumb will kill Catherine out of sheer frustration and spite if she delays the rescue to summon help. Confronted with human skin outfits on dressmaking dummies and an arm sticking out of a bathtub, Starling remains admirably focused. Gumb slips on his nightvision glasses, represented by a green filter, turns off the lights and prepares for the kill.

Demme didn't want the showdown between Starling and Gumb to carry a feeling of triumph when the latter drops dead. The director felt satisfied that audiences didn't cheer Starling's gunplay. Violent death should not be a source of celebration, even in the case of a butchering psychopath like Jame Gumb. As Demme explained to Saskia Baron: '...even the idea of an essentially good person murdering an essentially bad person is not that palatable: you wish that there could be another solution to a confrontation like that.' The director also wanted to keep the audience on tenterhooks until the next scene, where Starling is shown safely back at the FBI academy: 'the feelings which might have been released by a cheer would be channelled into a more emotional place.'

This whole sequence, which should have been a *tour de force* to match Lecter's escape, instead demonstrates the problems inherent in faithful book-to-film adaptations. In the novel, Thomas Harris makes it clear why Gumb doesn't just shoot Starling in the head as she blunders through the darkness. Coveting Starling's 'glorious' hair, the killer is no hurry to risk damaging this prize scalp. Excited at the chance of hunting his 'prey' in the pitch-black room, Gumb is also intrigued by the novelty of stalking an armed target. Aside from a subjective shot of Gumb's hand reaching out to Starling's hair and face, the movie doesn't convey this. Jodie Foster argues that Gumb simply doesn't regard Starling, a mere 'thing', as a serious threat, service weapon or not, but this is hard to discern from the film itself. Thomas Harris gives Gumb's death a certain poignancy. As a Malaysian Luna Moth settles on the mortally wounded Gumb's infrared light, the dying killer gets his last words: 'How... does... it feel... to be... so beautiful?' There is a sense of sad, wistful longing here, lending Gumb a strange sense of dignity lacking in the film.

Jodie Foster's passion for the role of Clarice Starling is evident throughout *Silence of the Lambs*. Given her fight to get the part, it seems churlish to criticise Foster's earnest performance, or point out that she's a little old for a trainee FBI agent. Her accent, initially criticised by Jonathan Demme, is perhaps overdone, Starling at times sounding like a close female relative of Elvis Presley. Foster herself seemed in no doubt that the character represented a major achievement for movies in particular and womankind in general. 'She faces things about herself that are ugly and while facing them she solves the crime. This is hero mythology and that has never been applied to a female character in film, ever.' Foster went further, suggesting that Hollywood now had a duty to follow her precedent: 'It's the responsibility of the studios in some ways to start developing female heroes and educating the audiences about them.' This is an admirable sentiment, yet characters of Starling's calibre are likely to remain rare, even in the female action hero subgenre. For every Ellen Ripley or Clarice Starling, there is a Barb Wire or Red Sonja.

"WE'VE NEVER COME ACROSS ANYTHING LIKE HIM, THANK GOD."

Along with Jonathan Demme, and Roger Corman, Anthony Hopkins felt that evil characters should always have an attractive quality, surface or otherwise. At the same time, the actor describes his version of Hannibal Lecter as 'a brilliant, complex piece of machinery, a killing machine, a killing instrument'. Hopkins even suggests that the Doctor is, to some extent, acting involuntarily: '...a man who is locked in the monstrosity of his own mind'. Aside from the HAL computer influence, Hopkins characterised Lecter's voice as 'a combination of Truman Capote and Katharine Hepburn', which would probably not flatter either.

Anyone who has seen *The Silence of the Lambs* will recall the actor's gleeful, yet controlled delivery of the famous line: 'A census taker once tried to test me. I ate his liver with some fava beans and a nice chianti.' Hopkins follows the wine with an ad-libbed slurp. Jodie Foster's Clarice Starling looks understandably freaked by this relished admission. Screenwriter Ted Tally deserves some credit here, as *Lambs'* best-known, most-quoted line of dialogue is changed from the original book, where Lecter admits to eating the man's liver with 'a big Amarone'.

Anyone doubting Lecter's dark charisma and intellectual brilliance need only compare him with his appointed keeper. Doctor Chilton, a grade 'A' piece of slime in Thomas Harris's book, is even less appealing in the movie. Slick of hair and tongue, Chilton's level of personal and professional incompetence verges on the risible. Ted Tally's script gives Chilton Jack Crawford's response to Starling's question about Lecter: 'He's a monster'. Having supposedly studied Lecter for years, Chilton is no closer to understanding his prisoner. Tally also has Chilton leave his metal pen behind in Lecter's cell, instead of the anonymous researcher in the book. Demme needlessly zooms in on the pen, ensuring that the audience grasps its significance. In both cases, the pen is transformed by Lecter into a handcuff key. Talking to the television news cameras in Memphis, Chilton boasts of his 'unique insight into Lecter's mind'. This man is just asking to be eaten.

Hannibal Lecter's all-important entrance in *Lambs* is well handled by Demme and Hopkins. Brian Cox's Doctor Lecktor lay slumped on his bunk, face to the wall, apparently oblivious to visitor Will Graham. Hopkins opts to have Lecter standing up, alert and expectant, facing the glass wall of his cell as Starling approaches. His smart blue boiler suit looks freshly laundered, as if Lecter was dressed for company. Lecter is curiously reptilian in his steady, deliberate movements, his eyes always staring, probing. Framed largely in close-up, the Starling-Lecter exchanges to have a real intensity. Relishing the chance to probe another subject, Lecter licks the front page of the questionnaire brought by the trainee agent.

ABOVE: Anthony Hopkins as Dr Hannibal Lecter in *Silence of the Lambs* (1991).

ABOVE: Jack Crawford (Scott Glenn) and Clarice Starling (Jodie Foster) in Washington DC. *The Silence of the Lambs* (1991).

ABOVE: Trainee FBI agent Clarice Starling meets fully qualified psychopath Dr Hannibal Lecter in *The Silence of the Lambs* (1991).

LEFT: Dr Chilton (Anthony Heald) taunts Lecter (Anthony Hopkins) in *The Silence of the Lambs* (1991).

ABOVE: Jack Crawford (Scott Glenn), Hannibal Lecter
(Anthony Hopkins) and Clarice Starling (Jodie Foster).
The Silence of the Lambs (1991).

ABOVE: Jodie Foster as trainee FBI agent Clarice Starling in *The Silence of the Lambs* (1991).

LEFT: Jame Gumb (Ted Levine), aka celebrity serial killer 'Buffalo Bill', in *The Silence of the Lambs* (1991).

ABOVE: Anthony Hopkins signs a copy of *The Silence of the Lambs*.

LEFT: Hopkins with his Best Actor BAFTA award, March 1992.

LEFT: Hopkins celebrates his Oscar triumph.

ABOVE: Anthony Hopkins declares a full house
outside the Odeon cinema in London's Leicester Square.

For all the psychological banter, *Silence of the Lambs* depicts
Hannibal Lecter as a full-fledged supernatural monster. As Starling and
Chilton approach the entrance to Lecter's corridor, the screen is suffused
with red light. This is a descent into hell. Howard Shore's score features
disembodied voices that merge with the cries of inmates, the wails of
the damned. In Thomas Harris's books, and the *Manhunter* film, Lecter
occupies a stark, clinical white cell. Demme places the character in a
medieval dungeon, dark, dank and full of ghoulish promise. This is
gothic horror territory, bearing about as much resemblance to reality
as Castle Dracula in the Universal and Hammer films. Similarly, the
humble, if reinforced, Memphis police cell of the novel becomes a vast,
elaborate cage centred in the middle of a large room. Demme shot these scenes
in the suitably austere Soldiers and Sailors Memorial Hall, in Allegheny.

The 'creature of the night' angle is reinforced during Starling's
second visit to Lecter. The Doctor is glimpsed in near darkness, his
eyes reflecting sinister points of light. To emphasise Lecter's unnatural
appearance, Demme and cameraman Tak Fujimoto employ the same
kind of downlighting used by Michael Mann and Dante Spinotti in
Manhunter. *Lambs* also elaborates on Lecter's facial restraints, the
equipment that prevents him from biting out more tongues and eyes.
Trussed up in his cell while Chilton gloats, the Doctor's lower face is
fitted with a wire guard, his nose pressed down like a stockinged bank
robber's. For the Memphis trip, Lecter wears a designer mask that covers
his face from nose to chin, the broad nose-piece giving him a bestial
look. In the novel, Lecter is simply decked out with a standard issue ice
hockey goalminder's mask. It is possible that Demme and his costume
designer felt this would be too close to *Friday the Thirteenth*'s mass
murderer Jason Vorhees, who had worn a hockey mask since Part III
of the series. The mask would also have obscured Anthony Hopkins's
face. The actor had his own ideas about how Lecter should look in the
Memphis scenes. The costume designer intended to outfit Hopkins in
an orange boiler suit, clothing normally associated with supervillains'
henchmen in the James Bond films. Hopkins wanted to be dressed in white,
feeling that it lent Lecter both a deceptive serenity and a clinical coldness.

While Hannibal Lecter's dialogues with Clarice Starling offer an
element of enlightenment along with the snide and painful personal

remarks, other characters get only verbal abuse. The film rewrites Lecter's brief, if memorable, exchange of words with Senator Ruth Martin. In the original Thomas Harris version, the Doctor scores points for sly cruelty, mocking the maternal instincts of a mother who fears her only child is about to meet with the worst, grisliest fate imaginable:

> LECTER
> Did you nurse Catherine?

> SENATOR MARTIN
> Pardon me? Did I...

> LECTER
> Did you breast-feed her?

> SENATOR MARTIN
> Yes.

> LECTER
> Thirsty work, isn't it...?

In the movie, Lecter responds to the Senator's affirmation with 'Toughened your nipples, didn't it?', which seems crude by comparison. Ted Tally's script elaborates on this nipple angle, Lecter unwilling to let a good thing go: 'Amputate a man's leg and he can still feel it tickling. Tell me, ma'am. When your little girl is on the slab, where will it tickle you?'

Confined to a cell much of the time, Lecter gets to star in the film's most accomplished set-piece, the Memphis jailbreak. Listening to Bach's 'Goldberg Variations' on tape, the Doctor leaves a copy of *Bon Appetit* magazine on display, a hint of things to come. His two police guards don't stand a chance once the handcuff key does its work. Demme employs a striking low-angle track-in shot as Lecter, face bloodied, methodically beats Lieutenant Boyle (Charles Napier) to death with his own nightstick. Pausing while he listens to the Bach, Lecter returns to business: 'Ready when you are, Sergeant Pembry.' Boyle's eviscerated body ends up hanging from the cage, carefully backlit, his arms raised in a pseudo-winged effect. Demme appears to be paying homage to *Red Dragon*, as well as giving his favourite supporting actor an unforgettable exit. The police believe they've got Lecter trapped in a lift shaft, yet the audience knows by now that the Doctor is too smart to be so easily cornered. The sequence is undermined only by an implausible payoff: Lecter escapes from the building by disguising himself with Sergeant Pembry's uniform and carefully severed face. This uncomfortably literal 'face-mask', which passes the scrutiny of the police, the SWAT team and the ambulance crew, defies belief. When Leatherface obliges his unfortunate 'girlfriend' Stretch to don a recently detached male face in *Texas Chain Saw Massacre Part 2*, she doesn't suddenly take on the man's appearance.

Anthony Hopkins has described his performance in *Silence of the Lambs* as 'theatrical', which is often taken as a euphemism for overstated or even rampant ham. Hopkins's curious, much imitated accent for Hannibal Lecter resembles a cross between a courtly Southern gentleman and Roddy McDowall's spooky older brother. The actor claimed he didn't want to be become obsessive about perfecting the voice, concentrating his energies on getting the overall character right. This is fair enough, yet at times Hopkins's vocal performance seems careless, lapsing into an English accent on certain words. An effective display of cultured villainy, his Hannibal Lecter is also a shameless piece of show-off acting, demanding the viewer's attention with all the subtlety of a bite in the face. Reviewing Anthony Hopkins's performance in *Magic*, *Observer* critic Philip French suggested that the star was 'a fine actor in danger of becoming an irritatingly mannered one... crazy too soon and too obviously.' While Hopkins's portrayal of Lecter is far superior to his demented ventriloquist, it displays a lack of confidence in the character's inherent fascination. Brian Cox's Lecktor affected to be deeply uninterested in *Manhunter*'s other characters. Hopkins's Lecter is always performing the psycho role, whether for Clarice Starling, Senator Martin or his police guards in Memphis. The decision to have Hopkins play Lecter with an American accent seems puzzling, given Brian Cox's undisguised British tones. It is possible that Orion boss Mike Medavoy, having lost his battle to cast Robert Duvall, insisted that Lecter at least sound like a native. Jonathan Demme let Barbara Steele keep her English accent in *Caged Heat*.

Whatever the flaws in his performance, Anthony Hopkins did succeed in turning Hannibal Lecter into one of the cinema's best known, and possibly best loved, monsters. He also got an official seal of approval from a real criminal profiler. Mary Ann Kraus, Jodie Foster's FBI liaison, felt that Hopkins's Lecter was utterly convincing: 'He made my skin crawl. I have learned to live with the reality but the fiction on the screen disturbed me. There are people like that out there.' Kraus's FBI colleague John Douglas begged to differ: 'We've never come across anything like him, thank God.' Discussing the two screen interpretations of Hannibal Lecter with Kate Hardie, Brian Cox remained both tactful and suitably enigmatic: '...the difference between Anthony Hopkins's performance and my performance is that Tony Hopkins is mad and I am insane!'

For all the power of the leading performances, the 'twist' ending to *Silence of the Lambs* seems a bit of a gimmick. Graduating at the FBI academy, Starling is praised by the normally reticent Crawford: 'Your father would have been proud today.' She then gets a cheery phone call from Bad Father Hannibal Lecter, decked out in dark glasses and a long brown wig.

Thomas Harris goes into more detail about Lecter's escape. Following the Memphis jailbreak, the Doctor checks into the Marcus Hotel, St Louis as one 'Lloyd Wyman', the name of a victim whose wallet and car he appropriated at Memphis Airport. The Marcus Hotel is situated opposite the Myron and Sadie Fletcher Pavilion of St Louis City Hospital, described by Harris as 'one of the world's foremost centres for craniofacial surgery'. In need of a good disguise, Lecter can wear a facial bandage without drawing attention to himself.

The movie skips this episode, Lecter suddenly springing up again with jack-in-the-box glee. Calling Starling from a tropical airport, Lecter signs off with an excruciating joke: 'I do wish we could chat longer but... I'm having an old friend for dinner.' On cue, Doctor Chilton walks down the steps from an aircraft, as smug and feckless as ever. As Lecter walks down the road after Chilton, the camera pulls back and up. While *Manhunter* ends with a freezeframe, *Silence of the Lambs*' closing credits roll over a moving street scene, Lecter long out of view when the screen finally fades to black. Thomas Harris's book is more understated, Lecter writing to Starling from the Marcus Hotel, prior to his departure overseas. Lecter also sends notes to Barney, his favourite hospital orderly, and Frederick Chilton, his least favourite 'expert' psychologist. Unlike Starling and Barney, Chilton is assured of a visit in the very near future.

"I DON'T SEE IT AS A GORY FILM."

During the late 1980s, Orion Pictures enjoyed major hits with Paul Verhoeven's gleefully ultra-violent science fiction satire *Robocop* (1988) and Kevin Costner's pro-Native American, pro-environment western *Dances with Wolves* (1990). Picking up an impressive seven Academy Awards at the 1991 ceremony, including the coveted Best Picture and Best Director, *Wolves* would eventually gross $177 million in North America. Even this surprise hit, enhanced by the Academy seal of approval, couldn't save Orion Pictures, whose occasional box-office successes were countered by a string of flops.

By the time *Silence of the Lambs* completed post-production, Orion was so heavily in debt it could no longer afford the extra millions necessary to release its films. Reasoning that *Lambs* stood a better chance of commercial success than most of its other products, the studio scraped together the necessary cash for distribution. Running out of options, Orion subsequently made a deal with Columbia-Tristar, selling the rival studio the North American video rights and all foreign rights to Orion's next 50 films for $175 million. Some completed films, notably Tony Richardson's downbeat drama *Blue Sky* (1991/94), starring Jessica Lange and Tommy Lee Jones, were shelved indefinitely.

Orion released *The Silence of the Lambs* on 13 February 1991, a day before Saint Valentine's Day. Publicity for the film included the punchy taglines: 'Prepare yourself for the most exciting, mesmerising and terrifying two hours of your life!'; 'The only way to stop a killer is by going into the mind of a madman' and 'To enter the mind of a killer she must challenge the mind of a madman.'

Sent out on the promotional rounds, Jodie Foster enthusiastically endorsed the movie: '...I don't see it as a gory film. It's quite sensitive and deals with the problem of serial murders effectively without going into grand gore.' Most reviewers agreed with her, *Variety* praising the movie as 'A mesmerizing thriller that will grip audiences from first scene to last.' Despite the often repellent subject matter, *Silence of the Lambs* provoked remarkably little criticism for a film dealing with murder, torture, cannibalism, extreme violence against women and human flesh wardrobes. The ever-strict British Board of Film Classification had no problem with *Lambs*, passing it uncut as an '18' release on 8 January 1991. The most contentious element was the script's perceived homophobia. There were protests from sections of America's gay community that the character of Jame Gumb represented a particularly despicable example of Hollywood's tendency to demonise homosexuals. That said, the demonstrations that accompanied the film's release were as much concerned with Jodie Foster's supposed sexual preferences as the movie itself. This controversy did little to dampen *Lambs'* audience appeal, and it became the third-highest grossing film of 1991. In the United States and Canada alone, *Lambs* took $130.727 million. The movie's worldwide box-office take of $250 million equalled that of Tim Burton's mega-hyped, mega-hit *Batman* (1989) two years earlier.

In Britain, the film grossed an impressive £17 million, scoring a smash hit on a par with the vastly more expensive *Robin Hood: Prince of Thieves* (1991) and *Terminator 2: Judgment Day* (1991). As Jonathan Demme put it: 'it's great to know that, finally, you've made a movie that's seen by a lot of people.' Oddly, *Lambs* did only average business in Japan, perhaps because the cultural tolerance for extreme graphic violence in entertainment made the film's catalogue of murder, mutilation and cannibalism seem like standard fare.

The overseas reviews for *Silence of the Lambs* were largely favourable. *Guardian* critic Derek Malcolm felt that *Lambs* transcended its nominal genre to serve as a full-blown allegory: 'An exceptionally good film... in which the horror genre is elevated into the kind of cinema that can at least be argued about as a treatise for its unsettling times.' *Monthly Film Bulletin* reviewer Lizzie Francke described Hopkins's Lecter as a 'renaissance man turned mediaeval gargoyle'. Others were not so convinced by either film or star. Referring to the 'unprecedented media hype' around *Lambs*, *Evening Standard* critic Alexander Walker suggested that Hopkins looked 'a mite too fit, sleek, fresh and self-enraptured' to really convince in the role. A fan of *Manhunter*, Walker preferred Brian Cox's earlier screen incarnation of Lecter, 'grislier to look at' and exhibiting 'a gamier relish'. Walker also picked holes in *Lambs'* plot, notably the strange lack of security cameras around Lecter's Memphis cage. All things considered, the film stacked the cards too heavily in Lecter's favour. Only seen attacking men, the Doctor did not even exhibit the standard serial killer misogyny, a marked contrast to Jame Gumb.

Brian Masters, author of a book on British serial killer Dennis Nilsen, attacked *Silence of the Lambs* for its supposed lack of morality. Artists have a responsibility to their public and '...with this film one's moral perceptions are being smothered in the name of entertainment.' Writing in the *New Statesman and Society*, Anne Billson offered a more balanced take on *Lambs*: 'not so much a film, more a case history in how to take a tasteless subject and make it acceptable to a middle class audience.'

Once *Silence of the Lambs* had established its place in the public consciousness, the parodies came thick and fast, if not necessarily funny. The hardcore porn industry, not known for its lavish production schedules, got in on the act first, with one Jerry Butler taking the title role in *Hannibal Lickter* (1992). Both *The Simpsons* and the British *French and Saunders* comedy show offered small screen take-offs, though the latter seemed too impressed with its recreation of Lecter's 'dungeon' cell to bother with actual jokes. Academy Award winning actor F Murray Abraham did a brief turn as Dr Hannibal Lecher in *National Lampoon's Loaded Weapon 1* (1993).

The most elaborate film parody of *Lambs* came in the dubious form of *The Silence of the Hams/Il silenzio dei prosciutti* (1993). An Italian-American co-production, the film was virtually a one-man show, co-produced, scripted and directed by its star, popular Italian television comic Ezio Greggio. Even allowing for some loss of humour in translation, the result seemed utterly desperate. Billy Zane starred as trainee FBI agent Jo Dee Fostar, with former Mel Brooks collaborator Dom DeLuise as Dr Animal Cannibal Pizza. The other character names, notably Sharon Bone and Inspector Putrid, suggested that Greggio had run short of inspiration very fast. The only mild surprise in the film was the basic plot, which largely ignored *Lambs'* script in favour of spoofing the 30-year-old *Psycho*. Martin Balsam, whose private investigator had memorably encountered Norman Bates's 'Mother' at the top of a staircase, agreed to reprise his old role. Time and abysmal dialogue rendered this direct 'homage' a little sad. The supporting cast included such formerly respected names as John Astin, Shelley Winters and Henry Silva, not forgetting comedian Phyllis Diller and *Police Academy* stalwart Bubba Smith. This is a fairly impressive haul for a television star barely known outside his native country. Perhaps the film's Italian executive producer, politician and television mogul Silvio Berlusconi, carried more weight. Greggio even roped in the noted horror directors Joe Dante, John Carpenter and John Landis for cameo appearances, along with a brief turn from DeLuise's old compadre Mel Brooks. Greggio's American co-producer on the film was Julie Corman, wife of Roger Corman. Given her husband's past collaborations with *Lambs* director Demme, not to mention his acting role in the film, this seems a little disloyal.

The awards for *Silence of the Lambs* came as thick and fast as the spoofs. Jonathan Demme won a Silver Bear for his work on the movie at the 1991 Berlin International Film Festival. In 1992, the Director's Guild of America handed out awards to Demme and his producers Ron Bozman and Kenneth Utt. Screenwriter Ted Tally also did well out of *Lambs*, picking up a Writer's Guild Award and an Edgar Allan Poe Award, or 'Edgar'. The film received several Foreign Press Association Golden Globe nominations, Jodie Foster winning for Best Actress in a Drama. Nominated for Best Actor in a Drama, Anthony Hopkins lost out to Nick Nolte, who'd made a big impression in Barbra Streisand's *The Prince of Tides* (1991). Even those who regarded the latter movie as a vanity project for director-star Streisand rated Nolte's performance as a man confronted with a long-suppressed trauma when his sister becomes suicidal. Both Foster and Hopkins were subsequently honoured at the 1992 British Academy of Film and Television Awards (BAFTA) ceremony.

When it came to the Academy Awards, still the biggest and most influential movie trophy contest, *Silence of the Lambs* seemed a long shot at best. The Academy of Motion Picture Arts and Sciences tended to favour films that were prestigious, uplifting and box-office hits. For all the hot reviews, *Lambs* only really scored in the last category. Horror movies had long been the lowest of the low among the cinema's popular genres, just a notch above pornography in the opinion of many. Even if the film passed itself off as a less disreputable thriller, few examples of this genre had picked up Oscars. In recent years, *Fatal Attraction* (1987) had been nominated for Best Picture, Best Director, Best Original Screenplay, Best Actress and Best Supporting Actress. This potential slew of top awards amounted to exactly nothing on the night. Bernardo Bertolucci's *The Last Emperor* took the Best Picture award, while *Fatal Attraction* alumni Adrian Lyne, James Dearden, Glenn Close and Anne Archer lost out to, respectively, Bertolucci, Mark Peploe and Bertolucci, Cher, for *Moonstruck*, and Olympia Dukakis, also for *Moonstruck*. Clearly, this was the year of oriental epics and feelgood Italian-American romances, not adulterous husbands and headcase one-night stands who boil pet rabbits.

Genre[s] aside, many felt that *Silence of the Lambs* had been released too early to stand a realistic chance of Academy Award nomination. Academy members do not have particularly long-term memories and tend to focus on films released in the autumn period. Hitting the cinemas over a year before the relevant Awards hand-out in March 1992, *Lambs* was already ancient history. Handing out trophies at the 1991 ceremony, Anthony Hopkins and Jodie Foster fully realised that the current buzz around their performances in the film could soon evaporate into air. On the bright side, *The Godfather* and *Annie Hall* were the two Academy Award winning exceptions that proved the rule.

Orion's dire financial situation did not prevent the company from mailing hundreds of video copies of *Lambs* to Academy members. Jeffrey Daumer's arrest in the summer of 1991 served as a grim reminder that serial killers were sadly not confined to works of fiction. On a more positive note, Anthony Hopkins' fine performance in the recently released Merchant-Ivory drama *Howards End* (1992) brought a flurry of highly favourable press notices. More to the point, Hannibal Lecter seemed firmly lodged in the public consciousness, endlessly quoted and mimicked months after *Silence of the Lambs* disappeared from the cinema screens. Badly in need of revenue, Orion had given the film a very early video and cable television release in October 1991, enabling viewers to renew their acquaintance with Lecter in the comfort of their living rooms.

The Academy Award nominations were announced in mid-February 1992. *Silence of the Lambs* picked up a total of seven nominations, including the big four: Best Picture, Best Director, Best Actor and Best Actress. There were also nominations for Best Adapted Screenplay, Best Editing and Best Sound. On the verge of bankruptcy, Orion allocated a campaign budget of $350,000 for *Lambs*. The other Best Picture nominees were *Beauty and Beast*, *The Prince of Tides*, *JFK* and *Bugsy*, all 1991 releases. Of these four, only one could really be described as first rate. Disney's animated feature *Beauty and Beast* confirmed *The Little Mermaid*'s promise that the company had found its cartoon feet again after years of half-hearted projects. The first animated film to be nominated for Best Picture, *Beauty and the Beast* made Academy history yet remained a long shot to actually take the award. *The Prince of Tides* had a serious, Oscar-worthy subject and tone, yet the Barbra Streisand factor had proved problematic in the past. Oliver Stone's *JFK*, a dynamic and provocative piece of conspiracy speculation, suffered from media cries of foul over its rewriting of recent, and well known, American history. *Bugsy*, a whitewashed biopic of the deeply nasty gangster Benjamin Siegel, simply wasn't very good. On the night, Elizabeth Taylor and Paul Newman presented the Best Picture award to *Lambs* producers Edward Saxon, Kenneth Utt and Ron Bozman.

In the Director category, Jonathan Demme faced competition from Barry Levinson, for *Bugsy*, Ridley Scott, for *Thelma and Louise*, John Singleton, for *Boyz N the Hood* and Oliver Stone, for *JFK*. Scott's avowedly feminist road movie had been another sleeper hit, a return to form for the director after the deeply crass culture-clash police thriller *Black Rain* (1990). Demme was handed his award by Kevin Costner, Best Director winner the previous year for *Dances with Wolves*.

Leaving aside the question of *Lambs'* horror movie status, Anthony Hopkins knew his chances of taking the Best Actor Award were slender. There had been British Best Actor wins for the past two years running, Daniel Day Lewis for *My Left Foot* in 1990, and Jeremy Irons for *Reversal of Fortune* in 1991. A third successive win for a British performance seemed unlikely, even with an American accent in an American-made film. Many felt Orion should have set their sights slightly lower, pushing for Hopkins to be nominated in the less fiercely contested Best Supporting Actor category. His fellow Best Actor nominees for the 1992 award were Robert De Niro, for *Cape Fear*, Robin Williams, for *The Fisher King*, Warren Beatty, for *Bugsy*, and Nick Nolte once again. Up against this formidable line-up, Hopkins was well aware that he couldn't match his rivals for Hollywood clout.

None of the other movies had been out-and-out hits, however, either with the critics or the paying public. Martin Scorsese's *Cape Fear*, a remake of the arguably superior 1962 film, looked like a slick, commercial star vehicle, rather than a deeply-felt personal work on the level of *Taxi Driver*. De Niro's character, psychotic rapist Max Cady, rivalled Hannibal Lecter for unpleasant habits, biting a chunk out of one female victim's face. Decked out with long, stringy hair and biblical body tattoos, Cady was a caricature villain, lent presence and dynamism by De Niro's enthusiastic playing. *The Fisher King* marked Terry Gilliam's Hollywood rehabilitation after the commercial disaster of *The Adventures of Baron Munchausen* (1989) and displayed the director's trademark quirkiness at half strength. Cast as Professor Parry, an academic driven insane by his wife's murder, Robin Williams overdid the heartstring tugging and the cuddly/lovable act. *Bugsy* notably failed to join *The Godfather* in the pantheon of great gangster movies. In the title role, Warren Beatty merely looked smug. Even *Prince of Tides* star Nick Nolte had trouble generating audience identification for his rape-traumatised football coach. None of these movies displayed the nominated stars at their best. None of the characters they portrayed registered the startlingly screen impact of Hannibal Lecter. Neither De Niro, already a Best Actor winner for *Raging Bull* (1980), nor Williams, were seen as serious contenders by the bookmakers. Nick Nolte remained the favourite for the award, closely followed by Warren Beatty. Anthony Hopkins came in third at four-to-one against.

At the start of the 1992 Academy Awards ceremony, celebrity host Billy Crystal was wheeled on stage at the Dorothy Chandler Pavilion, wearing a Hannibal Lecter-style mask. Crystal then walked out into the audience to where Anthony Hopkins sat, shaking the actor by the hand. Nevertheless, Hopkins claims to have remained sceptical about his chances until the Best Actor nominations were read out by actress Kathy Bates. Only then did he suddenly feel that the award would be his. Handed the gold-plated statuette, a tearful Hopkins said hello to his mother, watching the ceremony on television back in Wales.

Jodie Foster's competition for the Best Actress award didn't seem quite as fierce, though there was an element of luck here. Susan Sarandon and Geena Davis, the acclaimed stars of *Thelma and Louise*, had both been nominated in the category, which would almost certainly split their votes. The other nominees were not seen as serious contenders. Laura Dern's performance in *Rambling Rose* attracted favourable notices, though the film scored as a critical rather than a commercial success. A Deep South tale of passion and repression, *Rambling Rose* featured a scene where the teenage Rose is masturbated by a thirteen year old boy, material as controversial as *Lambs*'s flesh-eating. British film censor James Ferman thought the scene contained some of the best acting he'd ever seen, yet still felt obliged to cut it under the strict UK child protection laws. Bette Midler had been given a token nod for her powerhouse performance in *For the Boys*, a heavy-handed $40 million piece of bittersweet showbiz musical nostalgia that flopped. Academy Award historian Anthony Holden suggests that Foster's chances were further boosted by the recent success of her directorial debut, *Little Man Tate* (1991). Casting herself as the single parent mother of a genius child, Foster reaffirmed her commitment to flawed yet positive characters determined to rise above their deprived backgrounds. Handed the award by Michael Douglas, Foster's acceptance speech included the words: 'Thanks to the Academy for embracing such an incredibly strong and beautiful feminist hero that I'm so proud of.'

Silence of the Lambs' Academy Award sweep made big news, especially Anthony Hopkins's Best Actor win. Hopkins was the first male star to take the award for playing a villainous character since Marlon Brando's *Godfather* win two decades earlier. Furthermore, *Lambs* was only the second horror film to net its leading man a Best Actor trophy, following Fredric March's award for his performance in Rouben Mamoulian's 1932 *Dr Jekyll and Mr Hyde*. Curiously, Hopkins had recently played the same role as March in the *Desperate Hours* remake.

Silence of the Lambs' haul of the major Academy Awards was equalled only by *It Happened One Night* (1934) and *One Flew Over the Cuckoo's Nest*. Completing the quintet of wins, Ted Tally picked up the award for Best Screenplay based on material from another medium, beating out Agnieszka Holland for *Europa, Europa*, Fannie Flagg and Carol Sobieski for *Fried Green Tomatoes at the Whistlestop Cafe*, Oliver Stone and Zachary Sklar for *JFK*, and Pat Conroy and Becky Johnston for *The Prince of Tides*. In a bittersweet gesture of triumph,

Orion splashed out $50,000 on a post Academy Awards party at top LA nightspot Rex II Ristorante. Inevitably, *Lambs'* comprehensive sweep of the major Academy Awards attracted some adverse criticism. *Los Angeles Times* critic Kenneth Turan argued that: 'Giving Best Picture to as bloody and non-inspirational a film as this [is] some kind of first in the Academy's long and curious history.' Nobody took much notice.

The moral and critical sniping aimed at *Silence of the Lambs* barely registered with Orion Pictures. The company was far more concerned with impending financial disaster. Like Dino de Laurentiis before them, Orion's executives had bankrolled too many non-commercial projects too fast. Desperate for cash, Orion had brought *Lambs'* video and cable television release forward to October 1991, reasoning that the Halloween season always brought a brief upturn in the demand for horror-related titles. Two months later, on 15 December 1991, the company filed for Chapter 11 bankruptcy, its debts estimated at anything between $300 million and nearly $1 billion. Orion's creditors included both Jodie Foster and Jonathan Demme, the director owed over $350,000. Four months after the Orion Pictures Corporation went bust, *Silence of the Lambs* enjoyed its Academy Award bonanza.

PART THREE

HANNIBAL COOKS

The wickedness herein I took from my own stock.
THOMAS HARRIS, *Hannibal*

He may eat people, but he has feelings, too.
ANTHONY HOPKINS on Hannibal Lecter

Aside from vastly increasing the number of applications to the FBI Academy, *The Silence of the Lambs'* box-office success helped pave the way for a new horror sub-genre, the high-class serial killer movie. Not only did these films offer lavish production values, premiere behind-the-camera talent and big name actors, they also had Something To Say About The Age We Live In. Or so the pressbooks would claim. The rural psycho-lovers road movie variant made two notable appearances: *Kalifornia* (1993), with Brad Pitt and Juliette Lewis, and *Natural Born Killers* (1994), with Woody Harrelson and Juliette Lewis. Oliver Stone's *NBK*, a supposed satire on the media's amoral glamorisation of serial murder, found itself accused of the same crime, with reports of copycat killings.

More urban serial killers featured in the similarly upmarket *Jennifer 8* (1992), *Se7en* (1995), *Summer of Sam* (1999) and *American Psycho* (2000). In *Jennifer 8*, written and directed by Bruce Robinson, the victims are all blind women, though jaded Los Angeles cop Andy Garcia takes a very long time to nail the obvious culprit. David Fincher's surprise hit *Se7en* plays with the Seven Deadly Sins, as Wise Old Cop Morgan Freeman and Ambitious Newcomer Brad Pitt search for their man in murky, rain-swept city streets that reek of decay and corruption.

Spike Lee's *Summer of Sam* uses the real-life 'Son of Sam' murders as a backdrop for an examination of the tensions within New York's Italian-American community during the late 1970s. Mary Harron's *American Psycho*, adapted from the infamous book by Brett Easton Ellis, tells the story of thrusting Wall Street broker Patrick Bateman (Christian Bale), who just can't get enough of dissecting young women.

Whatever their individual merits, none of the above films featured the kind of heroic female characters called for by Jodie Foster, following her triumph as Clarice Starling. In *Se7en*, for example, nominal co-star Gwyneth Paltrow had the token role of policeman Brad Pitt's loyal, stay-at-home wife. Paltrow's biggest contribution to the film involved being decapitated, off-screen, by Kevin Spacey's well-spoken killer, who then hands Pitt her head in a box. There were, however, stronger women's roles in *Copycat* (1995), with Sigourney Weaver (psychologist) and Holly Hunter (detective); *Kiss the Girls* (1997), with Ashley Judd (doctor); *In Dreams* (1998), with Annette Bening (psychic artist), and *The Bone Collector* (1999), with Angelina Jolie (beat cop). For the *Scream* trilogy (1996, 1997, 2000), a self-referential, self-parodying *homage* to the slasher movie, writer Kevin Williamson and director Wes Craven provided a plucky teen heroine in the form of Neve Campbell. The Williamson-scripted *I Know What You Did Last Summer* (1997) failed to repeat the trick, Jennifer Love Hewitt appearing sympathetic only because her friends were so unpleasant and deserving of violent death.

Amid all these daughters of Clarice Starling, there was no further sign of the Special Agent herself. For all *The Silence of the Lambs'* huge success and the inevitable demand for a sequel, neither Starling nor Lecter could return until Thomas Harris came up with another book. Prior to the release of the *Lambs* movie, Harris had signed a deal supposedly worth $3.5 million for a third Lecter novel and an unspecified follow-up. Originally expected to finish the book in late 1993, Thomas Harris showed no signs of rushing the latest instalment of the Lecter saga. In late 1994, the author's British publisher, Heinemann, announced that it expected to receive the manuscript in time for a late 1995/early 1996 publication. In the event, Harris went over schedule by nearly six years.

Finally published in June 1999, *Hannibal* broke sales records in the

United Kingdom, becoming the fastest-selling hardback adult fiction title of all time. Book reviewers who normally shunned mere thrillers acclaimed Harris as a literary genius who effortlessly blurred the line between popular fiction and 'serious' literature. Stephen King reclaimed his position as Harris's Supreme Celebrity Champion: '...one of the two most frightening popular novels of our time, the other being *The Exorcist... Hannibal* is the third and most satisfying part of one very long and scary ride through the haunted palace of abnormal psychiatry...' There were a number of dissenters, both among the critics and the paying public, who found the book's storyline rambling, its violence unpleasant and the finale risible. When it came to turning *Hannibal* into a movie, these reservations would resurface with a vengeance.

"CHARMING, WITTY, SEDUCTIVE, SEXUAL – AND LETHAL"

Seven years on from Doctor Lecter's jailbreak, all is not well in the world of American law enforcement. As the Federal Bureau of Investigation approaches its ninetieth birthday, the Quantico Academy has folded for lack of funding. The Bureau of Alcohol, Tobacco and Firearms rents office space from the Reverend Sun Myung Moon, head of the Moonie sect. Even Lecter's old prison, the Baltimore State Hospital for the Criminally Insane, is now closed and awaiting demolition. Squeezed by budget cuts, the FBI is obliged to participate in multi-departmental operations, its agents working in high-risk situations with unfamiliar, inexperienced, non-Bureau officers. Stuck in a career rut, former FBI star Clarice Starling is part of such a team that raids a drug factory, only to find their quarry forewarned and forearmed. Forced to shoot five people dead in the ensuing bloody fiasco, Starling is labelled the FBI's 'DEATH ANGEL' by the ever-popular *National Tattler*. Still reeling from the public relations disaster of the Waco siege, where members of the Branch-Davidian religious cult were wiped out by gunfire and flames, the FBI does not need any more bad press.

Older, wiser and a great deal sadder, Clarice Starling still feels oppressed by the casual sexism of the male-dominated FBI. Travelling to the drugs raid location, she is the only female member of the scratch assault team. 'Starling felt pierced and lonesome in this goat-smelling surveillance van crowded with men.' Only slightly scarred physically by Jame Gumb, with a gunpowder burn on her cheekbone, Starling has come to realise that her FBI career suffered long-term harm because of the 'Buffalo Bill' case. Starling's rescue of Catherine Martin earned the lasting appreciation of the now ex-Senator Martin, but stirred jealousy and resentment within senior government circles. Starling's main nemesis in the corridors of power is Deputy Assistant Inspector General Paul Krendler, from the Department of Justice. Having unsuccessfully attempted to bed the woman who beat him to Jame Gumb, Krendler's frustrated lust for Starling only increases his hatred of her. As Harris puts it: 'it was Krendler's nature to both appreciate Starling's leg and look for the hamstring.'

Pitted against HIV-positive drug queenpin Evelda Drumgo, who uses her own baby as a body shield, Starling has little choice but to gun down the mother in full view of a television news helicopter. Abandoned by her department in the glare of hostile media coverage, she is offered up as the FBI's scapegoat, or sacrificial lamb, 'fresh, bleeding meat'. Temporarily reprieved when Hannibal Lecter surfaces after years of silence, Starling's run of luck is short-lived. Taking his instructions from a powerful benefactor, Paul Krendler sets Starling up, framing her for planting a coded warning to Lecter in a newspaper. The official hearing to determine Starling's guilt is no more than a formality: '...the proceeding went forward with the dispatch of an eighteenth-century amputation.' Approaching 33 years of age, the supposed lifespan of Jesus Christ, Clarice Starling seems about to join him in martyrdom. Hannibal Lecter, who once sketched Starling as the crucified Christ, certainly appreciates the parallel.

Despite the Doctor's understandably low profile, interest in Hannibal 'The Cannibal' Lecter is as strong as ever. There are websites devoted to Lecter and a flourishing, if irregularly supplied black market in Hannibal 'souvenirs'. Posing as one 'Doctor Fell', Lecter is currently curator at the Palazzo Capponi, in his beloved Florence. Reading of Clarice Starling's public 'disgrace', Lecter sends a letter of encouragement, on his usual mauve notepaper: 'You are a warrior, Clarice. The enemy is dead, the baby safe. You are a warrior.' Starling will prove Lecter right, opting to rescue the Doctor from cruel vigilante 'justice' as vile as any of Lecter's own crimes. Alienated from the FBI and disgusted that the corrupt Krendler is colluding in Lecter's murder, Starling decides to follow her own instinct for right over wrong: '*The world will not be this way within the reach of my arm.*'

Hannibal Lecter's fixation on Clarice Starling has not diminished since their last encounter at the Memphis jailhouse. As the Doctor plays Bach on his clavier, he looks at a *National Tattler* picture of Starling. Lecter subsequently cuts out the photograph, glues it to a piece of finest parchment and adds the body of a winged lioness. Back in the United States, Lecter carefully breaks into Starling's prized Mustang car while she is out running. Sitting in the driver's seat normally occupied by Starling, Lecter wraps his tongue around the leather steering wheel cover and savours Starling's scent as if it were the finest wine.

Early on in *Hannibal*, Thomas Harris seems about to make some spectacular, theological revelation of Lecter's true identity. A Romany Gypsy pickpocket, recruited as part of an operation to kidnap the Doctor, recoils from Lecter's gaze with horror: 'That is the Devil. Shaitan, Son of the Morning, I've seen him now.' Anthony Hopkins had arrived at the same conclusion while preparing for his role in *The Silence of the Lambs*: 'Lecter is a personification of the devil, and I have always perceived the devil as very charming, witty, seductive, sexual – and lethal.' In the event, Harris opts for something more corporeal, even playing down Lecter's unusual physical traits. The left hand's sixth finger, never very convincing, is now gone, surgically removed in Brazil.

We discover aspects of Lecter's personality that do not quite tally with his character in *Red Dragon* and *The Silence of the Lambs*. While incarcerated, the Doctor encouraged fellow inmate 'Multiple' Miggs to throw sperm at a female visitor, Doctor Chilton's fiancée. So much for Lecter's avowed loathing of discourtesy. It is possible that this incitement spurred Miggs to further sperm-throwing, including the handful that ended up on Clarice Starling. Which might explain why Lecter seemed so agitated at the time, the Doctor's mischief-making going further than he wished.

Revisiting the Baltimore State Hospital for the Criminally Insane, in search of Lecter's medical records, Starling makes a gloomy tour of the derelict building. Walking into Lecter's old cell, she is almost disappointed by the lack of his presence: 'The cell was as empty of its former occupant as a snake's shed skin.' The big revelation about Hannibal Lecter centres on a nightmare incident from his wartime childhood, when he and his young sister were left alone after the death of their parents. Mischa Lecter is first alluded to with a casual reference, 'long dead and digested', hinting that Lecter ate her himself. Having played on his readers' cynical expectations, Harris proceeds to reveal that nothing could be further from the truth. In 1944, frozen and starving German deserters from the Eastern Front raided the bombed-out Lecter family estate in Lithuania. Concerned only with brute survival, the soldiers rounded up the local children and ate them one by one.

Deemed too scrawny for a decent meal, the six-year-old Lecter fought in vain as the younger, chubbier Mischa was taken away. Hearing the terrible sound of an axe, Hannibal prayed for his sister to be returned to him. All he got was a glimpse of her milk teeth in the 'reeking stool pit' used by the soldiers. Lecter's faith in God vanished at this point. Compared to Divine cruelty, biting out a nurse's eye or eating a census taker's liver are minor misdemeanours: 'his own modest predations paled beside those of God, who is in irony matchless, and in wanton malice beyond measure.'

Associating Mischa with the image of a wounded deer, another item on the deserters' menu, Lecter still screams out loud at the memory of her murder, the sound of his anguish 'thin and rising'. Compared to poor Hannibal Lecter, Francis Dolarhyde and Jame Gumb had it pretty damn easy. Perhaps concerned that Lecter seems too sympathetic too early, Harris briefly reintroduces Senator Ruth Martin to remind readers of the Doctor's bad side. Questioned by Starling over the telephone, Senator Martin refers to Lecter's taunts about her breast-feeding Catherine: 'he just sucked down my pain'. Throughout the book, Harris sporadically refers to Lecter as 'the monster', yet the term carries little conviction. Cannibalism pushed to one side, Hannibal Lecter is now a hero.

Back in the United States, Lecter settles in Maryland, near Muskrat Farm, the family mansion of a surviving victim. In no hurry to settle unfinished business, the Doctor shops, takes in the best New York concerts and watches Clarice Starling run in the forest. Lecter's 'whimsical' attachment to Starling proves to be his undoing. Having beaten a hit squad in Florence, Lecter is finally grabbed in the less decorous surroundings of Starling's local Safeway car park, hardly gourmet territory. For a regular imbiber of Batard-Montrachet wine, $125 a bottle, this is undignified.

"A CREATURE OF THE DEEP, DEEP OCEAN..."

In the considered opinion of Will Graham and Jack Crawford, any surviving victim of Hannibal Lecter would be justified, if not legally sanctioned, in seeking vengeance against the Doctor. In the case of Mason Verger, Thomas Harris clearly disagrees. The heir to a meat-packing fortune and some heavyweight political influence, Verger is one of only two living Lecter victims. Vast inherited wealth or not, Verger's sorry plight should merit at least a little sympathy. A former patient of the Doctor, Mason Verger was treated to a special Lecter cocktail of amyl nitrate, methamphetamines and LSD. Lecter then persuaded the tripping Verger to cut off his own face with a shard of broken mirror. Verger fed most of the facial slices to his pet dogs but ate the nose himself, informing Lecter that it tasted like chicken. As an encore, Doctor Lecter broke Verger's neck.

Survival, in Verger's case, is a relative term. Occupying a respirator 24 hours a day, his paralysed body is an inert ruin, only his tongue, an eye and one hand, 'like a pale spider crab', still functioning. Housed in a specially built annexe to the family mansion, Verger lives in darkness, kept company by his giant pet eel. Moving around its tank in an endless figure of eight, the eel has more living space than Verger. Working with tongue-operated controls, Verger's pitiful existence seems like a living death. Refusing to just shrivel and die, he has hatched an elaborate scheme of revenge against Lecter. Drawing on his family business expertise, Verger plans to have Lecter eaten alive, feet first, by specially bred pigs. Nasty, perhaps, but with a cunning element of grisly poetic justice.

Unfortunately, the Lecter versus Verger contest is hopelessly slanted in the Doctor's favour, no mean feat given Hannibal's track record. A serial abuser of children, including his younger sister, Mason Verger was a foul, twisted specimen of inhumanity long before he encountered Lecter. Taking a break from the meat-packing business, Verger served as a travelling executioner for Ugandan dictator Idi Amin, performing beheadings and crucifixions as required. Verger only agreed to see the esteemed psychiatrist Hannibal Lecter as part of a plea-bargain deal to beat child molestation charges. Ever the show-off, he was demonstrating a favoured auto-erotic asphyxiation technique with a noose when Lecter gave him the drug cocktail.

Making no secret of his bias towards Lecter, Thomas Harris seems to relish detailing Verger's loathsome appearance, drawing a clear parallel with his pet eel: 'Mason Verger, noseless and lipless, with no soft tissue on his face, was all teeth, like a creature of the deep, deep ocean.' Despite his immobile state, Verger's child abuse has continued by other means. Children from deprived, welfare-dependent families are summoned to a special playroom that adjoins his chamber. Attempting to scare selected children, Verger shows them his face, then cruelly taunts them with threats, stealing the resultant tears to drink with his Martini cocktail. This is a fairytale monster of the most dubious kind.

Clarice Starling's one visit to Verger's chamber of horror recalls her first encounter with Lecter in *The Silence of the Lambs*. This time around, there is no hint of a connection between the characters. Claiming to be a 'saved' Born Again Christian, Verger punctuates his rambling conversation with regular 'Hallelujah!' cries. This religious conviction appears to be genuine, if distasteful, Verger musing on the inefficiency of the Divine plan: 'Clearly He needs some help in directing the blind fury with which He flogs the earth.' Franklin, a black child summoned to Verger's bedside, has the latter well sussed: 'You a mean old doo-doo. An you ugly too.'

Every supervillain needs a lackey and Paul Krendler suits Mason Verger's requirements very nicely. Neither an Inspector General nor even an Assistant Inspector General, Deputy Krendler is hungry for political power. With Verger's patronage, he can successfully run for Congress. Crass in the extreme, Krendler dismisses Hannibal Lecter's cultured tastes as 'All this artsy-fartsy stuff'. Any man so interested in opera and fine wines has to be gay. While Lecter plays Bach on the piano to

concert standard, Krendler can barely pick out the theme tune to the
Dragnet television show.

Lacking Mason Verger's vast resources, both financial and
intellectual, Krendler has done his best to make the world a nastier place.
In the case of Clarice Starling, this is very personal. Having rejected
Krendler's drunken advances, Starling stirred up bitter resentment with
the jealousy he already felt over her 'triumph' with the Jame Gumb case.
When Starling finally confronts Krendler over his systematic long-term
sabotage of her career, the Deputy merely confirms her suspicions:
'Don't flatter yourself, Starling... this town is full of cornpone country
pussy.' Thomas Harris employs elementary psychology to explain
Krendler's deep-seated hatred of this particular 'cornpone'. Many
years previously, a girl resembling Starling accused the bashful young
Krendler of being 'queer' after he failed to become aroused during a
back-seat fumble. Harris has pulled a cunning, if dubious, narrative
trick in *Hannibal*: next to the repulsive trio of Verger, Krendler and
Verger's fame-hungry pet psychologist Doctor Doemling, Hannibal 'The
Cannibal' Lecter seems almost noble. The revelation that Lecter really is
of noble birth is perhaps gilding the lily.

The lengthy Florence-based section of *Hannibal* largely centres on
the intricate cat and mouse games played by Lecter, or 'Doctor Fell',
and Italian policeman Rinaldo Pazzi. Middle-aged and disillusioned,
Pazzi has a career history to match Clarice Starling's fall from FBI grace.
A few years back, Pazzi had been lauded by his superiors and the Italian
media for tracking down Il Mostro, 'The Monster', a serial killer who
preyed on young couples in the backstreets of Florence. Like Francis
Dolarhyde in *Red Dragon*, Il Mostro took his inspiration from a painting,
in this case Botticelli's 'Primavera'. Unfortunately, the culprit was freed
on appeal, Pazzi accused by the defence lawyers of planting evidence.

Disgraced and disillusioned, Pazzi now has a lead on Lecter's
whereabouts, which he sells to Mason Verger after a brief wrestle with
his conscience. Conveniently, Pazzi spent time at Quantico studying
the FBI's serial killer profiling techniques and saw Lecter's sketches
of Florence. Harris devotes a lot of pages to Pazzi's ingenious plan for
taking Lecter alive, which finally seems redundant. For all his elaborate
scheming, Rinaldo Pazzi never stands a chance of outwitting Hannibal

Lecter. One of Pazzi's ancestors was hanged from the Palazzo Vecchio for conspiring against the Medicis. Demonstrating the cyclical nature of history, especially history of the unpleasant kind, Lecter dangles Pazzi from the same window of the Palazzo. After five centuries, man's capacity for inventive barbarity remains reassuringly constant: 'his neck broke and his bowels fell out.'

Surrounded by hostile forces in *Hannibal*, Clarice Starling is notably short of friends, Doctor Lecter excepted. Ardelia Mapp, her fellow FBI graduate and housemate, is still on hand, yet does little other than lament the unfairness of Starling's plight. The figure of Jack Crawford, Starling's former boss, drifts like a ghost through the narrative, melancholy and ineffectual. On the verge of retirement, Crawford is offered a Deputy Director post if he stays out of the Starling witch-hunt. Displaying an integrity otherwise lacking in the higher echelons of the FBI, Crawford refuses to be bribed.

Still in mourning for his late wife Bella, Crawford's strongest passion is his enduring hatred for Lecter. As he explains to Starling: 'In the present political climate, if the doctor's caught he'll get the needle.' It's hardly necessary for Harris to add: 'The prospect of death for Dr Lecter pleased him mightily.' Suffering a heart attack just as Starling is placed on trial for abetting the fugitive Lecter, Crawford's failing health seems of little consequence either to the narrative or himself. His death from cardiac arrest, referred to long after the event in the book's closing pages, only serves to confirm that Starling no longer has any need for Crawford's paternal guidance.

Another *Lambs* character hovering on the sidelines of *Hannibal* is Barney, the efficient and wise hospital orderly, who warned Doctor Chilton that the Memphis police would not be able to handle Lecter. Sharing the benefits of his classical education, Doctor Lecter introduced Barney to Socrates, Suetonius and Gibbon during their many night-time conversations. Since the closure of the Baltimore State Hospital for the Criminally Insane, Barney has assembled an impressive, if legally questionable collection of Lecter memorabilia, which he steadily sells off at private auction. There are signed papers, books and, best of all, the Doctor's restraining mask, still encrusted with flecks of authentic Lecter saliva. Hannibal Lecter would surely be impressed by this ingenious small-scale private enterprise. But, displaying a disappointing lack of loyalty, Barney signs up with Mason Verger, giving him information on Lecter and Starling.

"ALL WE ASK IS THAT
YOU KEEP AN OPEN MIND"

Epic in scope and painstakingly detailed, *Hannibal* is ultimately inferior to both *Red Dragon* and *The Silence of the Lambs*. In expanding and reworking the format that made the first two books a success, Harris has lost the focus and urgency of his earlier work. One curious aspect of *Hannibal* is its half-hearted attempt to reflect contemporary issues. Along with the internet, government budget cuts and the Unabomber, there is scandal in the White House. Not wanting his epic to date too fast, Harris avoids mentioning Bill Clinton and Monica Lewinsky by name, though thoughts of misdirected sperm would strike a chord with Clarice Starling. Harris appears genuinely concerned by America's weapons-freak subculture, dismissing the patrons of a dingy gun show as 'scruffy, squinty, angry, eggbound'. Bad diet creates bad attitude, though apparently not in Hannibal Lecter's case. The humour is sometimes heavy-handed, Starling's associates on the failed drug raid including Agents Burke and Hare. Lecter does his own body snatching during the course of the narrative, though for the best possible reasons.

The Florence episode often sidetracks into pure travelogue and gory historical anecdotes. Having conducted extensive, first-hand research, Thomas Harris does not wear his learning lightly on this occasion. Dante references fall thick and fast, often in untranslated Italian. Cultural elitism aside, there are elements of both self-indulgence and lazy repetition to this section of the book. All the Italian characters seem to point with their chins. Aside from stating some obvious themes about the links between money, politics, religion and violence, much of the Florence sojourn seems redundant. Harris also appears preoccupied with noble lineage. Hannibal Lecter's own father was a Count, with ancestry dating back to the 10th century. Lecter had a similarly distinguished Italian mother, which explains his fascination with Florentine history and culture.

The cultural allusions are not confined to medieval Italy. William Blake's painting 'The Ancient of Days', also known as 'God Creating the Universe', hangs in the reception area of Mason Verger's chamber. While 'The Great Red Dragon and the Woman Clothed With the Sun' was a central motif in *Red Dragon*, this time around the Blake reference seems an empty flourish. Employing a prose style to match Hannibal Lecter's striking elegance, Harris comes up with some memorably bizarre phrases, notably: '...excitement leaped like a trout in the public trousers.' The first edition of *Hannibal* also contained an unusual number of typos for a major publication, Paul Krendler's distinctive ears printed as 'cars' more than once. (Perhaps this betrayed the haste to meet an early publication date.)

While most of the supporting figures in *Hannibal* are functional character sketches, Margot Verger, Mason's sister, is a grotesque caricature. A stereotyped butch lesbian, the musclebound Margot has screwed up her body with steroid abuse: her voice is deep, her hairline receding and her ovaries shrivelled. Mason Verger sexually abused his sister as a child, forcing her to perform masturbation and fellatio on him. Suffering a broken left elbow during one of these episodes, the adult Margot has aggressively reclaimed her body and her sexuality. Suppressing the feminine side that she associates with weakness and vulnerability, Margot's masculine transformation has exacerbated rather than repaired the physical and mental damage inflicted by her unrepentant brother. Thomas Harris seems to be insinuating that Mason Verger's many crimes include making his sister gay, a strikingly reactionary and homophobic attitude.

Margot briefly bonds with Verger employee Barney, the two of them working out together in the gymnasium. She soon offers him $5 million to help out with a little scheme. Just as Mason Verger plans to murder Hannibal Lecter, so Margot Verger plots to kill her brother, first extracting his sperm to impregnate her girlfriend with a legitimate Verger heir. When Barney declines to assist, Margot performs the task herself with the help of a cattle prod. Grabbing hold of Mason's prized pet eel, Margot inserts the creature's head into her brother's mouth, its snapping teeth biting into his tongue. Mason drowns in his own blood, a deserving victim of perverse phallic symbolism. Brutal fratricide apart, Margot

Verger seems a fine candidate for surrogate parenthood, possessed of a strong maternal instinct, a long term loving relationship and extreme wealth that just got much bigger. Even Doctor Lecter tips his hat to her.

While Mason Verger abused his sister, Hannibal Lecter loved Mischa and has mourned her throughout his adult life. Dispensing with the dark mystery that made Lecter so fascinating in *Red Dragon* and *The Silence of the Lambs*, Thomas Harris now wants the reader to share Hannibal's pain. Mischa Lecter loved the colour purple, especially her big brother's eyes. Hannibal's intense, 'preternaturally knowing' manner, which disturbed the Lecter family servants, never bothered her. In Clarice Starling, Lecter sees an echo of Mischa, and perhaps even a way for his sister to return from the dead. Both orphaned at an early age, Hannibal and Clarice belong together, two lost souls in need of healing.

Hannibal has two successive climaxes, the first a swine-frenzied shootout that recalls some of Sam Peckinpah's 'ballets of blood'. Inside Mason Verger's spacious barn, the captive Lecter is tied and suspended in a crucified position, an obvious piece of symbolism that takes in both the birth and death of Christ. Displaying near magical powers, Lecter later walks unharmed through the pigs bred solely to devour his living, bleeding flesh. The assembled swine do not even attempt to attack Lecter: 'he faced them and they smelled no fear.' Hit by two powerful tranquillizer darts, Lecter's rescuing angel Clarice Starling is herself delivered from the pigs by the Doctor, who later sucks the drug from her puncture wounds. Neither vampire nor monster, Doctor Lecter is now a healer.

Back at Lecter's Maryland retreat, Hannibal and Clarice engage in mutually beneficial psychotherapy sessions. Just as Lecter is still haunted by the spectre of Mischa, so Starling has yet to deal with her feelings for her murdered lawman father. Using a combination of deep hypnosis and hypnotic drugs, Lecter arranges a fantasy encounter between father and daughter. Freed from all inhibitions, Starling expresses the negative feelings she'd always suppressed: the anger and resentment at her father's wasteful death, Mr Starling 'too goddamned stupid' to deal with a couple of petty thieves. There is an obvious parallel between Mr Starling's shoddy treatment by the town authorities and Clarice Starling's own frustrated career at the FBI: 'He should have told those town jackasses to stuff the job.' Having recently disinterred Mr Starling's remains, along with his belt buckle and bullet-torn hat, Lecter lays out the bones on a bed. Starling weeps over her father's skull, her tears splashing the cranium. This somewhat Jacobean grief-therapy encounter seems to do the trick, Clarice Starling finally at peace with herself.

While Lecter guides Starling on her path to self-awareness, a process begun during their first encounter in *The Silence of the Lambs*, the Doctor knows he cannot control or 'own' her. 'He could feed the caterpillar, he could whisper through the chrysalis; what hatched out followed its own nature and was beyond him.' The celebratory dinner party which follows is easily *Hannibal*'s most controversial section. Given one more mind-altering injection by Lecter, Starling sits down to a Belon oyster starter. The main course is a delicious combination of black truffle, shallots, caper berries, brioche and the fresh brains of Assistant Deputy Inspector General Paul Krendler. Tied to a 'stout oak armchair', the anaesthetized but fully conscious Krendler is fed 'a parsley and thyme infusion' to improve his flavour. Ever the prepared gourmet chef, Lecter has already cut through the top of Krendler's skull with a specially purchased autopsy saw. Departing from his clinical culinary description, Thomas Harris is unable to resist a truly awful pun: 'All we ask is that you keep an open mind.'

With Krendler chattering away, Lecter expertly cuts slices from the 'pinky-gray dome', dredging them lightly in seasoned flour. Harris's admiration for Lecter's gastronomic virtuosity is clear: 'he sautéed the slices until they were just brown on each side.' Even the notoriously philistine Krendler is impressed: 'Smells great!' As Lecter and Starling munch their way through Krendler's brains, the effect is more light ironic comedy than gross-out horror. Citing the example of Oliver Twist, yet another literary orphan, Starling asks for '*MORE*', duly supplied by Lecter: 'A second helping consumed most of the frontal lobe, back nearly to the premotor cortex.' Having literally devoured her arch-enemy, the embodiment of all the bigoted, chauvinistic establishment forces that stifled her career and attempted to ruin her life, Clarice Starling seems the better for it. A consummate host, as always, Lecter scrapes the leftovers from her plate into Krendler's newly emptied cranium.

Following a brief discussion of Mischa Lecter, Stephen Hawking, the Rule of Disorder and Clarice Starling's place in the universe, Harris takes his leading characters into bodice-ripping Black Lace territory. Clarice places mouth-warmed Chateau d'Yquem, a favourite Lecter tipple, on her breast for Hannibal to lick: 'a thick sweet drop suspended from her nipple like a golden cabochon and trembled with her breathing.' Still pondering the possibility of resurrecting Mischa through Clarice, Hannibal opts to take a different route. Harris relates how Lecter 'went on a knee before her chair, and bent to her coral and cream in the firelight his dark sleek head.' Here is Thomas Harris manufacturing purple prose out of the school of Barbara Cartland.

As a perverse sado-erotic fantasy, the Lecter-Starling coupling in *Hannibal* wins points for imagination and attention to detail. In terms of credible character development, Clarice Starling bears little relation to the person encountered in *The Silence of the Lambs*. On the other hand, *Lambs* concerned Starling's attempt to find her place in the 'real' world. This time around, she comes to rest in Hannibal Lecter's world.

Thomas Harris rounds off his epic saga with an epilogue. Three years on from the Krendler dinner, Hannibal and Clarice tour the cultural highspots of the South American continent. Having begun to remodel his features back at the Marcus Hotel in St Louis, Lecter is now at least two faces ahead of the image on the FBI's 'Most Wanted' bulletin. No longer dreaming of Mischa, Hannibal seems happy with Clarice, whose devotion to Lecter is unprompted by hypnotism or narcotic stimulation. These partners in bliss are best left to their own devices, or so Thomas Harris suggests: 'We'll withdraw now... For either of them to discover us would be fatal.'

"MORBIDITY OF THE SOUL"

Long before *Hannibal* hit the bookshops, the people behind *The Silence of the Lambs* film dropped strong hints about returning for a sequel. Jodie Foster felt that Jonathan Demme's movie had equalled Thomas Harris's achievement of blending the popular with the cerebral: 'I loved *Silence*. It's a movie that's stuck with me... It's both very complex and very literary; and at the same time great entertainment.' According to Buddy Foster, the star talked enthusiastically of a possible follow-up, citing Clarice Starling as her favourite screen role. Interviewed for *The Sun* newspaper shortly after *Lambs'* release, Anthony Hopkins spoke eagerly of reuniting with Foster and Demme for a sequel. 'However, we must wait for the author Tom Harris to finish the story. You cannot rush him.' According to Foster, Hopkins mentioned the sequel whenever they met. Jonathan Demme appeared just as enthusiastic on Academy Awards night 1992, telling the assembled press: 'I want to make a sequel so bad.' Thomas Harris also seemed keen for Foster, Hopkins and Demme to reunite on a film sequel, sending all of them copies of the finished *Hannibal* manuscript when he finally delivered it to his publisher. In the cases of Foster and Demme, their enthusiasm for a new Lecter movie suddenly waned.

Having passed on the film rights to *The Silence of the Lambs*, Dino de Laurentiis did not intend to let the third Hannibal Lecter saga elude him. Dismayed by *Manhunter's* poor box-office performance, the producer didn't even bother to read Thomas Harris's follow-up to *Red Dragon* ('Big mistake'). When Harris and Orion Pictures approached de Laurentiis about the proposed film version of *Lambs*, he reportedly granted them the rights to Hannibal Lecter for free.

Still active in Hollywood during the 1990s, the producer hadn't enjoyed many recent box-office hits. The year after *The Silence of the Lambs* swept the Academy Awards, the best de Laurentiis could manage was *Body of Evidence* (1993), notable only for the scene where murder suspect Madonna drips candle wax over defence lawyer Willem Dafoe's groin. By the end of the decade, de Laurentiis had hit better commercial form with the successful World War II adventure *U-571* (1999), yet Hannibal Lecter remained an elusive prize. While the *Manhunter* deal that gave the producer first refusal on all new Thomas Harris books remained effective, it counted for little when the author's novel output stayed stuck at a total of three. There were even rumours that de Laurentiis had pressured Thomas Harris to write the third Lecter book, the producer determined to get a hit movie out of the character. De Laurentiis confirmed that, throughout the 1990s, he'd visited Harris once or twice a year at the author's Miami and Sag Harbor homes, discussing the new novel over a friendly dinner of prime liver.

The name of the new Thomas Harris book had remained a closely guarded secret pre-publication, and the long-projected film version acquired a series of unofficial titles. These included the portentous *Morbidity of the Soul*, which didn't sound like a box-office winner, and the equally uninspiring *Manhunter 3* and *Silence of the Lambs 2*. In May 1999, media reports claimed that de Laurentiis was close to buying the film rights for an impressive $9 million. This would be the biggest book-to-film deal ever, a major gamble when none of the *Lambs* people had committed to the sequel. Even with the rights secured, the producer would have to pay out serious money to bring the movie to the screen. The third Lecter film had an estimated budget of $100 million, nearly five times the cost of *The Silence of the Lambs*. Aside from the book rights, de Laurentiis would probably have to fork out around $15 million a piece for Jodie Foster and Anthony Hopkins, plus $5-10 million for Jonathan Demme.

Despite his reputation for blowing multi-million dollar budgets on over-inflated flop epics, Dino de Laurentiis had always been cost-conscious when it came to hiring the talent for his films. Approaching Yul Brynner to play the title role in the biblical epic *Barabbas* (1962), the producer expressed horror at the star's salary demands, claiming that Brynner thought he really was the King of Siam. While employing the behind-the-camera talent from *The Silence of the Lambs* for the new film seemed a logical move, it didn't necessarily represent real value for money.

Jonathan Demme's post *Lambs* work included the sentimental, Academy Award-winning AIDS drama *Philadelphia* (1993), which cemented his status as a leading Hollywood player early in the decade. Five years on, the much darker *Beloved* (1998), based on the novel by Toni Morrison, had done badly at the American box-office. Despite the involvement of co-producer and star Oprah Winfrey, a hugely popular figure on television, this tale of slavery, child murder and ghosts lacked easy audience appeal. Ted Tally's subsequent career, boosted considerably by the *Lambs* factor, had yet to produce a hit in the same level. Working as scriptwriter on the Demi Moore vehicles *Before and After* (1996) and *The Juror* (1996), Tally seemed unable to craft credible, strong female characters to match Clarice Starling. Then again, he didn't have a pre-existing Thomas Harris blueprint to work from.

No longer head of his own filmmaking empire, de Laurentiis intended to make the *Hannibal* movie in association with Hollywood giant Universal Pictures. This alliance between producer and studio doesn't appear to have been entirely voluntary. In June 1992, de Laurentiis had been involved in a court case with Universal over the film rights to the as-yet-unwritten sequel to *The Silence of the Lambs*. Universal Pictures chairman Tom Pollock claimed to have an oral contract with de Laurentiis, guaranteeing his studio first refusal on the sought-after property. According to Pollock, this deal dated back to 1991, when de Laurentiis made the flop Christian Slater cop comedy *Kuffs* (1992) for Universal. With both eyes firmly on the newly-released hit film version of *Lambs*, Pollock approached de Laurentiis about a prospective follow-up, aware that the Italian producer still had a first-look deal with Thomas Harris. Universal would pay half the cost of the film rights and a significant proportion of the production budget. In return, Pollock wanted the North American distribution rights for the film, de Laurentiis holding on to all foreign rights. Supposedly consenting to these terms, de Laurentiis declined to sign a written contract, claiming that he and Pollock had a gentleman's agreement. In a further twist to the case, former attorney Pollock had worked for de Laurentiis during the production of *Manhunter*. Faced with a $20 million damages claim, de Laurentiis eventually agreed to make Universal part of a *Hannibal* co-production deal. By the late 1990s, producer and studio were on good terms again, Tom Pollock no longer chairman at Universal. Making *U-571* in association with the studio, de Laurentiis had no problem reuniting with Universal for the long-awaited *Hannibal* movie. For the time being, he had to concentrate on actually obtaining the rights to the book.

While no-one contested the original de Laurentiis deal with Thomas Harris, some argued that the producer could only claim ownership of the Hannibal Lecter character. Metro-Goldwyn-Mayer claimed that it held all rights to the character of Clarice Starling, who post-dated the *Manhunter* deal, purchased from Orion Pictures when the latter went bankrupt. Even as she collected her Academy Award for *Lambs*, Jodie Foster worried that Orion faced financial ruin, later suing the company to get the money owed her. For the record, Orion still existed as a film production company. Following a successful reorganisation plan, which came into effect on 5 November 1992, the company formed a partnership with the Metromedia Company in July 1993 and returned to the movie business later that year. Orion aside, industry pundits predicted a major bidding war for the rights, de Laurentiis and Universal going head to head with MGM. Despite the latter's claim on Clarice Starling, Universal seemed the likely winner. In the event, the various parties agreed on a mutually beneficial co-production. MGM would distribute *Hannibal* in North America and Canada, while Universal handled the overseas markets. If *Hannibal* lived up to box-office expectations, everyone would go home happy.

This sense of elation did not extend to all the *Lambs* veterans. In mid-May 1999, after preliminary discussions with de Laurentiis in New York, Jonathan Demme announced that he wouldn't be directing the sequel, without giving a specific reason. A week later, Anthony Hopkins indicated that he was still willing to reprise his role as Lecter, depending on Demme's replacement. Hopkins had been through a brief period of self-flagellation over his role in *The Silence of the Lambs*, apparently after learning that children in his native Wales had seen the film on video. For all his appreciation of fine wines and medieval Florentine architecture, Hannibal Lecter did not offer a good role model for the kids: 'I don't want to encourage violence through my films.' In November 1994, *Dail Mail* columnist Baz Bamigboye reported that Hopkins had turned down an £8 million fee to reprise Lecter, citing fears of copycat violence. Closer inspection of the article revealed that no such decision had been made, the actor still waiting for Thomas Harris to finish his new book. Ever prudent, Jodie Foster declined to make any kind of commitment to *Hannibal* until she'd seen a finished script. Said to be unhappy about Demme's departure, Foster looked increasingly likely to bail out herself.

By early June 1999, Anthony Hopkins had still not signed on for *Hannibal*, though the actor was widely expected to reclaim the character, probably the best-known role of his career. De Laurentiis's desire to reunite the *Lambs* stars was tempered by their inflated price tags. Promoted to the Hollywood 'A' list by the success of *Lambs*, Jodie Foster and Anthony Hopkins were now both high-priced actors, making the 1991 film's modest $23 million budget a distant memory. Keen to have Hopkins back on board, de Laurentiis made it clear that he didn't think Foster's alleged $20 million salary demand was reasonable.

As the negotiations with Hopkins and Foster dragged on, details of Thomas Harris's new Lecter plot began to leak out. Jonathan Demme's official reason for rejecting the sequel lay with its 'lurid' storyline and allegedly 'excessive violence'. As the director had explained to Saskia Baron a decade earlier: 'I think that filmmakers definitely have [a] responsibility to portray violence... in a way that is not thrilling and glamorizing, as many movies do.' Advance word on the book certainly suggested that it was incredibly gruesome, making both *Red Dragon* and *The Silence of the Lambs* look tame by comparison. When *Hannibal* finally appeared on 8 June 1999, Thomas Harris's second sequel more than lived up to the pre-publication hype. The outlandish image of unholy lovers Lecter and Starling feasting on human brains sat uneasily with Jodie Foster's gutsy, compassionate portrayal of the latter.

Jonathan Demme's uneasiness with the material stemmed in part from his feeling that 'irresponsible' violent screen images could influence aggressive male behaviour, 'going out and performing real violence against other people.' From a creative point of view, Demme argued that no sequel to *Lambs* could hope to recapture the potency of the original. It is likely that he also felt wary about working for Dino de Laurentiis, the latter not being known for granting his directors full creative control over their movies. While Michael Mann had scripted and filmed *Manhunter* without front office interference, the final product was re-tailored according to de Laurentiis's dictates. Screenwriter Ted Tally echoed Demme's refusal to work on *Hannibal*. Tally particularly disliked the 'excessive' scenes involving face peeling and brain eating. Recording his commentary for the laserdisc release of *Lambs* in 1994, Tally also expressed dismay that Lecter had become 'a cuddly, camp figure'.

"I FOUND IT QUITE HUMOROUS"

With Jonathan Demme out of the picture, Dino de Laurentiis needed a new director who wouldn't seem an obvious second division substitute. When Universal put *Jaws 2* (1978) into production, no-one pretended that director Jeannot Szwarc was in the same league as Steven Spielberg.

De Laurentiis's first choice to replace Demme was British filmmaker Ridley Scott, whose erratic career was on the verge of being revived by his Roman epic *Gladiator*, another Universal release. Producer and director had briefly collaborated on the science fiction epic *Dune* (1984), Scott wisely bowing out during the early stages to make way for David Lynch. During the production of *U-571* on the island of Malta, de Laurentiis met up with Scott, the director working on the *Gladiator* set nearby. According to Scott, both de Laurentiis and Thomas Harris approached him about taking on the film version of *Hannibal*, prior to the book's publication. Once he'd been reassured that *Hannibal* wasn't another vast Roman epic production involving elephants, Scott became interested.

Educated at the Royal College of Art, Ridley Scott joined the BBC in the 1960s, working as a set designer, then a director on such diverse series as *Z Cars* and *Adam Adamant Lives!* Scott then moved into the more lucrative world of television commercials, his visual flair selling products ranging from instant coffee to Hovis sliced bread. Styling his first feature film, *The Duellists* (1977), in much the same way, Scott enjoyed a major hit with the science fiction shocker *Alien* (1979), made for Hollywood giant Twentieth Century-Fox. While the monster on the loose storyline offered nothing new, Scott's atmospheric, claustrophobic treatment of the material generated a relentless tension. The murky, dripping hardware of the spaceship *Nostromo* provided little reassurance as the ever-dwindling crew searched for the nightmare creature on their midst. Aside from H R Giger's striking, skeletal monster design, *Alien* offered an independent, resourceful female character in the form of Ellen Ripley (Sigourney Weaver).

Like Michael Mann and Jonathan Demme before him, Ridley Scott had spent long periods in the commercial wilderness. *Blade Runner* (1982), a melancholy science fiction tale of androids and android hunters, drew praise for its moody, rain-swept 'retro-noir' visual style without becoming a box-office hit. The ambitious, if flimsy fairy tale *Legend* (1985) was beset by disasters. After four years of pre-production work, the lavish forest set built for the film on Pinewood Studios' vast 007 Sound Stage burned to the ground. The delayed end result, full of artful backlighting, sunbursts and even soap bubbles, seemed too caught up in its own prettiness to bother with a strong storyline. Re-edited and re-scored for its American release, *Legend* never found an audience.

Scott attempted a Hollywood comeback with *Someone to Watch Over Me* (1987), a much more conventional thriller where blue collar cop Tom Berenger falls for upper class murder witness Mimi Rogers. Budgeted at a relatively modest $17 million, the film grossed only $4.5 million in the United States. While the Academy Award winning *Thelma and Louise* marked Scott's return to commercial and critical favour, the director seemed unable to sustain his success. Audiences proved uninterested in the Columbus anniversary spectacular *1492: Conquest of Paradise* (1992) and neither *White Squall* (1996) nor *GI Jane* (1997) were well received. Made at a time when historical epics were considered commercially suspect, *Gladiator* (2000) revived both the genre and Scott's career.

For all the glitches in Ridley Scott's filmography, the director seemed well qualified to take over the Lecter franchise. His impressive gallery of intelligent screen monsters included *Alien*'s nightmare extraterrestrial killing machine and the murderous yet sympathetic replicants of *Blade Runner*. Even *Legend* offered the demonic Lord of Darkness. Covered from horn to hoof in Rob Bottin's striking make-up design, *Rocky Horror* star Tim Curry had little left to act with apart from his voice. In addition to *Alien*'s Ellen Ripley, *Thelma and Louise* boasted strong, self-sufficient female leads, though the markedly inferior *GI Jane* seemed almost a caricature of 'feminist' heroics. *Gladiator* offered a fascinating, complex villain in the shape of the psychotic, patricidal, incestuous Emperor Commodus (Joaquin Phoenix).

Fortunately for Dino de Laurentiis, Ridley Scott did not share Jonathan Demme's reservations about *Hannibal*, as he explained to *EON* magazine: 'I read and loved the book... I found it quite humorous.' Hannibal Lecter struck the director as 'a very charming character'. The new Lecter movie would have a stronger vein of humour than the relatively po-faced *The Silence of the Lambs*, the Doctor as witty as ever between snacks. As Scott explained: 'I shall be very disappointed if I hear that people aren't smiling. When they're not screaming.' Having staged the famous chest-bursting sequence in *Alien*, Scott was no stranger to grossing out his audience.

Ridley Scott's decision to take over the Lecter franchise from

Jonathan Demme caused some comment. Rarely do big-name directors make sequels, especially sequels to someone else's film. Strictly speaking, *The Silence of the Lambs* was itself a sequel, to Michael Mann's *Manhunter*, though no-one at Orion Pictures would have admitted this at the time. Whether Scott considered himself to be making *Silence of the Lambs 2* or *Manhunter 3*, he had arrived on the pitch with the game already started.

There were a handful of precedents for this unorthodox career move. Sixty years previously, celebrated German emigré Fritz Lang had directed *The Return of Frank James* (1940), a Technicolor western far removed from his usual style. Recently contracted to Twentieth Century-Fox, Lang needed to prove his Hollywood bankability. Similarly, John Frankenheimer had revived a flagging career with the Fox-produced *French Connection II*. British director John Boorman, in need of a hit after *Zardoz* (1974), took on Warner's *Exorcist II: The Heretic* (1977), itself an infamous flop. More recently, Hong Kong action maestro John Woo agreed to direct *Mission: Impossible 2*, replacing Brian De Palma. Even David Cronenberg had a brief association with *Basic Instinct 2.*

Given Ridley Scott's public displeasure at being passed over for the first *Alien* sequel, 'not a very nice experience', the director laid himself open to charges of hypocrisy by taking on the new Lecter film. That said, Jonathan Demme had been offered *Hannibal* and turned it down flat, relinquishing his notional claim on the Lecter franchise. If nothing else, Scott's newly endorsed Hollywood status, and co-producer credit, gave him more leverage than most of Dino de Laurentiis's directors. While Michael Mann had been obliged to deliver a 119-minute cut of *Manhunter* to the cinemas, Scott could insist on a contractual right to go over the two-hour mark. In the event, the finished *Hannibal* would run for 132 minutes.

De Laurentiis's other co-producer on *Hannibal* was his wife, Martha de Laurentiis, née Schumacher. She had collaborated with her husband since *Ragtime* (1981), on which she worked as a production accountant. For *Hannibal*'s all-important screenplay, de Laurentiis hired the celebrated playwright David Mamet, paying out a cool $1 million fee. A Pulitzer Prize winner for his 1984 drama *Glengarry Glen Ross*, Mamet's film credits included *The Verdict* (1982) and *Wag the Dog* (1997), for which he received Academy Award nominations. As a writer-director, Mamet made an acclaimed movie debut with *House of Games* (1987), his more recent productions including *The Spanish Prisoner* (1997) and a screen adaptation of Terence Rattigan's *The Winslow Boy* (1999). No stranger to unashamed commercialism, Mamet had provided the scripts for *The Untouchables* (1987), *Rising Sun* (1993), *The Edge* (1997), which co-starred Anthony Hopkins, and *Ronin* (1998). Busy with his Hollywood satire *State and Main* (2000), writer-director Mamet agreed to fit the *Hannibal* screenplay into an already tight schedule. Thomas Harris, who had initially refused to change the book's finale for the film version, consented to devise something more palatable.

For the *Hannibal* movie, Ridley Scott recruited key members of his *Gladiator* crew: executive producer Branko Lustig, director of photography John Mathieson, editor Pietro Scalia, composers Klaus Badelt and Hans Zimmer, casting director Stephanie Corsalini and costume designer Janty Yates. A humble clapper loader on Derek Jarman's idiosyncratic biopic *Caravaggio* (1986), John Mathieson had worked on *The Hunger* television series, executive-produced by Ridley and Tony Scott, and the high-octane highwayman romp *Plunkett and Macleane* (1999), directed by Ridley Scott's son Jake. Pietro Scalia, who edited *GI Jane* for Scott, had won an Academy Award for his work on Oliver Stone's *JFK*. Klaus Badelt's credits included *Mission: Impossible 2*, another collaboration with Zimmer, and *The Hunger* tv show. German composer Hans Zimmer had worked with Ridley Scott on *Black Rain*, *Thelma and Louise* and *White Squall*, and scored Tony Scott's *True Romance* (1993). His previous horror credits included Wes Craven's *Scream 2*. For the movie's special make-up effects, de Laurentiis hired Greg Cannom, who'd provided some impressively grotesque creations for *Alien 3* (1992), *Bram Stoker's Dracula* (1992), *The Mask* (1994), *Thinner* (1996) and *Blade* (1998).

"WHEN THE POPE DIES..."

As the *Hannibal* production team came together, there was still a big question mark over Jodie Foster's participation in the film. While Dino de Laurentiis remained unimpressed by the star's salary demands, he couldn't deny her continuing Hollywood success. Since *The Silence of the Lambs*, Foster had appeared in *Sommersby* (1993), *Maverick* (1994), *Nell* (1994) and *Contact* (1996). Money aside, Jodie Foster wanted to see a finished script before she took negotiations any further. Dated 9 September 1999, David Mamet's 129 page first-draft screenplay made the expected radical alterations to the book. Unfortunately, they were not deemed to be changes for the better.

One dubious report claimed that Anthony Hopkins 'loved' the Mamet script, which persuaded him to put aside his doubts about Lecter and sign for the film. If so, the actor was in a minority of one. Universal rejected Mamet's draft almost immediately. The script lacked any real narrative drive and failed to develop the crucial relationship between Lecter and Starling, who didn't even meet until page 108. Prior to the last 20 pages, Mamet devoted too much time to supporting characters Mason Verger and Rinaldo Pazzi, who dominated the film at the expense of the supposed leads.

Unimpressed by the obvious flaws in the Mamet's narrative and characterisation, Jodie Foster also regarded the script as just 'too grisly'. Foster also felt that Harris's novel 'betrayed the essence of Clarice Starling' and Mamet's adaptation hadn't solved the problem. Universal executive Stacey Snider put a diplomatic gloss on the whole incident, claiming that Mamet's script 'gave us a terrific start, but it needed work'. Paid in full and assured a co-writing credit on the finished film, Mamet departed from the project. Ridley Scott denied any falling out with Mamet, explaining that the latter had no more free time to work on *Hannibal*.

The task of turning Harris's novel into a workable script passed to Steven Zaillian, described by Ridley Scott as 'one of the best three screenwriters in the business'. Probably best known for *Schindler's List* (1993), which netted him an Academy Award, Zaillian's high-profile credits included *Awakenings* (1990), *Clear and Present Danger* (1994), *Mission: Impossible* (1996), for which he provided the original story, and Martin Scorsese's *Gangs of New York* (2001). Zaillian's writing success had enabled him to turn producer-director for the courtroom drama *A Civil Action* (1998), starring John Travolta.

Originally offered first shot at adapting *Hannibal* for the screen,

Zaillian had declined. Citing prior work commitments, the writer also felt dubious about following *The Silence of the Lambs*: 'You can almost never win when you do a sequel.' Once David Mamet had been and gone, Zaillian changed his mind, picking up the same $1 million fee. As the writer explained, it could be very difficult saying no to Dino de Laurentiis.

Universal commissioned Zaillian to produce a complete rewrite of *Hannibal*, the studio looking for a finale that would placate Jodie Foster. Asked to comment on the discarded David Mamet script, Zaillian echoed Stacey Snider's tact, asserting that the Mamet draft was '...good but it wasn't the movie we want to do.'

Working closely with Ridley Scott, Zaillian spent nearly a month going through the Harris novel and the Mamet screenplay, deciding which characters and story details would have to be changed, rearranged or dropped altogether. Zaillian had accepted the *Hannibal* job on the condition that received a clear brief about the ending required. Consequently, Thomas Harris joined Scott and Zaillian in Los Angeles for the first few days of their script session. Initially reluctant to work on the screenplay, Harris found he enjoyed the experience enough to remain on hand during pre-production, offering Stacey Snider casting suggestions. After several weeks of close collaboration, Ridley Scott felt confident that Steven Zaillian could produce the necessary 'blueprint' for *Hannibal* the movie. Six weeks later, Zaillian had completed a first draft screenplay, soon followed by the final 128 page shooting script, dated 9 February 2000, that satisfied all Universal's requirements.

A lot of the changes from Harris's book were purely practical. Appreciating that the virtually motionless Mason Verger would be difficult to recreate on screen, no matter how gifted the actor, Zaillian gave the character a degree of mobility by placing him in a wheelchair. Aware of the possible controversy over the cannibal element, the writer eliminated some of the book's other unsavoury details, including Verger's paedophilia. A number of key supporting characters were dropped, including several who had appeared in *The Silence of the Lambs* film. Jack Crawford, who initially featured in the script, soon joined Ardelia Mapp in the character discard pile. On the other hand, Zaillian retained the marginal figure of 'Il Mostro', a real-life serial killer who terrorized Florence. New scenes included a gory flashback to the infamous nurse-biting incident described in both *Red Dragon* and *The Silence of the Lambs*.

Zaillian's biggest challenge with the *Hannibal* script was to find an acceptable substitute finale. Aside from the much-debated brain eating, Ridley Scott felt that Thomas Harris's ending just didn't work, Clarice Starling acting completely out of character. As the director explained to *Premiere* journalist Jill Bernstein, he didn't believe Lecter would even want to seduce Clarice Starling into his world: 'I think one of the attractions about Starling to Hannibal is what a straight arrow she is.' Interviewed by the *New York Post*, Scott recounted how he'd met Harris and explained his problem with the finale to the author: 'I just don't buy these two going off together, even with Clarice under the influence.' Harris didn't seem bothered by Scott's criticism and subsequently declared himself happy with Steven Zaillian's rewrite, approving the new, top secret finale. Despite the changes, Zaillian still felt that *Hannibal* was primarily 'a kind of bizarre love story' between Lecter and Starling.

In the event, Jodie Foster still didn't like what she read in the revised screenplay, especially in relation to Starling's character transformation: 'The original movie worked because people believed in Clarice's heroism. I won't play her with negative attributes she would never have.' Officially, Foster dropped out of *Hannibal* in favour of concentrating on her budding second career as a director, which had started out well enough with *Little Man Tate*, made for Orion Pictures, then stumbled a little with the uneven comedy-drama *Home for the Holidays* (1995). There were also suggestions that the *Hannibal* producers had offered Foster less money than Anthony Hopkins, which didn't go down well with the screen's original Clarice Starling.

Ridley Scott claims that he always half-expected Jodie Foster to reject *Hannibal*, the star agreeing to read the Steve Zaillian rewrite more out of courtesy than real interest. Feeling that the further adventures of Hannibal and Clarice stood little chance of equalling *The Silence of the Lambs*, Foster didn't wish to risk undermining one of her favourite screen characters with an inferior second instalment. Some observers suggested that Foster's problem with *Hannibal* lay more with the balance between the characters than the gore. In *The Silence of the Lambs*, Clarice Starling was the undisputed lead: the focus of the title, the storyline and the publicity. Even with the script revisions, *Hannibal* gave centre stage to Doctor Lecter, with Starling now his loyal back-up woman.

Having recently finished work on the epic historical drama *Anna and the King* (1999), Jodie Foster chose to concentrate her energies on a new directing project, *Flora Plum*. Inevitably, rumours surfaced that both Universal and Anthony Hopkins were deeply resentful of Foster's decision to pull out. Dubious of audience responses to a *Lambs* sequel without the original Clarice Starling, Universal reportedly considered scrapping the project. Only the runaway success of Ridley Scott's *Gladiator* convinced the studio that *Hannibal* could work without Jodie Foster on board. In public, Dino de Laurentiis took a pragmatic attitude to the loss of Foster: 'In Italy, when the Pope dies, you get another Pope.' Away from the media glare, the octogenarian film producer supposedly shared Hopkins's fury and outrage. De Laurentiis later claimed that Foster never read Steven Zaillian's script, the star refusing to turn a page until she was offered a $20 million fee and 15 per cent of the box-office gross. In any case, the producer possibly didn't really want Foster in the part of Starling at all. As de Laurentiis explained to Jill Bernstein: 'I don't believe Judy [sic] Foster from day one was right when I read the book.'

"A CERTAIN KIND OF *GRAVITAS*"

With the Clarice Starling role very publicly vacated, there was a flurry of rumours over Jodie Foster's replacement. Initially concerned that no big name actress would want to play a character so closely identified with another star, Universal had no shortage of interest in the part. Names mentioned included *Se7en*'s head-in-a-box victim Gwyneth Paltrow, Cameron Diaz, *Kiss the Girls* star Ashley Judd, Charlize Theron, *Bone Collector* co-star Angelina Jolie, Hilary Swank, an Academy Award winner for her gender-bending performance in *Boys Don't Cry* (1999), and *Ally McBeal* television star Calista Flockhart.

Somewhere near the top of the rumour list came Gillian Anderson, co-star of the hit television series *The X Files* (1994-), an astute blend of science fiction, supernatural horror, police procedural and conspiracy thriller. Anderson's FBI Special Agent Dana Scully owed more than a passing debt to Jodie Foster's Clarice Starling, in terms of profession, dress sense, dedication to the job and quiet authority. She also encountered her share of serial murderers, though several were neither human nor actually living in the accepted sense. Cited as the supposed favourite for the Starling role, Anderson was never a serious contender, as her *X Files* contract didn't permit her to play another FBI agent away from the series.

Australian actress Cate Blanchett seemed a more likely bet, thanks largely to her recent success in the title role of *Elizabeth* (1998), a hit combination of historical drama, political thriller and doomed romance. Universal named Blanchett as its number one choice to take over the role of Clarice Starling, only to discover that her work commitments ruled her out. Other supposedly hot contenders for the part included Helen Hunt, star of the hit television sitcom *Mad About You* and an Academy Award winner for her performance in *As Good As It Gets* (1997). Sarah Michelle Gellar, star of the cult teen-horror television show *Buffy the Vampire Slayer*, expressed a strong interest in the role. Gellar's film work included creditable performances in *Scream 2*, *Cruel Intentions* (1999) and *I Know What You Did Last Summer*, yet she never looked like a serious choice for Starling.

With shooting on *Hannibal* only a few weeks away, Dino de Laurentiis and Ridley Scott finally named Julianne Moore as their new Clarice Starling. Scott felt they'd found a worthy successor to Jodie Foster, explaining to Jill Bernstein that Moore had 'a certain kind of *gravitas*, an intelligence, which is very similar.' A gifted and prolific film actress, Moore lacked an established star image and remained relatively unknown to the general cinema-going public. Moore's career straddled popular hits such as *The Fugitive* (1993) and *The Lost World: Jurassic Park* (1997) and more weighty dramatic fare, including *An Ideal Husband* (1999) and *The End of the Affair* (1999), for which she received a Best Actress Academy Award nomination. She specialised in quirky, arthouse movies, notably Robert Altman's *Short Cuts* (1993), Louis Malle's *Vanya on 42nd Street* (1994), scripted by David Mamet, Todd Haynes' *Safe* (1995), Paul Anderson's *Boogie Nights* (1997) and the Coen Brothers' *The Big Lebowski* (1998).

Moore seemed to have few worries about her screen image, playing a cocaine-addicted porn star in *Boogie Nights* and casually displaying her pubic hair in *Short Cuts*. Impressed by Julianne Moore's 'chameleon' ability, Ridley Scott was more taken by another quality in the actress, as he explained to *Empire* journalist Adam Smith: '...she can be very normal, a real person. And I always saw Clarice as a real person and not a "star"'. Moore had also played supporting roles in the earlier de Laurentiis productions *Body of Evidence* and *Assassins* (1995), neither of them among her finest work.

Discounting Steven Spielberg's dinosaur sequel, Julianne Moore's only previous horror credit was Gus Van Sant's bizarrely pointless shot-by-shot remake of *Psycho* (1998), where she played the investigative sister of murder victim Marion Crane (Anne Heche). Asked about her reasons for accepting the part of Clarice Starling, Moore kept it simple: 'I couldn't refuse such an anticipated film.' Compared to Jodie Foster's alleged $15-20 million price tag, Julianne Moore only cost the *Hannibal* producers $3 million, her highest movie fee to date. Anthony Hopkins felt Moore was a 'perfect' choice for Starling, though he denied having any say in her casting. Ridley Scott later confirmed that he'd consulted with Hopkins over the choice of Julianne Moore, the actor reportedly replying: 'Oh, yes. Jolly good.'

Basking in the glow of his much coveted Best Actor Academy Award, Anthony Hopkins had rapidly consolidated his post *Lambs* status as both a serious character actor and a Hollywood-friendly box-office draw. An ill-advised appearance in the flop science fiction thriller *Freejack* (1992) was obliterated by his performances in the Merchant-Ivory production *Howards End* and Francis Coppola's *Bram Stoker's Dracula* (1992). In the latter, an amusingly overblown retelling of the classic vampire tale, Hopkins's Van Helsing led the righteous, if eccentric forces of good against Gary Oldman's moody, mannered Prince of Darkness. A decade on, the actors would clash once more in *Hannibal*, though this time Hopkins would have the sharper teeth. The star continued to alternate weighty dramatic films such as Merchant-Ivory's *The Remains of the Day* (1993) and Richard Attenborough's *Shadowlands* (1993) with slick, hugely lucrative action-oriented fare like *The Mask of Zorro* (1998) and *Mission: Impossible 2* (2000). Hopkins also lent his presence to a number of intriguing but less-successful films, notably *The Road to Wellville* (1994), *Nixon* (1995), *Surviving Picasso* (1996), *Amistad* (1997) and *Meet Joe Black* (1998), none of which seemed to hurt either his serious actor reputation or commercial status.

For all the tabloid stories to the contrary, it always seemed likely that Hopkins would reclaim the role of Hannibal Lecter in any film sequel. There were rumours that the *Hannibal* producers had another British actor, Tim Roth, lined up to take over the part if Hopkins bowed out. While Roth had an undoubted flair for camp villainy, well displayed in *Rob Roy* (1994), he was an unlikely substitute. More to the point, without Anthony Hopkins, a third Lecter film seemed a dubious proposition. So far as is known, no-one at MGM or Universal made enquiries about Brian Cox's availability.

Despite claiming that 'playing Hannibal was a matter of speaking in a monotone and not blinking,' Hopkins regarded Lecter as his joint all-time favourite role, alongside Richard Milhous Nixon, both 'characters that are isolated and never open to love or life'. Dino de Laurentiis had become worried about *Hannibal* after reading that Hopkins intended to retire from films. Having gone through an arduous experience making *Titus* (1999), a Shakespearean tale of mutilation, revenge and involuntary cannibalism, the actor expressed disillusion with the movie business. Contacted by de Laurentiis, Hopkins assured the producer that he would make an exception for Hannibal Lecter. Jonathan Demme's decision to drop out of the sequel did not overly bother the star, who regarded Ridley Scott as a 'wonderful' director.

Finally convinced that the new Lecter film would not be 'a tawdry follow-up' to *The Silence of the Lambs*, Anthony Hopkins signed on. The deal for *Hannibal* paid Hopkins an estimated $15 million in fees and profit share. Though not as grossed-out by the book as Demme, Foster and Ted Tally, Hopkins disliked Harris's ending to the 'interesting' *Hannibal*, welcoming the Steven Zaillian rewrite. Having re-watched his *Lambs* performance on videotape, the actor decided to portray a 'mellower' Hannibal Lecter this time around. At the pre-shooting press conference for the film, Hopkins announced that he wouldn't be using make-up for the character, letting his own advancing years and relative pallor do the work.

While the casting rumours around *Hannibal* inevitably centred on

Starling and Lecter, there was a third lead part to be filled: the crucial yet physically restricting role of Mason Verger. A memorable villain, the character required a heavy make-up job that would render the actor underneath unrecognisable, not the biggest attraction for a star name. After speculation that the part would go to James Woods, the producers settled on Anthony Hopkins's fellow British actor Gary Oldman. On balance, this seems the right decision. James Woods scored highly on twitchy neurotic villainy, amply displayed in *Once Upon a Time in America* (1984), and leering bigotry, as seen in *Ghosts of Mississippi* (1996), but Oldman had more of the grotesque flamboyance required for Verger. Following his mannered, high-camp turn as *Bram Stoker's Dracula*, Oldman joined the ranks of Hollywood's top British villains, putting on the accents as required. In Tony Scott's *True Romance* (1993), he played one-eyed white Rastafarian Drexl Spivey, a pimp 'n' pusher who blows away a few of his rival drug-dealers before being shot in the groin by the hero. Luc Besson's *Leon* (1994) saw Oldman steal much of the show as bent narcotics cop Norman Stansfield, who listens to Beethoven on his personal stereo while blowing away the family of a double-crossing subordinate. Oldman had also enlivened *Romeo is Bleeding* (1993), as another corrupt cop, Besson's *The Fifth Element* (1997), with a very strange haircut, *Air Force One* (1997), as a crazed terrorist, and *Lost in Space* (1998), as an intergalactic saboteur. Interviewed by *The Sunday Times*'s Garth Pearce, Ridley Scott explained the choice of Oldman: 'I thought, who can lie on his back, be helpless, wear a new face and still... make it all look real?'

The role of doomed policeman Rinaldo Pazzi went to veteran Italian actor Giancarlo Giannini, best known for his Academy Award-nominated performance in Lina Wertmuller's controversial World War II satire *Seven Beauties* (1976), which Giannini also co-produced. The actor's recent American credits included *New York Stories* (1989), *A Walk in the Clouds* (1995) and *Mimic* (1997). Giannini had previously acted in the mediocre de Laurentiis productions *Anzio* (1968) and *Once Upon A Crime* (1992), the 24-year gap telling its own story. The part of Laura Pazzi, Rinaldo's greedy, materialistic young wife, had been built up in the script from the original novel. Casting director Stephanie Corsalini selected Italian actress Francesca Neri for the role. Busy in her native film industry, Neri only had one American credit, the largely forgotten Cannon Films version of *Captain America* (1992).

Doctor Cordell Doemling, Mason Verger's pet psychologist, would be played by Slovenian actor Zeljko Ivanek, who'd previously appeared in Ridley Scott's *White Squall* and Steve Zaillian's *A Civil Action*. Active in American film and television for two decades, Ivanek's credits included *The Sender* (1982), where he played the telekinetic 'John Doe Number 83', *Donnie Brasco* (1997) and Lars Von Trier's love-or-hate-it musical *Dancer in the Dark* (2000).

For the role of ill-fated redneck deer hunter Donnie Barber, Ridley Scott made the offbeat choice of fellow director Adam Spiegel, better known as Spike Jonze. A music video *auteur* noted for his work with Bjork, Fatboy Slim and those white-rapper badasses the Beastie Boys, Jonze had recently scored a major feature film hit with the deeply strange *Being John Malkovich* (1999). No mere beginner in the acting stakes, he'd already lent his dramatic talents to *The Game* (1997) and *Three Kings* (1999).

Boyd Kestner, who appeared in Scott's *GI Jane*, signed on for the part of FBI Agent Mendez, who appears alongside Starling in the opening fish market shootout.

Aside from Lecter and Starling, only two other characters from *The Silence of the Lambs* reappeared in the film version of *Hannibal*: Department of Justice official Paul Krendler and Asylum orderly Barney. Reports that Diane Baker would reprise her role as Senator Ruth Martin proved to be unfounded, hardly surprising given the character's voice only 'cameo' in Thomas Harris's book. The role of Krendler, Starling's government nemesis, went to Ray Liotta, who replaced the late Ron Vawter in the part. Following his memorably nasty turn in Jonathan Demme's *Something Wild*, Liotta had played charismatic near-psychopaths in *Goodfellas* (1990), *Unlawful Entry* (1992) and *CopLand* (1997). Interviewed by Jill Bernstein, Liotta demonstrated a clear grasp of Krendler's bad attitude: 'He has the opportunity and the know-how to make Starling's life miserable, so that's what he does.' Completing a hat-trick of Lecter movie appearances, Frankie R Faison agreed to reprise his *Lambs* role as Barney. Third time lucky, Faison got to do a little more in *Hannibal* than he had in either *Manhunter* or *The Silence of the Lambs*.

While Jonathan Demme praised Faison's performance in *Lambs*, a lot of the actor's footage was cut in post-production. Of the entire *Lambs* cast and crew, only Frankie Faison rejoined Anthony Hopkins for the sequel.

"WHY EXACTLY DID YOU AGREE TO DO THIS FILM?"

Budgeted at a healthy $87 million, *Hannibal* began filming on Monday 8 May 2000 with five weeks of location work in Florence, capital of the Italian province of Tuscany. Questioned at the pre-production press conference held in the Palazzo Vecchio, director Ridley Scott confirmed that the film's ending would be very different from the book. Julianne Moore faced the media alongside Scott and Anthony Hopkins, despite having no scenes in Florence. Her comments on playing the new-look Clarice Starling revealed little: 'this is a different Clarice, she is older and more mature.' Sticking close to Thomas Harris's book, the Florence locations for *Hannibal* included the Palazzo Vecchio, the Ponte Vecchio, the Palazzo Capponi, the Piazza del Duomo and the Uffizi Galleria. The European shoot also took in several days' work on the island of Sardinia, where Mason Verger's special Lecter-eating pigs are bred, conditioned and 'rehearsed'.

Steve Zaillian joined the location filming for the first few days, undertaking minor script revisions in consultation with Ridley Scott. Part-way through the Florence shoot, Thomas Harris arrived in the city on unrelated business. During his lengthy stay in Florence to research *Hannibal*, Harris had been very taken with 'Il Porcellino', a life-sized bronze statue of a huge pig. Presumably the inspiration for Mason Verger's man-eating swine, 'Il Porcellino' also featured in the film version. While most tourists just rub the pig's nose for luck, Harris commissioned a full-size replica for his garden. When he returned to collect the statue, the *Hannibal* producers invited him to visit the set, where Thomas Harris met Anthony Hopkins for the first time. Harris's presence inevitably sparked rumours that the author had been summoned by the desperate producers to perform some major script surgery.

While the *Hannibal* production supposedly operated a closed set, barring all uninvited visitors, the enormous media and fan interest in the film made the policy difficult to enforce. Shooting on the Ponte Vecchio bridge was complicated by problems with crowd control and protests from local shop owners at the filmmakers showing the unlicensed street vendors. Faced with virtual blackmail, Ridley Scott reluctantly revised a scene, Inspector Pazzi buying a cheap metal bracelet from a 'respectable' shop rather than a street hawker.

Complaints about the *Hannibal* production were not confined to Ponte Vecchio retailers. The local Green Party protested at the decision to allow a trashy, gory horror movie to be shot in the historic city of Florence. The Popular Party echoed this condemnation of Hollywood exploitation: 'This film adds nothing to Florence's world prestige. We believe that instead the city would become the setting for morbid thrills and vulgar horror.'

There was an element of irony here. For all its cultural splendours, the city of Florence had an extremely brutal history, alluded to by Thomas Harris in his book. More to the point, the *Hannibal* producers were paying the Florence City Council good money to shoot in the prime tourist areas, handing out $25,000 just for three days filming on the Ponte Vecchio. Whatever the local resentment at the 'intrusive' film production, at least one local entrepreneur cashed in on the movie. Visitors to Florence were offered a new style 'celebrity' tourist guide: 'Hannibal Lecter. Visit the places of the city where he was.'

Back in the United States, the production team set up shop in Richmond, Virginia; Washington, DC; and Asheville, North Carolina, where the Biltmore Estate stood in for Mason Verger's Muskrat Farm. The climactic 'pig barn' scene was shot at the Montpelier estate in Virginia. The Washington locations included the Union Station, an imposing piece of architecture that Thomas Harris had somehow neglected to use in his book. The American location work lasted eight weeks, the *Hannibal* shoot wrapping on 1 September 2000, on schedule and on budget. In total, filming had taken 83 working days over 16 weeks, commendably brisk for a major big-budget production.

Like Jodie Foster before her, Julianne Moore had prepared for the part of Clarice Starling by spending time at the FBI's Quantico Academy. Even with this grounding, she found the grisly subject matter distressing and difficult to handle, meeting with her analyst throughout *Hannibal*'s production. As the sensitive Moore explained to *Vanity Fair* magazine: 'It's psychologically horrifying.' The actress seemed anxious to demonstrate that she'd given serious thought to both the film's theme and its wider implications: '*Hannibal* is the dark side that is part of everyone. That's OK but I don't want to sound as if I'm rationalising violence.' Moore also had physical problems with the film. Shortly before starting training for *Hannibal*, she broke a toe, which restricted her fitness programme. During production, Moore disliked using Clarice Starling's handgun, blanks or not, and felt very uncomfortable with the genuine wild boar used for the crucial barn rescue sequence. The pigs hired and trained for the *Hannibal* production were a dozen Canadian breeding boars, weighing up to 600 pounds each. Having looked at thousands of pigs all over North America, animal co-ordinator Sled Reynolds felt confident he'd found the biggest available.

For his part, Anthony Hopkins admitted to having been mildly grossed out while shooting the flashback scene where Lecter 'persuades' the drugged Mason Verger to shave off his own face and feed it to his dogs: 'That was one point I said to myself: "Why exactly did you agree to do this film?".' No fan of heights, Hopkins also felt uneasy filming the scene where Lecter disposes of Rinaldo Pazzi, the star obliged to push a stuntman over the balcony of the Palazzo Vecchio. On the whole, Hopkins and director Ridley Scott found they worked well together, both favouring minimal rehearsal time, a brisk shooting pace and as few takes as possible.

Reports from the set suggested that Ridley Scott wanted to play up the 'horror' atmosphere of *Hannibal*, using a spooky, surreal style some way from Jonathan Demme's relatively restrained handling of *The Silence of the Lambs*. Scott's meticulous attention to lighting had got him into trouble with cost-conscious executives during the production of *Blade Runner*. On this occasion, the time devoted to each camera set-up did not stretch the agreed schedule.

Kept busy by *Hannibal*'s high level of blood and guts, make-up artist Greg Cannom devoted much of his time to Mason Verger's hideously ruined face. Having worked with Gary Oldman on *Bram Stoker's Dracula*, Cannom knew the actor would relish the chance to outdo his vampire count. Both Oldman and Cannom were pleased with the end result, Cannom telling Jill Bernstein: 'It's really disgusting.' Cannom also supplied the animatronic boar that rips the face off one character, then pulls out his entrails. This mock skinning and disembowelling proved highly effective: 'People were getting sick. I don't think they will show much of it.'

With *Hannibal* near the end of its post-production stage, Orion Pictures resurfaced with a threat of legal action against the film. Displaying a certain ingenuity, if nothing else, the company claimed all rights to the Hannibal Lecter character traits in *The Silence of the Lambs* film that were not in Thomas Harris's original book. Thus if Anthony Hopkins reused any of his distinctive mannerisms, notably the fava beans 'slurp', Orion would sue MGM and Universal. Even if Orion lost the case, their claim rejected out of hand, this legal wrangle threatened to be the kind of pre-release publicity no-one wanted. Rather than risk a lengthy, expensive court case that could delay *Hannibal*'s release, MGM opted to make cuts to the finished film.

Despite these minor deletions, *Hannibal* enjoyed a series of successful previews in the United States. Audiences, sworn to secrecy over the movie's new ending, supposedly gasped in horror during some sequences. Observing one 600-strong audience from the back of the auditorium, Ridley Scott spotted only two walk-outs, an impressively tiny percentage. Gory or not, *Hannibal*'s more extreme scenes didn't trouble the British Board of Film Classification, which passed *Hannibal* as an uncut '18' release on 1 February 2001. In Australia, a number of reviewers protested at the film's 'lenient' MA (Mature Accompanied) rating, which permitted children under fifteen to see *Hannibal* with a parent or guardian. Back in America, the film received an equivalent 'R' rating, allowing viewers under sixteen into screenings if they were accompanied by an adult. Despite recent protests over Hollywood's alleged marketing of violent material at children, *Hannibal* escaped serious controversy on its home ground.

The publicity build-up around *Hannibal* easily matched Orion's promotional campaign for *The Silence of the Lambs* a decade earlier. MGM released the first teaser trailer for *Hannibal* to US cinemas on 5 May 2000, before the film even began shooting. Lacking any actual footage, the trailer did little more than remind audiences of Doctor Lecter, hardly necessary under the circumstances. The poster image for *Hannibal* featured Lecter's image looming out of the darkness, the right side of his face in shadow, the left dominated by a piercing red eye. The publicity lines made less-than-subtle reference to *The Silence of the Lambs*: 'Break the Silence'; 'The silence will be broken'; 'How long can a man stay silent before he returns to the thing he does best?' and 'The silence is broken'. Best of all: '*His Genius* UNDENIABLE *His Evil* UNSPEAKABLE *His Name...* HANNIBAL'.

MGM had to deal with some unplanned publicity when a number of media commentators wondered why Gary Oldman would not have his name on the credits. Star names cast in bit parts often go unbilled, both to increase the element of surprise and keep attention focused on the film itself. Recent examples of celebrity cameos included Jack Nicholson in *Broadcast News* (1987), Macaulay Culkin in *Jacob's Ladder* (1990) and Sean Connery in *Robin Hood: Prince of Thieves*. Cast as *Hannibal*'s third lead, Gary Oldman could hardly be described as a 'special guest star'. *Hannibal* PR man Graham Smith hastened to reassure the media that Oldman hadn't disowned the film. Smith explained Oldman's absence from the credits with practised diplomacy: 'Although he has a large part, it really is Anthony and Julianne's film. Gary was always going to appear anonymously but producer Dino de Laurentiis rather gave the game away when he announced Gary's participation last year.' The *Hannibal* producers ultimately decided to include the actor's name on the closing credits of the release print, putting an end to one of the worst kept movie secrets of recent times.

As MGM and Universal got the *Hannibal* publicity machine into gear, Anthony Hopkins offered his insights into the title character: 'He is not just a killer, he is the darkness in us all.' Elaborating on this view, Hopkins added: 'The new film is a dark romance about obsession – the hatred that Lecter's enemy feels for him and the strange, bizarre love he feels for Clarice.' Looking for a suitably high-profile, high-class launch venue, the distributors arranged for *Hannibal* to be shown out of competition at the 51st Berlin International Film Festival, held in February 2001, with Anthony Hopkins in attendance.

While *Hannibal* hardly needed any additional publicity, its impending release seemed to stir the Hollywood establishment into action. In January 2001, the Academy of Motion Picture Arts and Sciences announced that Dino de Laurentiis would receive the 36th Irving G Thalberg Memorial Award at the Academy Awards ceremony on 25 March. Established in 1937, the year after Thalberg's tragically early death, the award is given to 'creative producers whose bodies of work reflect a consistently high quality of motion picture production.' Whether this really applied in de Laurentiis's case is, perhaps, open to debate. Thalberg, head of production at MGM, favoured quality family entertainment derived from literary sources. Whatever its merits, *Hannibal* didn't quite fit into this category. Earlier de Laurentiis movies such as *The Bible*, *Kiss the Girls and Make Them Die* (1967), *The Stone Killer* (1973), *Mandingo* (1975), *Orca*, *Amityville II: The Possession* (1982), *Conan the Destroyer* (1984), *Red Sonja* (1985), *Silver Bullet* (1985), *The Desperate Hours* and *Body of Evidence* were also way off the family entertainment mark.

It is likely the Academy felt that the Italian producer, now in his early eighties, was reaching the end of his career and had earned a nod of recognition. De Laurentiis hadn't won an Academy Award since 1957, when he picked up the Best Foreign Film trophy for Federico Fellini's *Nights of Cabiria*. With the regular award nominations about to be announced, Ridley Scott also enjoyed a surge of favourable publicity, media pundits predicting a slew of Oscar nods for *Gladiator*.

MGM originally planned to release *Hannibal* in the United States on 14 February 2001, ten years and one day after *Silence of the Lambs*' US premiere. This astute combination of tenth anniversary 'gift' and grisly St Valentine's Day offering was soon scrapped, MGM bringing *Hannibal*'s debut forward five days to 9 February. Julianne Moore attended the film's New York premiere, held on 5 February, along with an assortment of celebrities, including David Bowie and Emma Thompson. *Hannibal* went on to gross just over $58 million in North America over its opening three-day weekend – easily a record for an R-rated movie. By 20 February, MGM declared that the worldwide total stood at a staggering $140 million. Universal were similarly pleased with foreign takings: $9.5 million for the first three days in the UK, $6.3 for the first three days in Germany and $9.2 million after ten days in Italy.

"A MATTER OF PERSONAL TASTE"

With her Best Actress trophy still warm in her hand, original Clarice Starling Jodie Foster declared: 'I really do think that *Silence [of the Lambs]* is one of those very rare films that accomplishes greatness in kind of every single area.' This is not a claim anyone is likely to make for *Hannibal*. After the years of waiting, the legal wrangles, the casting problems and accusations of gore-mongering, the record-breaking 'sequel' to *Silence of the Lambs* emerged to mixed reviews, a sad reflection of its source material's dubious quality.

During the British leg of her *Hannibal* media tour, Clarice Starling number two Julianne Moore discussed the sequel's difference in tone: 'this one has more of a sense of humour – it's a fantasy.' While the jokes are there, the air of unreality seems a serious flaw rather than an asset, the film existing in an undefined, featureless limbo, lacking any sense of identity. *Hannibal* unfolds with no real conviction to its characters or story, taking the viewer's interest for granted.

Interviewed by Sally Weale for *The Guardian*, Anthony Hopkins claimed that he anticipated his second Lecter movie being sniped at. 'I expected *Silence of the Lambs* to be a big hit; but I wasn't so sure about *Hannibal* because it's a sequel. I was waiting for the critics to gun us down.' The shooting started before Hopkins's words made it to the British news-stands. While the *Hollywood Reporter* dismissed *Hannibal* as 'a banal police procedural', the *San Francisco Examiner* seemed deeply offended by the film: 'a revolting experience... wilfully gross, and fundamentally stupid.' There were reports of cinema-goers fainting during the brain-eating scene, both in America and Italy. If *Hannibal* could gross out audiences in the land of *giallo* thrillers and zombie flesh-munching, it had to be something special.

Writing in *The Guardian*, US-based reviewer John Patterson declared himself unimpressed with Hannibal Lecter's big-screen comeback. Having enjoyed Ridley Scott's 'energetic, if faintly ridiculous *Gladiator*', Patterson felt that *Hannibal* by comparison seemed an overblown, 'curiously inert experience'. Reverting to the bad habits evident in *Legend, Someone to Watch Over Me, Black Rain* and *GI Jane*, notably 'cheesy aesthetics' and 'flaccid storytelling', Scott had come up with 'the *Godfather III* of Hannibal Lecter movies'. Noting the absence of Lecter's fava beans and chianti slurp, regular *Guardian* critic Peter Bradshaw described *Hannibal* as 'a *Guignol* horror comedy: sleek, fast-moving, more than a little absurd.'

The first action set-piece is a cliché compendium of slow motion, dissolves and plaintive strings as reluctant gunfighter Clarice Starling is forced to shoot down drug dealer Evelda Drumgo, the latter shielded by her own baby. Elsewhere, there are far too many lingering close-ups of flickering computer screens, as Starling and Inspector Pazzi search the world wide web for information on the elusive Doctor Lecter. Scott presumably didn't know how else to convey the thrill of the electronic chase to audiences. Searching for some meaningful symbolism, Scott offers a stuffed and mounted lamb's head, hanging above Clarice's prone body, a crude and largely meaningless touch. The director also throws in William Blake's 'Ghost of a Flea' painting, as a postcard supposedly sent from Lecter to Starling. Even as an obscure *Red Dragon/Manhunter* in-joke, this seems a half-hearted gesture.

Most disappointing of all, *Hannibal* lacks energy and passion. In fairness to Ridley Scott, the script 'blueprint' he values so much badly let him down in the case of *Hannibal*. Faced with an overlong, unfocussed source novel, Zaillian delivered a flimsy, cut-down version of the plot, which only draws attention to the story's absurdities. Filled with annoying, oblique references to excised incidents and characters, the *Hannibal* screenplay is barely coherent at times. On the plus side, the script wisely eliminates the 'bull dyke' character of Margot Verger, who would surely have drawn protests to match the controversy over Ted Levine's effeminate Jame Gumb in *Silence of the Lambs*. The Florence scenes still drag, however, Lecter's easy victory over Pazzi a foregone conclusion.

Whatever its overall failings, *Hannibal* might at least have recreated the tense, ambiguous Starling-Lecter relationship of *Silence of the Lambs*. Julianne Moore describes her Clarice Starling as 'very solemn, solitary and sad', yet the film seems reluctant to dwell on her victim status. Much of the time, she looks cool and in control, possessing what Peter Bradshaw terms a 'languorous sensuality'. For all his supposed power, nemesis Paul Krendler never seems a serious threat to Starling. Aided by intensive coaching from real-life FBI agent Melissa Thomas,

Moore handles both the action and the investigation with plausible efficiency. The scene where she washes Evelda Drumgo's HIV-positive blood from her baby carries the film's only genuine charge. The character of Starling remains woefully underdeveloped, however. Offering a toned-down version of the accent used by Jodie Foster in *Lambs*, Julianne Moore seems subdued and ineffectual in all other respects. Having Moore repeat some of Foster's lines from *Silence of the Lambs* on a tape recording does not convince us that she is the same person. There is nothing in the new Clarice Starling to explain why Hannibal Lecter is obsessed with her.

From the start, there is no doubt that this is Lecter's movie, the title *Hannibal* appearing in the Doctor's own fine handwriting. Given Anthony Hopkins's close association with the role, it is ironic that he came close to playing a different cannibal psychiatrist a decade earlier. Anticipating legal problems with Dino de Laurentiis over the film rights to Hannibal Lecter, early script drafts for *Silence of the Lambs* referred to the character as 'Gideon Quinn'. If nothing else, *Doctor Quinn, Cannibal*, might have prevented the emergence of television favourite *Doctor Quinn, Medicine Woman*. Now clearly older, Hopkins's Lecter dominates the film simply by turning up. Padding around his Palazzo Capponi apartment, Lecter cuts a distinctive figure with his black outfit, bare feet and fine cigar. A trained classical pianist, Hopkins certainly looks at home tickling the ivories amid all the architectural splendour. Hopkins does the required job with seemingly effortless ease, his charming ogre surveying the rest of humanity with amused contempt. There is some suggestion that Anthony Hopkins didn't want his character, or the film, to be taken too seriously: 'This time Lecter is kind of camp – so outrageous, you just have to laugh.'

Anthony Hopkins and Julianne Moore had previously acted together in the Paris-shot Merchant-Ivory biopic *Surviving Picasso*, an experience Moore described as 'exciting', though critics and audiences tended to disagree. Whatever the stars' professional relationship, their characters do not click onscreen, generating little chemistry. Moore has described Lecter as possessing 'his own personal morality', suggesting a level of insight sadly lacking in the script. Both she and Hopkins deserved better.

Discussing the bloody set-pieces in *Hannibal* with *Empire* journalist

Adam Smith, Ridley Scott explained: 'If the violence is organic, built into the structure, then you can actually get away with more.' Up until the dinner party, however, much of the film's gore is obscured by motion blur, fast-cutting and low resolution 'security camera'-style visuals. Even Inspector Pazzi's entrails splatter artfully on the pavement below his hanging body. There is nothing here to match *Alien*'s chest-bursting, skull-smashing monster, or even the scene in *Blade Runner* where replicant Rutger Hauer breaks Harrison Ford's fingers.

Of the token supporting characters in *Hannibal,* only Gary Oldman's high camp Mason Verger manages to register. Enduring a daily three-and-a-half hour make-up job that left him virtually blind, Oldman resembles a skinned cat who talks like James Stewart, an unusual combination. Verger's relationship with Doctor Doemling, now his 'personal physician', recalls nuclear power magnate Mr Burns and his besotted, crawling assistant Smithers in *The Simpsons.* Faced with a tricky situation after the pig-barn shootout, Doemling is convinced by Lecter to feed his boss to the hogs, unceremoniously tipping Verger out of his high-tech wheelchair. So much for loyalty.

Discussing *Hannibal's* climactic dinner party sequence with Jill Bernstein, Ray Liotta claimed that: 'If anything, it's more explicit than in the book.' Julianne Moore regarded the scene as 'a horrifying mixture of the sublime and the ridiculous', her character rendered semi-comatose by shots of morphine. Anthony Hopkins, on the other hand, claims to have laughed at the gory finale, which left him less than shaken. On balance, Hopkins's response seems the most appropriate. True, the sight of Paul Krendler's exposed brain is somewhat gross, yet there is no real horror built into the dramatic conflict within the scene. The radical rewrite of the climax loses what effectiveness the book possessed, Lecter now feeding just one tiny sautéed brain slice to Krendler himself. Reduced to a horrifed onlooker, the resolutely moral, non-cannibalistic Starling begs the Doctor not to do it. For certain scenes in the graphic open-brain footage, Ray Liotta made way for a passably realistic $70,000 animatronic dummy. As to the complaints about the scene being too much, Julianne Moore put it very well: 'The more gory aspects are a matter of personal taste, I suppose.'

With preview audiences and critics 'forbidden' from revealing the new finale, potential *Hannibal* viewers were led to believe they'd be getting something very special. Ridley Scott explained the rewrite to Jill Bernstein in the following terms: 'I think the ending is more tonal as to what could possibly be in her mind at that moment.' Still determined to apprehend Hannibal Lecter, Clarice Starling ends up pinned to a refrigerator, her 'glorious' red hair trapped in the door. Morphine-haze or not, Starling will not be so easily beaten and turns the tables on her quarry. Handcuffed to Starling, police car sirens drawing ever closer, Lecter reaches for a meat cleaver and cuts off his own hand, making good his escape. The Hannibal Lecter of *Red Dragon* and *Silence of the Lambs*, dedicated to self-preservation at all costs, would have cut off Starling's hand, both a souvenir and a tasty snack. If nothing else, *Hannibal*'s finale pays fitting homage to two vastly superior examples of British Gothic Horror cinema. The skull-sawing recalls one of Peter Cushing's more graphic operations in *Frankenstein and the Monster from Hell* (1974), while the hand-lopping is redolent of *Scream and Scream Again* (1969), where man-made vampire Keith (Michael Gothard) rips off his hand to escape from police handcuffs. Incidentally, just where did Starling conceal the handcuffs on her tight black evening dress? There are rumours that Scott filmed an alternative ending, approved by Thomas Harris, which Universal and MGM tested on preview audiences before deciding to stick with the director's preferred finale.

PART FOUR

TWIN DRAGONS

ontrary to Ted Tally's optimism and the mass of media coverage, Anthony Hopkins hesitated over reprising his Lecter role in the *Red Dragon* prequel/remake: 'I think we've gone to the line with *Hannibal*, with the jokes and the gore.' As with his earlier plan to retire from film-making, Hopkins seemed open to persuasion. In early February 2001, it emerged that Hopkins had approached Dino de Laurentiis with his own ideas for a third Lecter film. Interviewed on the *US Today* television show, Hopkins declined to give further details: 'I shouldn't say anything else about it.' There was an alternative rumour that Hopkins would play only a cameo role in the new film, presumably making way for a younger screen incarnation of Hannibal.

With Hopkins still undecided, Universal Pictures took a risk and green-lit the *Red Dragon* project, on the strength of Ted Tally's first-draft script. Budgeted at $90 million, the film was offered to director Michael Bay, who specialised in large-scale, high-tech action movies such as *The Rock* (1996), *Armageddon* (1998) and *Pearl Harbor* (2001). Bay didn't seem an obvious choice for a serial killer thriller and the director proved unreceptive to the idea. When Bay passed on *Red Dragon*, the job went to Brett Ratner, a music video veteran best known for the action comedies *Rush Hour* (1998) and *Rush Hour 2* (2001), with Jackie Chan and Chris Tucker. Ratner also directed *The Family Man*, a romantic fantasy starring Nicolas Cage as a Wall Street high flyer who learns that there's more to life than material success. None of these films suggested that Ratner was a talent to match Michael Mann, Jonathan Demme or Ridley Scott. Nor did he seem any more suited to the material than Michael Bay. Dino de Laurentiis hadn't even heard of Ratner or seen any of his films. A meeting with the director persuaded de Laurentiis that Ratner could deliver the film they wanted. Furthermore, he had a sound commercial track record and an ability to get the job done with minimal fuss. Ratner received $6 million for directing *Red Dragon*, a $1 million increase on his fee for *Rush Hour 2*.

Ratner found that his first major job on *Red Dragon* was to help convince Hopkins to return as Lecter. Meeting with the actor, Ratner discovered that Hopkins was concerned about the level of graphic violence, especially in the scene where Lecter attacks Will Graham. The director promised his star that he would rely largely on suggestion, keeping the explicit gore to a minimum. Reassured, Hopkins finally signed up for the film. A decade on from *The Silence of the Lambs*, Hopkins was appearing in a film set before its predecessor. It's rumoured that Hopkins' face was digitally rejuvenated for his early scenes in *Red Dragon*, removing wrinkles and crows feet. Hopkins was certainly asked to lose 30 pounds, his additional bulk already noticeable in *Hannibal*, which at least showed the older, better-fed Lecter.

The crew for *Red Dragon* included cameraman Dante Spinotti, who shot *Manhunter* and Brett Ratner's *The Family Man*. Ratner had assumed that Spinotti wouldn't be interested in a second film version of *Red Dragon*. Spinotti was intrigued by the challenge of telling the same story in a different style, the modernist look of *Manhunter* giving way to the neo-Gothic atmosphere of *Red Dragon*. Ratner also recruited production designer Kristi Zea, who worked on *The Silence of the Lambs* and *The Family Man*, and editor Mark Helfrich, who cut his teeth on action movies such as *Rambo: First Blood Part II* (1985) and *Predator*, before teaming up with Ratner for *Rush Hour*, *The Family Man* and *Rush Hour 2*. The score was composed by Danny Elfman, best known for the *Simpsons* theme and his collaborations with director Tim Burton, notably *Pee-wee's Big Adventure* (1985), *Beetle Juice* (1988), *Batman* (1989), *Edward Scissorhands* (1990), *The Nightmare Before Christmas* (1993), *Mars Attacks!* (1996) and *Sleepy Hollow* (1999). Elfman's non-Burton credits included *The Family Man*.

The first choice for Will Graham was Ethan Hawke, an actor put to good use in *Before Sunrise* (1995) and *Gattaca* (1997), an offbeat science fiction fable. When Hawke passed, the role went to Edward

Norton, who first came to notice in *Primal Fear* (1996), as an altar boy accused of murder. Norton quickly established himself as a forceful character actor of great presence, co-starring in *The People versus Larry Flynt* (1996), *American History X* (1998) and the modern classic *Fight Club* (1999). Norton's more recent credits included *The Score* (2001), opposite Robert De Niro and Marlon Brando, and the biopic *Frida* (2002), a vehicle for his then girlfriend Salma Hayek. He received $8 million for *Red Dragon*, a respectable fee for an actor who lacked Hollywood A-list status. Norton was 33, the same age as William Petersen when he made *Manhunter*.

The role of Francis Dolarhyde was linked to Sean Penn and *Family Man* star Nicolas Cage, who could both project an edgy intensity with an undercurrent of suppressed violence. Actors who auditioned for the part included Jeremy Piven, seen in *The Family Man* and *Rush Hour 2*. Ratner eventually cast British actor Ralph Fiennes, who made his film breakthrough with *Schindler's List* (1993), as vile Nazi camp commandant Amon Goth. Fiennes subsequently starred in *Quiz Show* (1994), *The English Patient* (1996) and *The End of the Affair* (1999), which also featured *Hannibal* actress Julianne Moore. His only major slip-up was *The Avengers* (1998), a big budget flop based on the classic 1960s TV series. Cast as iconic agent John Steed, Fiennes looked deeply uneasy beneath his bowler hat. 2002 also saw the release of David Cronenberg's *Spider*, in which Fiennes played a mental patient with extreme mother issues.

There was talk of Scott Glenn returning as FBI man Jack Crawford. After meeting with genuine FBI agents, Brett Ratner decided that the soft-spoken Glenn bore little resemblance to his real-life counterparts, who looked and behaved like New York cops (much like Dennis Farina in *Manhunter*). Ratner replaced Glenn with Harvey Keitel, a Brooklyn-born actor best known for Martin Scorsese's New York classics *Mean Streets* (1973) and *Taxi Driver* (1976). Keitel excelled at playing characters who were tough and often unbalanced yet also thoughtful and humorous. His career as a leading man peaked in the late 1970s, with starring roles in *The Duellists* (1977), the debut film of *Hannibal* director Ridley Scott, *Blue Collar* (1978) and *Fingers* (1978), all of which earned critical acclaim but little money. Keitel's talents were often wasted in his 1980s films, with the notable exception of Scorsese's *The Last Temptation of Christ* (1988), which cast him as an unusually sympathetic Judas Iscariot. He enjoyed a career renaissance in the 1990s, with major roles in Scott's *Thelma and Louise* (1991), *Reservoir Dogs* (1992), *Bad Lieutenant* (1992), *The Piano* (1993), *Pulp Fiction* (1994) and *From Dusk Till Dawn* (1996).

Ratner intended the role of Reba McClane for Tea Leoni, who co-starred in *The Family Man*. When Leoni proved unavailable, he cast British actress Emily Watson, exchanging Hollywood glamour for the latter's striking yet less conventionally attractive looks. Watson made an extraordinary film debut in *Breaking the Waves* (1996), cast as a naïve young woman who submits to sexual degradation at the hands of strangers to both please and 'save' her disabled husband. She went on to appear in *Hilary and Jackie* (1998), *Angela's Ashes* (1999) and *Gosford Park* (2001). Molly Graham was played by Mary Louise Parker, whose films included *Fried Green Tomatoes* (1991) and *Bullets Over Broadway* (1994). The small but crucial role of Freddie Lounds went to Philip Seymour Hoffman, who appeared in *Boogie Nights* (1997), *The Big Lebowski* (1998) and *Magnolia* (1999). Hoffman had been interested in playing Dolarhyde, a role already earmarked for Ralph Fiennes. According to Ratner, Hoffman discovered that his packed schedule ruled out a major role in *Red Dragon*, and he settled for the part of Lounds, receiving special billing. Hoffman's other 2002 releases included *Punch-Drunk Love*, with Emily Watson.

Ratner also cast Chinese-American actor Ken Leung, who appeared in *Rush Hour* and *The Family Man*. Leung's other credits included *Welcome to the Dollhouse* (1995), *Keeping the Faith* (2000), directed by and co-starring Edward Norton, and *AI: Artificial Intelligence* (2001). In *Red Dragon*, Leung played forensics expert Lloyd Bowman, the one member of Crawford's FBI team with significant screen time. Grandma Dolarhyde's voice was provided by Ellen Burstyn, star of *The Exorcist* (1973), while the Voice of the Dragon was Frank Langella, whose more sinister movie characters included *Dracula* (1979) and Skeletor in *Masters of the Universe* (1987). Burstyn went uncredited and Langella's vocal cameo would be dropped from the release print. While Ratner liked Langella's low key reading, the Dragon's voice almost a whisper, he felt the device was too hokey, detracting from Ralph Fiennes' anguished performance.

Frankie Faison and Anthony Heald returned as Barney and Doctor Chilton, playing younger versions of their *Silence of the Lambs* characters without any digital assistance, though Heald wore a wig. Faison upheld his record as the only actor to appear in all of the Lecter films. While Faison looks more or less the same in *Red Dragon*, bar some weight gain, Heald is noticeably older, underlining the skewed chronology. Heald's performance in *Red Dragon* is broader, perhaps to compensate for his less substantial role and a consequent loss of dramatic tension. Brett Ratner hoped that *Manhunter* director Michael Mann would make a cameo appearance. Mann proved unavailable, hardly a surprise given Dino de Laurentiis's public expression of contempt for his film.

Red Dragon was filmed over 77 days, starting on 7 January 2002. Most of the locations were in Maryland, including Baltimore, and California. Visitors to the set included Michael Jackson, who was treated like showbusiness royalty. As a joke, Ratner filmed a take where Dolarhyde informs Reba that Jackson is hiding in his attic. Given Jackson's bizarre public image, his presence in Dolarhyde's haunted world doesn't seem so weird. One exterior shot, of the Baltimore State Forensic Hospital, had to be taken from *The Silence of the Lambs*, as the building used was now part-demolished.

Red Dragon is more faithful to Harris's book than *Manhunter* and this may be its biggest problem. Announced as the definitive film version of the story, with 'official' Lecter Anthony Hopkins in place, *Red Dragon* is curiously muted, despite a heavyweight cast and strong technical credits. Brett Ratner had been unsure if he was the right choice for the film, its dark subject matter far removed from his previous work. On the evidence of the finished movie, his reservations were justified.

Ratner aimed to shoot *Red Dragon* in the style of *The Silence of the Lambs*. The latter influence is apparent only in the most obvious ways, highlighting Lecter's dungeon-like cell, restraining mask and blue prison uniform. Ratner cannot match Jonathan Demme's sense of pace, framing and composition or his skill with actors. Whatever its faults, *The Silence of the Lambs* gets under the viewer's skin while *Red Dragon* remains obstinately superficial. Ratner's direction is efficient yet impersonal, struggling to establish mood and atmosphere. The monotonous pace verges on the plodding, with minimal suspense or excitement and not even much sense of urgency. The closing moments of *Red Dragon*, leading into the earlier film, are treated as a humorous throwaway.

The visuals are more graphic than in *Manhunter*, with flashes of gore and female nudity. The film-makers tried to strike a balance between shocking the audience and grossing them out. While *Red Dragon* retains the book's 'secretor' line, dropped from *Manhunter*, Ratner cut a short scene where Graham states that Valerie Leeds was raped post-mortem. *Manhunter* remains the more unsettling experience, relying on mood and suggestion rather than overt shocks.

Ratner's key collaborators show professionalism rather than inspiration. Danny Elfman's conventional score verges on the anonymous, with little hint of his usual flair and imagination. Ted Tally's much-vaunted script is overemphatic and the dialogue sometimes awkward. Michael Mann's screenplay for *Manhunter*, which made significant departures from the book, is a much leaner piece of writing, with a surer sense of dramatic structure. For example, in *Red Dragon*, the do-as-god-does aspect is introduced too early, losing much of the impact it had in *Manhunter*. Graham's first visit to the incarcerated Lecter is now at Jack Crawford's suggestion, his former colleague clearly reluctant to make the trip. One of the strengths of Harris's book, and *Manhunter*, is that Graham makes the decision himself, re-entering the lion's – or dragon's – den of his own free will.

In the scene with the sleeping tiger, Reba uses a stethoscope to listen to its heart, rather than placing her ear against the animal's chest. It should be noted that under new animal protection laws, the tiger couldn't be sedated on set, as happened with *Manhunter*. Emily Watson was understandably nervous, especially when the tiger repeatedly got up mid-take. While the film-makers' caution on *Red Dragon* is understandable, the image – and its attendant subtext – no longer has the same resonance. One of the more effective touches comes early on, as the credits play over Dolarhyde's scrapbook, an ingenious means of accelerated narrative progression.

Edward Norton carries most of the film and emerges with points for effort rather than achievement. Norton clearly put a lot of thought into the role of Will Graham. Ted Tally's script had Graham visibly scared during his first encounter with the imprisoned Lecter. Norton rightly argued that an experienced agent like Graham would never show his fear to a prisoner. Brett Ratner agreed and Graham stayed outwardly cool throughout the scene. After Graham leaves Lecter, the sweat stains under his armpits give his true feelings away.

Norton captures Graham's earnestness and determination, but little of the passion, anger or intensity found in William Petersen's portrayal of the character. This is not to say that Petersen is a better actor than Norton. His success as the Graham-lite Gil Grissom in *CSI: Crime Scene Investigation* suggests he is a charismatic actor of limited range, ideally cast in macho-intellectual roles with undercurrents of sensitivity and inner pain. Norton, a more versatile performer, is simply miscast as Graham. He is further handicapped by an ill-advised blond dye job that screams 'fake!' Norton's best moment is the scene where Graham comforts Reba after her escape from the burning Dolarhyde house. Graham is sympathetic, reassuring and humorous, telling Reba that her hair is a mess. Norton also conveys the agent's brisk professionalism, Graham both compassionate and detached in the line of duty.

As a vehicle for Hannibal Lecter, *Red Dragon* is handicapped by its fidelity to the source novel. Harris wrote Lecter as a supporting character who played an important yet secondary role in the narrative. *Manhunter* opens with the unseen killer at the Leeds house and the early scenes are dominated by Will Graham. Lecter – or Lecktor – isn't even mentioned for the first 20 minutes, making his entrance shortly afterwards. *Red Dragon* screenwriter Ted Tally attempts to counter this problem with a lengthy pre-credits sequence, set in 1980, comprising three new scenes. Lecter is first seen at a concert by the Baltimore Symphony Orchestra, where a flautist's off-key playing offends him. A slow crane shot finds Lecter in the audience, his left eye twitching as he cringes at the musician's incompetence. The film then cuts to a dinner party, where Lecter serves a special course that delights his fellow Symphony Board members. Quoting from Horace, he watches his guests eat with a calm detachment. His visitors departed, the Doctor is clearing away when Special Agent Will Graham comes calling. In line with Hopkins' wishes, the fight that follows is low on gore, despite the multiple stab wounds

ABOVE: Hopkins shares a joke with a masked Billy Crystal, the host of the 64th Academy Awards in Los Angeles, March 1992.

LEFT: Director Jonathan Demme at the Academy Awards ceremony. Demme won the Best Director, Jodie Foster won Best Actress and Anthony Hopkins was awarded Best Actor on the night.

ABOVE: Anthony Hopkins was immortalised in wax by Madame Tussaud's in 1994.

RIGHT: Director Ridley Scott revitalised his career with *Gladiator* (2000), and further consolidated his reputation with the commercial success of *Hannibal* (2001).

RIGHT: *Hannibal*

ABOVE: Gary Oldman was buried under layers
of prosthetics to play the disfigured Mason Verger,
Lecter's vengeful nemesis, in *Hannibal* (2001).

LEFT: Julianne Moore and Anthony Hopkins at the
New York Premiere of *Hannibal,* February 2001.

ABOVE: Hopkins at the Hamburg premiere of *Red Dragon,* October 2002.

RIGHT: Anthony Hopkins and Ralph Fiennes at the New York premiere
of *Red Dragon,* September 2002.

ABOVE: Gaspard Ulliel as the young Hannibal Lecter, and Gong Li as Lady Murasaki Shikibu, in *Hannibal Rising,* 2007.

ABOVE: Director Peter Webber, producers Martha di Laurentiis and Dino di Laurentiis and stars Gong Li and Gaspard Ulliel at the New York premiere of *Hannibal Rising,* January 2007.

and bullet holes. Competently handled by Ratner, this crucial encounter – referred to in the book but not part of the narrative – falls strangely flat as dramatised on film. There's little tension or suspense and the element of surprise is non-existent.

By this point, Anthony Hopkins could have played Lecter in his sleep. Third time around, he delivers the expected goods without adding much to the character. In *The Silence of the Lambs*, Hopkins' Lecter shared the limelight with Jodie Foster's Clarice Starling. In *Hannibal* he was the undisputed star. In *Red Dragon*, Lecter remains a supporting figure, despite Hopkins' top billing and the extra scenes shoehorned into the narrative. Hopkins' dyed hair and ponytail (why?) are distracting, though his cold lizard stare and elegantly phrased contempt for humanity are undeniably effective.

Hopkins delivers some impressive grace notes. His line to Graham, 'How I'd love to get you on my couch', is loaded with multiple meanings, yet Hopkins makes it very matter of fact. Lecter acts hurt when Graham loses faith in him and somewhere within their twisted relationship the Doctor seems genuinely fond of his FBI associate, a 'remarkable boy'. Lecter gives Graham a reassuring pat on the shoulder, a neat touch suggested by Hopkins. Threatened with exposure, Hannibal is a tender butcher, considerate towards Graham as he plunges a blade into his chest. Stabbed with a handful of arrows, Lecter smiles to himself, still impressed by Graham's initiative and determination. In later scenes, Hopkins gives the incarcerated Lecter a childish sulk, moving from playful banter to cold fury in a matter of seconds. The Doctor is desperate for small victories over the man who put him away. Humiliating Doctor Chilton is just too easy for Lecter, even when confined to a straightjacket and restraining mask. Lecter's anger towards Graham is always tempered by a keen insight and sense of admiration, 'You stink of fear, but you're not a coward.'

Keen to get Lecter out of his cell, Ted Tally wrote a brief sequence set in an indoor exercise yard, Hannibal held on a chain leash. While this scene provides an effective shock cut, Hopkins' bulky figure does not suggest the diet of an institutionalised patient or prisoner. In another original scene, Lecter is served a gourmet dinner in his cell, a chef and waiter on hand. As the latter attends to the meal, Lecter looms into view inches from his face, mouthing a sincere 'Thank you'. Offered good material, Hopkins rises to the occasion. Elsewhere, he delivers Lecter-by-numbers.

What *Red Dragon* misses is the menace and passion of the younger, slimmer Lecter seen in *The Silence of the Lambs*. There's nothing to match Hopkins' sly delivery of the line, 'That new one, Buffalo Bill. What a naughty boy he is.' In the Demme film, he looks physically powerful, with no bulging waistline, and seems even crueller, coolly dismissing a murdered patient, 'His therapy was going nowhere.' This Lecter has more edge, perhaps because Hopkins had something to prove at the time. Active in films but by no means a star, he was disenchanted with his stage career and tired of marking time in *de luxe* TV soap operas. *The Silence of the Lambs* offered the chance of a Hollywood break that Hopkins grasped with all the ferocity of Lecter chewing on a face. Ten years later, this hunger was gone, sated by a slew of starring roles in big budget movies. Having nailed the character in *The Silence of the Lambs* – and walked off with an Academy Award – Hopkins can hardly be blamed for treating his Lecter reprisals as well-paid star turns.

The Dolarhyde house is the spooky rural mansion of Harris's novel. It's also the stuff of a thousand 'B' grade horror movies and has barely more impact here, despite the superior design and set dressing. Grandma Dolarhyde's disembodied voice is another horror cliché, a pale imitation of Mother's stern tones in *Psycho*. The business with the false 'Dragon' teeth, marginalised in *Manhunter*, is more explicit here. In one scene, Dolarhyde puts the teeth in and snarls while wearing a stocking over the top half of his head. The end result resembles a bizarre (unintentional?) homage to *Alien* (1979). It's regrettable that Dolarhyde is never this unsettling again.

Like Edward Norton, Ralph Fiennes worked hard at his role, putting on serious muscle. Norton was impressed by Fiennes's 'rich mellifluous voice', though this quality is toned down in *Red Dragon*. Fiennes' Dolarhyde is subdued, unsettling and socially inept, yet the actor seems an awkward fit for the role. As Tom Noonan proved in *Manhunter*, the part doesn't require movie star looks, which are arguably counterproductive. While Fiennes's prosthetic harelip is well-achieved, it doesn't detract from his handsome face. Fiennes's Dolarhyde conjures no sense of dread, rendering his nude shotgun antics bizarre yet devoid of menace. His spectacular tattoo, which took eight hours to apply, inspires curiosity rather than fear and trembling.

The Dragon slide show, a highpoint in *Manhunter*, is less effective here, despite the calibre of the actors. Philip Seymour Hoffman's Lounds isn't seen reading the note, one of Stephen Lang's finest moments in the earlier film. Hoffman is clad only in his underpants, while Fiennes is wearing a bathrobe, then nothing, giving the scene an air of gothic-camp more weird than frightening. The museum trip, dropped from *Manhunter*, is retained from the book, Dolarhyde devouring Blake's painting of 'The Great Red Dragon and the Woman Clothed with the Sun'. It's debatable whether or not this scene worked in Harris's novel. On film, it seems both risible and inconsistent, Dolarhyde leaving behind two living witnesses who can identify him. While Dolarhyde is arguably acting out of character, his feelings for Reba distracting him from his Dragon's mission, the sight of Ralph Fiennes coshing the cheerful gallery attendant and snacking on the shredded picture inspires only bemusement. Brett Ratner loved the scene and Fiennes insisted on chewing real paper, yet their enthusiasm doesn't translate into the *tour de force* moment so clearly intended. Fiennes saw Dolarhyde as a monster with a soul. While he captured the latter aspect of the character, his family-slaughtering serial murderer just isn't monstrous enough.

The double climax is reasonably faithful to the book during the scenes at the Dolarhyde house. The showdown between Graham and Dolarhyde is radically changed from the novel, as Ratner, de Laurentiis and Tally all felt that Graham should be more heroic. Moving the action from the beach to the Graham house, the film gives Will Graham the moment of glory denied him by Harris. This sequence is well-handled, Graham using Grandma Dolarhyde's words – as recorded in the scrapbook – to unsettle her horribly damaged grandson. The mix of knife and gunplay recalls Graham's fight with Lecter at the start of the film. This time around, the FBI man isn't so vulnerable, despite the threat to his young son. In the interests of gender equality, Molly delivers the *coup de grace*, clearly signalled by her earlier target practice. Wounded but not disfigured, Graham holds on to his life, his family and his sanity. As with *Manhunter*, the softened ending eschews the bleakness of Harris' book, delivering a more conventional yet dramatically satisfying conclusion.

The US reviews for *Red Dragon* were mixed, yet often favourable. *Chicago Sun-Times* critic Roger Ebert praised director Brett Ratner and his cast:

> To my surprise, he does a sure, stylish job, appreciating the droll humor of Lecter's predicament… Ratner doesn't give us as much violence or as many sensational shocks as Scott did in *Hannibal*, but that's a plus… This movie, based on Harris's first novel, has studied *Silence of the Lambs* and knows that the action comes second to general creepiness…As the 'Tooth Fairy' figure, named Francis Dolarhyde, Ralph Fiennes comes as close as possible to creating a sympathetic monster.

Variety's Todd McCarthy echoed the sentiment:

> Hannibal Lecter scores again in *Red Dragon*. Even to the multitudes familiar with every detail of Thomas Harris's first installment of the Lecter trilogy, as well as with Michael Mann's estimable first screen version *Manhunter,* Brett Ratner's faithful, immaculately-appointed new telling of the inescapably creepy tale will be an intense, unnerving experience. An outstanding cast… lends a classy veneer to this sure-fire commercial attraction.

Village Voice critic Michael Atkinson begged to differ, dismissing *Red Dragon* as an 'utterly unnecessary remake of *Manhunter*… Hopkins devotes most of his concentration to trying not to blink and intoning cannibal puns… Norton is far too young, Method-y, and earnest for his role… Every rental of the Mann instead is a vote for Hopkins's retirement.' Reviewing the film for the *San Francisco Chronicle*, Edward Guthmann felt the high calibre cast was slumming. 'Amazing, isn't it, how even world-class actors like Fiennes, Watson and Mary Louise Parker are so easily seduced? *Red Dragon* is a grisly, amped-up thriller that doesn't challenge or dignify their talent, but it obviously has the potential to expand their profile and boost their asking price.'

British critics were unimpressed, by and large. Writing in *The Guardian*, Peter Bradshaw damned *Red Dragon* with faint praise. 'It's more satisfying than the Lecter-at-large story of *Hannibal*, but the whole serial-killer thing is now very, very tired.' *Observer* critic Philip French wondered if 'Hopkins wants to wipe away the memory of his fellow Celt, Brian Cox, a cult villain since his performance in *Manhunter*, and aims to make Hannibal all his own.' The end result, in French's view, was 'a decent enough entertainment that sticks closely to the novel... Edward Norton is too preppy, not inward enough as the FBI man. Ralph Fiennes is barking mad in a Heathcliff mode as the Tooth Fairy. Anthony Hopkins's acting is all glowering, self-conscious charisma as Lecter.'

The Independent's Jonathan Romney, no fan of *Manhunter*, characterized Brett Ratner as 'a faceless director springing from the anonymity trap by appropriating the cast-off surfaces of earlier Thomas Harris adaptations... *Red Dragon* isn't the real thing, just a prelude to it... Overall, a terrible slowness prevails: Ratner directs like a shopper weighed down by a cartload of de luxe ingredients.' Romney also saw major problems with the casting, 'As played by the narcissistically moody William Peterson [sic], *Manhunter*'s Graham came across like an upmarket hairdresser with a hard-knuckle Hemingway streak. He was infinitely preferable, though, to Edward Norton, anaemic and weaselly with his uninflected drone.' Romney did praise 'Hopkins's success in restoring dignity to a character who was halfway to being as facetiously ingratiating as Jack Nicholson's Joker'. *Time Out* critic Peter Watts saw a film running on empty:

> Where Mann and Demme steered the hokum away from
> dull genre generalities, Ratner's point-and-film literalness
> churns out a thriller by rote, shorn of the psychological
> dogfighting that distinguished the first two films...The
> cast look brilliant on the fly poster, and might as well have
> remained there for all the depth they bring to the film.

Red Dragon premiered in the US on 30 September 2002, going on general release four days later. In Britain, the film opened on 11 October

2002. Once the film was in release, Anthony Hopkins announced that *Red Dragon* was definitely his last outing as Doctor Hannibal Lecter. Hopkins seemed to be in tune with the general feeling that Lecter had exhausted his potential as a movie icon. While *Red Dragon* took the number one spot during its opening weekend – in the US and 40 other countries – the total box-office gross was disappointing. The film took a modest $92.9 million in the US and £9.5 million in the UK. *Hannibal*, released a year earlier, made $165 million in the US and £21.4 million in the UK. Perhaps Lecter fatigue was beginning to set in. Fans of the *Silence of the Lambs* film had waited ten years for a sequel, only to be offered two in quick succession. It didn't help that neither *Hannibal* nor *Red Dragon* were the equal of *Lambs*. *Red Dragon* also compared unfavorably with *Manhunter*, now an established cult classic. Worldwide, *Red Dragon* took around $200 million, barely enough to cover its production, marketing and distribution costs once the theatre owners' percentage had been deducted. While television and home video sales put the film into profit, it hardly qualified as a blockbuster. Was there still life in the Hannibal Lecter franchise? Dino de Laurentiis certainly hoped so. His next Lecter project would be without Anthony Hopkins, yet the producer held an ace up his sleeve. Thomas Harris was working on a new Lecter novel.

PART FIVE
FINE YOUNG CANNIBAL

Hannibal Rising (2006) chronicles the adventures of the young Lecter, expanding on the flashback in *Hannibal*. Some Thomas Harris fans felt that revealing Lecter's origins reduced the character's mystery and appeal. An entire book explaining his background and formative influences could backfire badly, damaging the Lecter brand-name. Having created the world's number one literary cannibal, Harris seemed in danger of losing sight of what made the character work.

For the first time, Harris would also script the film version of his book. According to Martha de Laurentiis, Dino de Laurentiis was surprised when Harris asked to write the script. Relatively few authors adapted their work for another medium and even fewer made a success of it. Novels and screenplays were very different forms and skill in one field rarely transferred to the other. Whatever his reservations, de Laurentiis wasn't going to turn Harris down. While this would have stirred excitement a few years – and books – earlier, the *Hannibal Rising* project smacked of an opportunistic package deal. Unusually, the screenplay would be completed before the novel, Harris putting the book aside to concentrate on the film version. Far from being a stand-alone literary work, the *Hannibal Rising* book seemed more of an afterthought, albeit one guaranteed to sell in the millions.

Determined to keep the Lecter franchise rolling, Dino de Laurentiis began pushing the movie in 2003. The book was announced on 28 October 2004 by Harris's UK and US publishers, William Heinemann and Bantam Press. The fourth Lecter novel was scheduled to appear in the Autumn, or Fall, of 2005. At this stage, the title was *Behind the*

Mask. Much of the story was set in France, in and around Paris. Harris researched some of the background details with the Brigade Criminelle of the Paris police, based in the Quai des Orfevres. Most of Lecter's killings were based on real-life murders Harris had covered as a young crime reporter.

The original title was dropped, initially in favour of *Young Hannibal*, which invited comparison with Mel Brooks's comedy horror classic *Young Frankenstein* (1974). Other rumoured titles included *Behind the Mask: The Blooding of Hannibal Lecter*, *Hannibal 4* or *IV*, *The Lecter Variations* and *The Adventures of Young Hannibal Lecter*. The final choice of *Hannibal Rising* seemed both more fitting and suitably enigmatic.

True to form, Harris overran his schedule, though only by a year or so. According to a report in *The New York Times*, Harris didn't deliver the manuscript until August 2006. This left his publishers little time to have the novel ready for a pre-Christmas launch, the peak period for book sales. *Hannibal Rising* was treated as a major event, shrouded in secrecy. Reviewers had to sign a legal document promising not to discuss the book until publication day. In mid-November, Chapter Six of *Hannibal Rising* was released on the book's official website, in both print form and as an audio file read by Harris himself. Advance copies of the novel were strictly limited and sent to reviewers two days prior to the official release, putting critics just one day ahead of the wider reading public. Harris declined to grant interviews, arguing that the book should speak for itself. *Hannibal Rising* hit the bookshops on 5 December 2006, late in the day for a blockbuster novel aimed at the Christmas market.

Hannibal Rising opens in Lithuania during the early 1940s. The eight-year-old Hannibal Lecter is a good natured, if preternaturally bright child who lives with his aristocratic parents and younger sister in the family castle. In harmony with nature, he enjoys a daily stand-off with a black swan that swims in the castle moat. Showing respect for the creature, Hannibal competes with the swan on its own terms, using branches to create an intimidating wing span. This blissful existence is brought to an abrupt end, as the Lecter family flee from the German sweep across Eastern Europe towards Russia. Taking refuge in the estate's hunting lodge, they are safe for a while....

Hannibal Rising sees Thomas Harris as adrift as his young hero.

The confident prose style, assured background detail and precision storytelling of *Red Dragon* and *The Silence of the Lambs* are seldom to be found here. Even the lurid excesses of *Hannibal* are more memorable than the join-the-dots vendetta narrative that makes up *Hannibal Rising*. In some ways, it seems almost appropriate that the prequel to the earlier Lecter books should be the most uncertain of the series in tone and style, yet this probably wasn't the author's intention.

Harris remains partial to literary allusion, opening with a quote from poet Philip Larkin, 'Time is the echo of an axe/Within a wood.' Axes and woods figure heavily in the narrative that follows, though Harris struggles to match Larkin's ominous lines. There are regular gobbets of untranslated German, French and Japanese, Harris assuming a high level of erudition among his readership or a willingness to consult the appropriate dictionaries and online resources. Lest he become too highbrow, Harris throws in a reference to Lawrence Welk, a band leader and light entertainer who was a fixture on American television from the 1950s to the 1980s. Noted for his accordion and bubble machine, Welk isn't exactly a household name outside – or within – the United States.

The symbolism is heavy-handed, notably the death of the black swans from Castle Lecter, their flight to safety cut brutally short. The death's head imagery recalls the moths of *The Silence of the Lambs*, while the Lecter family pennant features a wild boar, a clear nod to *Hannibal*. Critic Ali S Karim draws comparisons with the Brothers Grimm, whose unsettling fairy tales often feature innocent children lost in dark and dangerous woods. Lecter's ancestor is named Hannibal the Grim, suggesting that Harris was conscious of the influence. While Karim sees this section of the book as 'a monstrous fairy tale', it lacks the resonance of the Grimms's work, the Gothic horror elements sitting uneasily with the all-too-believable wartime atrocities.

As with *Hannibal*, Harris doesn't wear his learning lightly, composing sentences such as 'A veil slid across her eyes like the nictitating goggles of a hawk.' Is he expanding the reader's vocabulary, or just showing off with big words? Perhaps he is merely compensating for the lack of confidence and authority in *Hannibal Rising*. Harris is operating in unfamiliar territory and it shows. For all his research, the first half of the book offers little more than the revelations that war is hell and Nazis are not nice people. Harris stumbles over the dialogue, using inappropriate Americanisms with scant regard for the characters or setting. Did World War II Russian tank commanders employ the phrase 'lock and load', or Lithuanian looters tell their colleagues to 'Get your ass out there'? *Hannibal Rising* has an air of contractual obligation absent from Harris's earlier books. At times, it reads more like a blueprint for a screenplay than a novel. A curious use of present tense resembles script directions. Reflecting the project's genesis, *Hannibal Rising* is a 'novelisation' of the forthcoming film.

The characterization tends towards the perfunctory. Hannibal's mother, Simonetta, is an intriguing yet distant figure: 'her bright maroon eyes reflected the light redly in sparks.' This is very similar to the description of Lecter in *Red Dragon*. A pleasing homage or perfunctory retread of tried and tested ingredients? Mrs Lecter plays baroque counterpoint on the piano, yet otherwise exists only as a victim-in-waiting. The infant Hannibal is a child prodigy *par excellence*, reading from age two and studying Euclid's *Elements* from age six. His young sister Mischa brings out the best in him. He blows bubbles for Mischa through her baby bracelet, mercifully ignorant of what is to come. Hannibal's Jewish tutor Mr Jakov sees early on that there could be trouble ahead, 'To remember is not always a blessing.'

The first of Hannibal's bad memories is implanted when he witnesses the death of his mother during a Stuka bomber attack, 'lying in the yard, bloody and her dress on fire'. Despite Hannibal's rejection of God, his visions of dead relatives recall descriptions of Christian martyrs, their pure beautiful bodies sliced, bespattered and burnt. Simonetta Lecter is more icon than person, a holy relic treasured in her son's famous memory palace. Hannibal's nemesis is Nazi collaborator Vladis Grutas, who loots and murders under cover of a Red Cross ambulance. Having survived the Stuka attack, Hannibal and Mischa are at the mercy of a man without conscience or morality. Grutas's law of survival is brutally simple, 'We have to eat or die'. Anyone familiar with *Hannibal* knows where this is going, though Harris takes his time getting there. Mischa's fate is hardly a secret, yet Harris treats it as a shocking revelation.

Traumatised by the events in the hunting lodge, Lecter suffers partial amnesia and nightmare flashbacks. A near-mute, he functions only in terms of brute survival. The fabulous Lecter intellect and spirit survive, albeit damaged, and young Hannibal undergoes a transformation more complete and terrible than anything dreamed of by Francis Dolarhyde or Jame Gumb. Harris describes Lecter's epiphany in terms of the fragility and deception of innocence and faith in a higher power, 'He would conduct his life beneath the painted ceiling of his childhood. But it was as thin as Heaven, and nearly as useless. So he believed.' Prophetically, Hannibal's image of Mischa takes the form of dismembered body parts, 'an excellent chalk and pencil drawing' of his sister's hand and arm.

The teenage Hannibal is adopted by his uncle Robert Lecter, an artist who lives comfortably in post-war France with his Japanese wife, the Lady Murasaki Shikibu. Harris falls over himself conveying the grace, beauty and radiance of the latter. His prose becomes not so much overwrought as almost surreal: 'Lady Murasaki was in the water. In the water was Lady Murasaki…' Is this a bold stylistic device or just a bizarre typo? Hannibal finds a kindred spirit in Murasaki. Having lost most of her family when the atom bomb hit Hiroshima, she knows the value – and necessity – of nurturing and healing. Murasaki believes that young Lecter can follow her back into the daylight, 'Hannibal, you can leave the land of nightmares.' Harris fans know full well that this won't happen, rendering Lecter's relationship with his aunt – and stepmother – a pointless exercise in well-spoken mind games and underplayed mutual attraction. It doesn't help that Murasaki caters to all the clichéd western fantasies of oriental exoticism and eroticism. Harris is clearly taken with the character but he doesn't bring her to life.

While Murasaki offers spiritual healing to Hannibal, he also submits to the probing of psychiatrist Dr Rufin. This line of enquiry is a dead end, though Lecter shares his recurring nightmare image of baby teeth in a stool pit (no surprise to readers of *Hannibal*). Lecter has already chosen his path, initially as a self-appointed protector of the small, weak and vulnerable. Where he failed with Mischa he will succeed on behalf of others, sometimes with lethal force. His first kill is Paul the Butcher, a racist Nazi collaborator with a foul mouth. Why? He insulted Lady Murasaki with a coarse gynaecological reference. In Hannibal's view this merits a death sentence and Harris makes little attempt to argue otherwise. The butcher is also indirectly responsible for Robert Lecter's death from heart failure, yet this seems a mere detail in Hannibal's view. Hannibal's skill with a samurai blade draws the attention of Parisian Police Inspector Popil. Like Lecter, Popil lost family members during World War II and now specialises in hunting fugitive war criminals. Having served under the Vichy government, which collaborated with the Nazis, Popil carries his own burden of guilt, though Harris shows minimal interest in the character.

It's clear from the start that Popil is no match for Lecter. Hannibal beats a polygraph test and Lady Murasaki – though disconcerted by her nephew's actions – aids the cover-up of his guilt. Harris offers a token exploration of moral relativism, skewed heavily in Lecter's favour. Now a medical student, Hannibal witnesses the state-sanctioned execution of a murderer and collaborator. The latter is decapitated by guillotine, just as Lecter removed the butcher's head with clinical precision. Is there a difference, Harris asks, between legally ordained law enforcement and vigilante justice, when both end in the death of the guilty?

Hannibal's interludes with the now-widowed Murasaki suggest a budding if chaste romance. As she puts it, 'I see you and the cricket sings in concert with my heart.' Lecter responds in kind, 'My heart hops at the sight of you, who taught my heart to sing', evoking the Troggs' pop classic 'Wild Thing' rather than classical Japanese poetry. All this is mere calm before the storm. Now attending the Lycee school in Paris, Lecter draws the face of Vladis Grutas without knowing his name. To Lecter, Grutas is simply Blue-Eyes, the killer of children who haunts his dreams. The former Nazi thug and freelance looter is now living in France as 'Victor Gustavson', dealing in drugs and prostitutes, with a little stolen art on the side. A born entrepreneur, Grutas is a big fan of high quality consumer goods, especially American refrigerators and Bosendorfer pianos. Lecter knows Grutas or Blue-Eyes as another kind of consumer, the cold monster who ate Mischa's flesh.

Enrolled in medical school at an improbably young age, Lecter is given to Biblical musings, wondering if God intended to eat Isaac once Abraham had killed him? Returning to Lithuania and the family hunting lodge, Lecter finds Mischa's remains in a bath tub. Performing a burial service, he offers her an atheist valediction, 'Mischa, we take comfort in knowing there is no God. That you are not enslaved in a

Heaven, made to kiss God's ass forever. What you have is better than Paradise. You have blessed oblivion. I miss you every day.' Is Hannibal seeking 'blessed oblivion' for himself once his hunger for vengeance is satisfied? The actions of the middle-aged Lecter suggest a man driven by an appetite for physical and mental stimulation that renders all matter – human or otherwise – an inconsequential plaything.

It should be said that the depiction of Lecter in *Hannibal Rising* is sometimes inconsistent with the earlier books. As Karim points out, Lecter's increased age – from six to twelve – at the time of Mischa's death, and lack of an extra finger, are obvious examples. He is kind to animals, whether swans or horses, whereas *Red Dragon* states that he tortured and killed them as a child. This raises a number of questions. Did Harris forget these details while writing *Hannibal Rising*? Did he not check that they tallied with earlier books? Or did he simply not care? Similarly, did the editors and proofreaders on *Hannibal Rising* miss these errors? Did they consider them unimportant? Were they wary of questioning Harris's judgement? Or did they not have time to cross reference these details, thanks to Harris's late delivery and the looming publication date?

Hannibal is offered the chance of a new life in Japan with Lady Murasaki, who promises 'If you are scorched earth, I will be warm rain.' He must choose between a 'normal' loving relationship – between aunt and nephew or stepmother and stepson? – and the path of bloody vengeance. If this supposed dilemma carried any weight or conviction, *Hannibal Rising* would be a more substantial piece of work. As things stand, the weak characterisation of Murasaki and the reader's foreknowledge of Lecter's destiny render his choice a foregone conclusion. Hannibal is tempted briefly, it seems, but there's no contest, 'I already promised Mischa'. Harris rounds off this sequence with one of his weirdest sentences: 'The damned in chains beneath his chest marched off across his diaphragm to hell beneath the scales.' This image would work better without the anatomical references, 'The damned in chains... marched off...to hell beneath the scales.' Hannibal's – and Harris' – fixation on body parts overwhelms the novel on almost every level.

Grutas's subordinates are easy prey for Lecter, garrotted or drowned according to the circumstances but always decapitated. Drawing out the suspense, Harris makes Grutas more elusive. Hannibal's first attack on Grutas fails, the would-be avenger captured. Held over a bathtub, Lecter nearly meets the same fate as Mischa, saved only by a well-timed explosion. With one bound, give or take, our hero is free to fight another day.

As Lecter and Grutas head for the inevitable showdown, Inspector Popil looks poised to play a more significant role in the narrative. Harris chooses not to pursue this path, leaving the dogged policeman on the sidelines. Popil should at least be a sympathetic figure, tracking down war criminals – and battling inner demons – much as Hannibal does, albeit within the constraints of the law. Yet he becomes Lecter's adversary and even resorts to brutality, striking the arrested Hannibal with 'a small rubber sap'.

While Popil wants Lecter incarcerated in an asylum, not imprisoned or executed, his sense of justice and fair-play are of little consequence. He serves mainly to offer a summary of Lecter's mental state for readers who might be in doubt, 'The little boy Hannibal died in 1945 out there in the snow trying to save his sister. His heart died with Mischa. What is he now? There's not a word for it yet. For lack of a better word, we'll call him a monster.' Harris places Popil on a level with fellow lawman Jack Crawford in *The Silence of the Lambs*: well-meaning, dogged, yet lacking in inspiration and ultimately ineffectual.

Having tracked Grutas to his lair, Lecter is caught out once again by his arch enemy. For a supposed genius and master strategist Lecter becomes remarkably careless at the most crucial moments. Perhaps Harris wants to emphasis that the young Hannibal's mind can still be clouded by emotion, a flaw the older Lecter would suppress. Once again, Hannibal is saved by a blatant contrivance, a variation on the bullet stopped by a medal, bible, pocket watch or cigarette case. The climactic dreadful revelation is effective, if blindingly obvious in retrospect. Readers unfamiliar with the book or film may want to skip the next few lines:

> I know I'm going to miss her
> I went and ate my sister

As expected, Hannibal slays Grutas but loses Murasaki, who departs with the question 'What is left in you to love?' Clarice Starling found the answer in *Hannibal*, though many readers were unconvinced.

Hannibal Rising ends with our (anti-)hero now based in the United States, enrolled at The John Hopkins University, in Baltimore, Maryland. Having slain the last of Mischa's killers during a brief jaunt to Canada, Lecter heads back south to his new home in the USA. As Hannibal relaxes in his comfortable train seat, Harris echoes Popil's earlier diagnosis of Lecter's ice cold 'monstrosity'. 'Hannibal had entered his heart's long winter. He slept soundly, and was not visited in dreams as humans are.' Lecter is at peace, yet emotionally dead and no longer part of the human race. Which is where we came in.

The reviews for *Hannibal Rising* were mixed, falling way short of the baffling euphoria that greeted *Hannibal*. Writing in *The New York Times*, Terrence Rafferty felt Harris was working on autopilot. 'So Hannibal has risen again, smoothly, but without, it seems, measurably elevating the pulse rate of his creator. Although this isn't a terrible novel, it never feels like a necessary one.' *Telegraph* critic Will Cohu was unimpressed:

> The dot-to-dot simplicities of this book, its fatuous psychology, its sketchy detail and curt characterizations seem less of a novel than a draft of a screenplay. More than anything Harris has previously written, it seems influenced by the Hollywood dream of a villain with whom the audience can side, a man whose evil is little more than the antique version of Judeo-Christian justice. But if Lecter is just, then we need not fear him. Hannibal has been consumed by the niceties of plot; you cannot have your cannibal and eat him.

Writing in the same paper, novelist Tibor Fischer liked what he read, despite some reservations:

> This latest volume is the final stage of rehabilitation for Hannibal Lecter; he is still frightening, but no longer evil. He has become an extreme Sir Galahad, righting wrongs in a brutal and excessive way.... Lecter has become the person many of us would like to be: a cool,

urbane, erudite, artistic polyglot who takes no rubbish, who dispatches anyone boorish or annoying, and who is never found wanting for a quip or a telling retort. The Renaissance man, with attitude.

Fischer felt Harris fell down in his research. 'One wonders how Count Lecter and his family have apparently led such an untroubled life in a country which had already been under occupation by Stalin's Soviet Union, a system not noted for its fondness for the nobility.' On balance, Fischer regarded *Hannibal Rising* as a worthy addition to the Lecter canon. 'You know the destination, but that doesn't mean the journey isn't bracing. It isn't *The Silence of the Lambs*, but fans of Harris will be delighted with *Hannibal Rising*. I was.'

Guardian reviewer Steven Poole felt Harris had drifted into slick formula. 'After the brilliantly taut and claustrophobic procedurals earlier in the series, Harris has finally morphed into an upmarket version of Dan Brown.' Fellow *Guardian* critic John Crace felt downright cheated. 'Hannibal smiled. He had got away with his greatest crime to date. A bestselling thriller with no thrills at all.' *Independent* critic Boyd Tonkin awarded points for grisly entertainment value but little else:

> As a stylist, the over-lauded Harris indulges in a low-temperature elegance that mimics the clinical 'detachment' of his subject…Why, beyond the vast pulling power that Hollywood bestows, has a talented but limited crime writer attracted such preposterous praise? The silliest swooning has come from literary types who mistake Harris's incessant high-culture chatter for genuine artistic ambition.

Writing in *The Times*, Erica Wagner felt that Harris – and his editor – had become careless on several levels. Pointing out the linguistic, grammatical and geographical errors in the book, Wagner argued:

> …in a book that takes on the issues of collaboration in France during the war, as well as the looting of European art, mistakes simply indicate laziness (not least on the

part of the publisher; this is simple stuff to check). And, quite possibly, one wouldn't mind, if that laziness didn't otherwise permeate the book. In the circumstances this may seem a bad pun, but nothing quite comes alive.

There were notable exceptions to the general condemnation. *Independent* critic Mark Timlin, who found *Hannibal* disappointing, was full of praise for the follow-up. '*Hannibal Rising* is spot on. It's a superb work of blood and violence where the horrors of war are beautifully, if that's the right word, described, as Hannibal is forced into becoming the cannibal that will later be his trademark.' In terms of sales, the negative reviews hardly mattered. As expected, *Hannibal Rising* was a huge success worldwide. The hardback version was on the *New York Times*' bestseller list for over 15 weeks, while the paperback edition enjoyed a 30 week run.

Barely two months after *Hannibal Rising* appeared in bookshops, the film version opened in cinemas. At the time it was felt that this rapid follow-up would benefit both novel and movie, the latter reviving interest in the former while riding on its tidal wave of publicity. The major challenge facing the producers of *Hannibal Rising* was finding a new Hannibal Lecter. No amount of digital magic could make Anthony Hopkins look 20 years old. The substitution of Julianne Moore for Jodie Foster in *Hannibal* had been only a qualified success and most fans still regarded Foster as the definitive Clarice Starling. In this instance, the change of actor hadn't been crucial, as *Hannibal* was first and foremost a vehicle for Anthony Hopkins. The wrong choice of lead for *Hannibal Rising* would doom the film to failure.

At least eight actors shot screen tests for the role, including Canadian Hayden Christensen, best known as the moody Annakin Skywalker in *Star Wars Episode 2 – Attack of the Clones* (2002) and *Star Wars Episode 3 – Revenge of the Sith* (2005). While these movies hardly stretched Christensen's talents, he showed his dramatic ability in such films as *The Virgin Suicides* (1999). The producers also considered former child actor Macaulay Culkin, who achieved superstardom in *Home Alone* (1990) and *Home Alone 2: Lost in New York* (1992), only to see his career evaporate a few years later. While Culkin still acted on occasion, the star quality he possessed as a child had diminished with adulthood. Crossing the Atlantic, the casting directors looked to the UK, which supplied Lecter #1 Brian Cox and Lecter #2 Anthony Hopkins. Candidates included Hugh Dancy, seen in *Black Hawk Down* (2001), *King Arthur* (2004) and *Basic Instinct 2* (2006), Rupert Friend, from *The Libertine* (2004) and *Pride and Prejudice* (2005), Dominic Cooper, best known for *The History Boys* (2006), Tom Sturridge, who appeared in *Vanity Fair* (2004), and Tom Payne, future star of the hit TV series *Skins* (2007-).

The producers decided that the young Lecter should be more European than American or British. The role went to Gaspard Ulliel, a French actor born in 1984 in Boulogne-Billancourt, Hauts-de-Seine. Ulliel had an early ambition to be a film director, studying cinema at the University de Saint-Denis. He worked as a professional actor from the age of 12, despite a visible scar on his left cheek, the result of a dog attack when he was six. Ulliel's film credits included *Le Pacte des loups/The Brotherhood of the Wolf* (2002), as a shepherd boy attacked by a mysterious beast. He went on to play Audrey Tatou's love interest in *A Very Long Engagement* (2004), which also featured *Silence of the Lambs* star Jodie Foster. Wary of comparisons with Anthony Hopkins, Ulliel hesitated over accepting the role. After repeated viewings of Hopkins's Lecter films, especially *The Silence of the Lambs*, Ulliel decided he could bring something new to the character.

Lady Murasaki was played by Chinese actress Gong Li, who achieved stardom with her debut film *Red Sorghum* (1987). She went on to appear in *Ju Dou* (1990), *Raise the Red Lantern* (1991), *Farewell My Concubine* (1993), *Temptress Moon* (1996) and *2046* (2004), all of which enjoyed successful 'arthouse' releases in the West. Li made her American debut in *Memoirs of a Geisha* (2005), cast as another Japanese character. While Gaspard Ulliel spoke excellent English, Li wasn't fluent in the language, usually learning her dialogue phonetically. Li wanted to appear in *Hannibal Rising*, but was committed to making *Miami Vice* (2006), Michael Mann's disappointing revamp of his 1980s TV series. Dino de Laurentiis agreed to put *Hannibal Rising* on hold until Li became available. Shooting in Miami, Li had the chance to meet local resident Thomas Harris and discuss – via an interpreter – the role of Murasaki.

In line with Hollywood tradition, the lead villains were played by British actors, in this instance Welsh and Scottish. The role of Vladis

Grutas went to Rhys Ifans, who gave a strong performance in the otherwise vacuous *Twin Town* (1997), before coming to wide notice in *Notting Hill* (1999), as Hugh Grant's slovenly flatmate. Ifans made his US debut in the Adam Sandler comedy *Little Nicky* (2000). Tall, lean and gangly, Ifans wasn't obvious leading man material, playing supporting roles in *The Shipping News* (2001) and *Enduring Love* (2004). He also lent his talents to *Garfield: A Tail of Two Kitties* (2006). Ifans auditioned for *Hannibal Rising* with the scene where Grutas captures Lecter after the botched bathroom assassination attempt. A fan of the Lecter books, and most of the films, Ifans saw Grutas and Lady Murasaki as twisted father and mother figures for the young Hannibal. Kolnas was played by Kevin McKidd, who co-starred in *Trainspotting* (1996) only to see Ewan McGregor steal most of the thunder. McKidd subsequently appeared in *The Acid House* (1998), *Topsy-Turvey* (1999), *De-Lovely* (2004) and *Kingdom of Heaven* (2005). He had a rare starring role in the cult horror movie *Dog Soldiers* (2002), surviving an onslaught of werewolves.

Not all the British actors in *Hannibal Rising* were cast as bad guys. Inspector Popil was played by Dominic West, seen in *Richard III* (1995), *Surviving Picasso* (1996), opposite Anthony Hopkins, and *Spice World* (1997). After playing a bit part in *Star Wars Episode 1 – The Phantom Menace* (1999), West won more substantial roles in *Chicago* (2002) and *Mona Lisa Smile* (2003). He achieved TV stardom in the US cop show *The Wire* (2002-), as Detective James McNulty. While filming *Hannibal Rising*, West was also working on *The Wire* and *300* (2006), a packed schedule.

Hannibal Rising was directed by Peter Webber, a British film-maker with a background in television documentaries. Webber made an acclaimed feature debut with *Girl with a Pearl Earring* (2003), based on the novel by Tracy Chevalier, starring Colin Firth and Scarlett Johansson. He met with Dino de Laurentiis at the latter's Los Angeles office and committed to *Hannibal Rising* after seeing just ten pages of Harris's rough draft.

Polish production designer Allan Starski had worked on *Man of Marble* (1977), *Man of Iron* (1981) and the French co-production *Danton* (1983). His later credits included *Schindler's List* (1993), *The Pianist* (2002) and *Oliver Twist* (2005). The score was composed partly by Japanese musician Shigeru Umebayashi, noted for his work on such

Chinese films as *In the Mood for Love* (2000), *House of Flying Daggers* (2004), *2046*, which co-starred Gong Li, *Fearless* (2006) and *Curse of the Golden Flower* (2006), also featuring Li. *Hannibal Rising* was edited by Pietro Scalia, who worked on *Hannibal* and *Memoirs of a Geisha*.

Hannibal Rising was budgeted at a modest $50 million, reflecting the lack of star names in the cast and the absence of Anthony Hopkins, the franchise's big selling point. The film was an Italian-French-British-Czech Republic co-production, with no American finance. The US rights were acquired by the Weinstein Company in partnership with MGM.

Filming began on 7 October 2005. Most of *Hannibal Rising* was shot in and around Prague, in the Czech Republic, a favourite destination for cost-conscious filmmakers. The producers had delayed filming for nearly a year until Gong Li became available. In the event, shooting on *Miami Vice* overran and *Hannibal Rising* started filming without her. Li couldn't join the production until late December and the film had to be rolling before the Czech winter descended. The first scene shot was Hannibal's killing of the butcher, which required the kind of weather that could pass as a French summer's day.

Peter Webber asked Gaspard Ulliel to spend a day observing and assisting with autopsies at the Prague medical school. Cast as a genius medical student, Ulliel had to look comfortable around cadavers – real or fake – and medical instruments. Ulliel volunteered to go back for a second day, which both reassured and disconcerted Webber. They'd clearly chosen the right actor for young Lecter but was he getting too much into character?

To lighten the atmosphere, Ulliel brought a fart machine to the set, which Peter Webber had to confiscate after three days. Rhys Ifans was accidentally stabbed filming his death scene, though the wound was minor. Thomas Harris's script ran way over length for a standard feature film. At Dino de Laurentiis's request, Webber shot the screenplay as written and the first cut of *Hannibal Rising* was three hours long. The theatrical version was reduced to two hours, Webber declaring himself happy with the result.

While *Hannibal Rising* (the movie) is no masterpiece, it's superior to the novel and, arguably, a better film than either *Hannibal* or *Red Dragon*. The fifth Lecter movie is a dark fairytale of revenge that barely connects with the earlier films yet is none the worse for it. Webber opens with a symbolic spider web in a backlit forest. The infant Hannibal plays with Mischa on a jetty, blissfully ignorant of the horrors to come. The film is technically proficient and effectively handled, though the pace is rushed in the early and late stages, settling down in between. The flashbacks are fairly well used, though little vital information is conveyed. There are several striking images: Mischa waving to a Russian tank commander, the burning of the Lecter family album, a Josef Stalin mosaic (cut from the cinema version), Hannibal's impassive face amid a row of hanging masks.

The visual style tends towards the muted. Webber employed a technique known as 'bleach bypass' to strip the colour from the war-time scenes. This desaturated look – almost *de rigueur* in WWII dramas since *Saving Private Ryan* (1998) – is used to good effect here. Webber watched *The Guns of Navarone* (1961) and *Where Eagles Dare* (1968) to get the 'juicy Nazi atmosphere' he wanted, yet *Hannibal Rising* has little in common with these gung ho classics. The French scenes were inspired by the 'neo-noir' work of director Jean-Pierre Melville, especially *Le Samourai* (1967), which features Alain Delon as a near-mute hitman.

There is an element of overkill, so to speak. Mrs Lecter hides her pearls inside a stuffed boar's head, the beast 'devouring' the family jewels, then says to Hannibal 'Pearls before swine'. Enough already. The three wise monkeys in Lecter's attic apartment – See No Evil, Hear No Evil, Speak No Evil – are similarly redundant. Webber also lapses into cliché, such as the Kendo lessons in the snowy landscape. Compared to the novel, the script is more streamlined, losing an entire subplot involving stolen art treasures. Supporting characters such as tutor Mr Jakov are also gone and the story progression is accelerated, dropping Hannibal's adoption by his uncle. Lecter crosses the Soviet border and makes his own way to Paris, where Lady Murasaki has already been widowed for a year.

The film tones down some of the more contentious elements. Mrs Lecter's death is less gruesome, in marked contrast to the later bloodletting. In the novel, Lecter is barely thirteen when he kills the butcher. The producers felt this would be unacceptable in a film, and the act is committed by the adult Hannibal. This adjustment of Lecter's age

creates problems in earlier scenes, Gaspard Ulliel too old to convince
as a teenager. Mischa is buried without a eulogy from Hannibal, losing
the 'blessed oblivion' and the denunciation of God. Were the producers
concerned about offending Christians?

The film is more successful than the book at depicting the progression
in Hannibal's violent tendencies. He has the opportunity to kill a sleeping
prefect bully but shows restraint, merely breaking the latter's ankle
in a bear trap. The moral relativism is also better handled in the scene
with Louis, the Nazi informant who betrayed Jewish children when he
was tortured. Resigned to his date with the guillotine, Louis has one
last question for Popil. 'Inspector, where were the police?' Popil has no
answer, as Hannibal is quick to remind him.

The film makes good use of the German folk song 'Ein Mannlein
Steht Im Walde', 'A little man who stands in the woods' , which appears
in Engelbert Humperdinck's opera *Hansel and Gretel*. Harris features the
song in the novel, without providing any context or even a translation.
The image of innocent children lost and alone in a dangerous forest has
obvious resonance for *Hannibal Rising* and the song becomes more
sinister with each rendition. In place of a child-eating witch, we have
child-eating Nazi collaborators turned murderous looters. Instead of
burning the witch in her own oven, Hansel/Hannibal slashes, stabs,
decapitates, garrottes, drowns, impales and devours the monsters who
stole his sister, his childhood and his humanity. The song continues 'ganz
still und stumm', 'all calm and quiet'. We already know that Lecter's
later life will be anything but calm and rarely quiet.

The performances are generally sound, though the supporting actors
have little to do. As Lady Murasaki, Gong Li offers a melancholy
beauty and a low key portrayal that accommodates her limited grasp of
English. In Li's view, Murasaki has the self-control that Lecter lacks.
When the butcher insults Murasaki, grabbing her ass, her desire for
revenge is outweighed by her responsibility towards Hannibal, who
needs a peaceful environment (or so she believes). Webber and Ulliel
saw Murasaki as both healer and mentor for Hannibal, giving him the
tools for revenge while imploring him to take a different path. A mixed
message, some would say.

Rhys Ifans is a high class villain with a believable East European accent, though his camper moments recall Gary Oldman's bent cop in *Leon* (1994). Webber intended Ifans to have a moustache and shot several tests. The idea was rejected, as Ifans looked too much like Leslie Phillips, best known for his smooth-talking cads in scores of British comedies. Webber felt that Ifans went over the top in some scenes and it's hard to disagree. Vain to the point of narcissism, Grutas has his chest shaved by a captive woman while he relaxes in the bath. As Grutas explains to Lecter, 'I love myself…', and Ifans's performance leaves this in no doubt.

As the young Hannibal Lecter, Gaspard Ulliel is lean, moody and increasingly menacing. Gong Li felt Ulliel had the cold eyes and colder smile needed for Lecter. Ulliel barely speaks for the first 40 minutes and his precise, halting diction suits the character. Alienated from his fellow war orphans and refugees, Lecter shows no respect for social niceties. As the headmaster at the Soviet young person's institution remarks, 'Hannibal, you do not honour the human pecking order.'

When Hannibal dons his first mask, taken from a suit of samurai armour, he becomes a grinning grotesque, a demon poised to strike. The doomed butcher is shown a drawing of his severed head, art shortly to be imitated by life. By the half-way point, Lecter's insanity is established beyond all doubt, the vengeful Hannibal smirking through his gore spattered face and tasting his victim's blood. Lecter threatens to become more creepy than his enemies and it's a tribute to Ulliel's performance that he pulls back from the edge on several occasions.

The fight between Lecter and Kolnas (Kevin McKidd) is well staged. As the one villain with a wife and family, Kolnas shows twinges of conscience, his new life as a respectable restaurateur haunted by ghosts from the past. Shown mercy by Lecter, Kolnas rejects this one-time-only offer, his foolish head skewered by a Japanese dagger. The last vicious plot twist turns Lecter super-nutzoid, with some face-biting to match Robert De Niro's antics in *Cape Fear* (1991). Martha de Laurentiis felt Ulliel resembled Anthony Hopkins. While Ulliel captures some of Hopkins' intensity and stillness, his Lecter is a creature apart from the Hopkins version. If we remain unconvinced that this young Hannibal will grow up into the Hopkins incarnation, the fault lies with Thomas Harris, not Ulliel.

The teaser trailer for *Hannibal Rising* pushed all the expected buttons:

> You know his name
> You know his methods
> You know his appetites
> But you could never imagine
> How it all began

Anyone familiar with the book, or even the novel *Hannibal*, already knew how it all began. Later trailers opted for a different approach:

> Born into war
> Driven into madness
> Hungry for revenge

Most critics had little appetite for *Hannibal Rising*. *Variety*'s Dennis Harvey damned the film with faint praise:

> This upmarket slasher is a well-produced but slow-moving thriller that never quite roars to life…. On its own terms this story works better on celluloid than it did on the page. Nonetheless, *Rising* emerges as a bit of a wet fuse, never especially involving or suspenseful…. While Ulliel will no doubt peeve those looking for a junior Hopkins act-alike, he does bring intelligence and poise to a role that strays too little from one menacing, supercilious note.

San Francisco Chronicle critic Peter Hartlaub offered a measured assessment of the film's strengths and weaknesses:

> *Hannibal Rising* isn't a classic, but it's entertaining and a surprisingly fitting addition to the franchise…. Creating a prequel to a great film [*The Silence of the Lambs*] with none of the original actors or director spells almost certain doom for a drama. That *Hannibal Rising* isn't complete trash is a monumental accomplishment. Ulliel tries his

best to be a respectable Hannibal…but it's a losing battle
from the start, in part because the actor looks nothing like
Hopkins…. Peter Webber directs with a steady hand and
consistent tone, whether it's a frenetic battle scene or a
slow-building confrontation at a market.

The *New York Times'* Terrence Rafferty, who dismissed the book as
Harris-lite, felt the film had more to offer. 'Peter Webber's *Hannibal
Rising* tells the oddly stirring story of the apprenticeship in homicide
of young Hannibal Lecter…. He's still pretty scary and still reasonably
amusing, though the new Hannibal, 22-year-old Gaspard Ulliel, doesn't
spit out his killer bons mots with quite the hissing panache of Mr Hopkins.'

Writing in *The Observer*, Philip French saw *Hannibal Rising* as a
comedown for its director. 'Peter Webber directed Scarlett Johansson
in the charming movie about Vermeer's muse, but sadly, this murky
thriller is more of a pig's ear than a pearl earring.' *Guardian* critic Peter
Bradshaw felt that the background story for Lecter was misguided. 'How
much more interesting – and scary – to have given Hannibal a perfectly
happy boyhood with not the smallest occasion for anger or violence.'

Hannibal Rising was released in the US and the UK on 9 February
2007. The film had a poor opening weekend, taking $13 million and
£1 million respectively. Bad reviews and worse word-of-mouth kept
audiences away. *Hannibal Rising* grossed just $27.66 million in the
US and £2.52 million in the UK. For the first time since *Manhunter*, a
film featuring Hannibal Lecter had flopped at the box-office. While the
Michael Mann movie is now well regarded, *Hannibal Rising* is unlikely
to acquire a cult following in years to come.

Hannibal Rising may have been hurt by misleading advance publicity.
According to Peter Webber, the US TV trailer assembled by the
Weinstein Company used new footage of sex and violence that wasn't
in the film. Audiences expecting a sleaze and gore-fest were bound to
be disappointed. Perhaps the reason for the poor box-office returns was
much more simple: a Hannibal Lecter film without Anthony Hopkins had
negligible popular appeal. It's also notable that *Red Dragon*, Hopkins'
last bow in the role, performed below expectations. If audiences were
losing interest in the character, a follow-up with or without Hopkins

stood little chance of reversing this decline. Recasting the part with a younger, little known actor was a gamble that didn't pay off. Despite the impressive book sales, *Hannibal Rising* the film had fallen to earth at speed.

While there's a considerable gap between the ending of *Hannibal Rising* and the start of *Red Dragon*, further adventures of the young or mature or middle-aged Lecter seem unnecessary. According to rumour, Thomas Harris plans to supply them anyway, chronicling Hannibal's bloody exploits up until his arrest by Will Graham. Perhaps it's best to leave Doctor Lecter alone now. As Harris suggests at the end of *Hannibal*, 'We can only learn so much and live.'

FILMOGRAPHY

MANHUNTER 1986

Red Dragon Productions/De Laurentiis Entertainment Group
Theatrical running time: 119 minutes

Executive producer: Bernard Williams; Producer: Richard A Roth;
Director: Michael Mann; Screenplay: Michael Mann, based on the
novel *Red Dragon* by Thomas Harris; Director of photography: Dante
Spinotti (Technicolor/JDC-Scope); Editing: Dov Hoenig; Production
design: Mel Bourne; Art direction: Jack Blackman; Original music:
The Reds, Michel Rubini; Casting: Bonnie Timmermann; Costume
design: Colleen Atwood; Makeup artist: Stefano Fava; Unit production
managers: Jon Landau, Peter R McIntosh, Bernard Williams; First
assistant director: Herb Gains; Second assistant directors: Nathalie
Vadim, Michael Waxman; Set dresser: John D Kretschmer; Property
master: Charles Stewart; Music editor: George A Martin; Sound effects
editor: Charles E Smith; Special effects co-ordinator: Joe Digaetano;
Visual consultant: Gusmano Cesaretti; Stunt co-ordinator: Bud Davis;
Stunts: Jack Carpenter, Bud Davis, Mike Haines, Chuck Hart, Bernard
Johnson, Larry Modlin, Don Pulford, Dennis Scott, Deborah Shuckman;
Still photographer: Gusmano Cesaretti; Gaffer: John C Ferguson; Music
engineer: Greg Fulginiti; Camera operators: Enrico Lucidi, Michael
Mann; Script supervisor: June Randall; Focus puller: 'a' camera:
Marco Sacerdoti.

Cast: William Petersen (Will Graham); Kim Greist (Molly Graham);
Joan Allen (Reba); Brian Cox (Doctor Lecktor); Dennis Farina (Jack
Crawford); Stephen Lang (Freddie Lounds); Tom Noonan (Francis

Dollarhyde); David Seaman (Kevin Graham); Benjamin Hendrickson (Doctor Chilton); Michael Talbott (Geehan); Dan E Butler (Jimmy Price); Michele Shay (Beverly Katz); Robin Moseley (Sarah); Paul Perri (Dr Sidney Bloom); Patricia Charbonneau (Mrs Sherman); Bill Cwikowski (Ralph Dandridge); Alex Neil (Eileen); Norman Snow (Springfield); Jim Zubiena (Spurgen); Frankie Faison (Lt Fisk); Garcelle Beauvais (Young Woman Housebuyer) [role cut from theatrical release print]; Joanne Camp (Mother on Plane); David A Brooks (Mr Leeds); Lisa Ryall (Mrs Leeds); Chris Elliott (Zeller); Gary Chavaras (Guard); Chris Cianciolo (Attendant); Ken Colquit (Husband Housebuyer) [role cut from theatrical release print]; Ron Fitzgerald (Storage Guard #1); Dennis Quick (Storage Guard #2); David Meeks (Dr Warfield); Sherman Michaels (Technician); Robin Trapp (Secretary #1); Lisa Winters (Secretary #2); Daniel T Snow (State Trooper); Cynthia Chvatal (Airport Waitress); King White (SWAT Man); Mickey Lloyd (Atlanta Detective); Dawn Carmen (Child on Plane); David Fitzsimmons (Bill); Robert A Burton (Doctor); Steve Hogan (Helicopter Pilot); Mickey Pugh (Lear Jet Technician); Kin Shriner (Mr Sherman) [role cut from theatrical release print]; John Posey (Mr Jacobi); Kristin Holby (Mrs Jacobi); Greg Kelly (Jacobi Boy #1); Brian Kelly (Jacobi Boy #2); Ryan Langhorn (Jacobi Boy #3); Hannah Caggiano (Sherman Child #1); Lindsey Fonora (Sherman Child #2); Jason Frair (Leeds Child #1); Bryant Arrants (Leeds Child #2); Christopher Arrants (Leeds Child #3); Melvin Clark, Renee Ayala, Dana Dewey, Stephen Hawkins, Leonard Johnson, Keith Pyles, Michael Russell, Michael Vitug, Pat Williams, Charles Yarbaugh (SWAT Team Members); Bill Smitrovich (Lloyd Bowman); Peter Maloney (Dr Dominick Princi); Michael D Roberts (The Runner).

THE SILENCE OF THE LAMBS 1991

Strong Heart/Demme/Orion
Theatrical running time: 118 minutes

Executive producer: Gary Goetzman; Producers: Ron Bozman, Edward Saxon, Kenneth Utt; Associate producer: Grace Blake; Director:

Jonathan Demme; Screenplay: Ted Tally, based on the novel by Thomas Harris; Director of photography: Tak Fujimoto (DeLuxe); Production design: Kristi Zea; Art direction: Tim Galvin; Editing: Craig McKay; Music: Howard Shore; Costume design: Colleen Atwood; Casting: Howard Feuer; Set decoration: Karen O'Hara; Hair stylist: Alan D'Angerio; Special makeup effects: Carl Fullerton, Neal Martz; Makeup artist: Allen Weisinger; Unit production manager: Kenneth Utt; First assistant director: Ron Bozman; Additional first assistant director: Steve Rose; Second assistant director: Kyle McCarthy; Second second assistant director: Gina Leonetti; Assistant props: Sean Foyle, Loren Levy; Master scenic artist: Eileen Garrigan; Key scenic artist: Frederika Gray; Storyboard artists: Kalina Ivanov, Karl Shefelman; Assistant art directors: Gary Kosko, Natalie Wilson; Set dressers: Ed Lohrer, Kenneth Turek, Edward West; Property master: Ann Miller; Stand-by scenic artist: Paula Payne; Assistant set decorator: Diana L Stoughton; Construction co-ordinator: S Bruce Wineinger; Sound effects editor: Ron Bochar; ADR recordist: David Boulton; Apprentice sound editor: Missy Cohen; Assistant ADR editor: Randall Coleman; Foley artist: Marko Costanzo; Assistant music editor: Susan Demsky; ADR boom operator: Kay Denmark; Apprentice sound editors: Bill Docker, Stuart Levy; Sound re-recording mixer: Tom Fleischman; Assistant music recording engineer: Peter Fuchs; Sound recordist: John Fundus; Assistant sound editor: Brian Johnson; Foley editors: Frank Kern, Steven Visscher, Bruce Pross; Sound designer: Skip Lievsay; Dialogue editors: Marissa Littlefield, Fred Rosenberg, Jeffrey Stern, Phil Stockton; Boom operator: Dennis Maitland; Sound re-recordists: Douglas L Murray, Sean Squires; Production sound mixer: Christopher Newman; Music editor: Suzana Peric; Assistant music editor: Nic Ratner; Assistant sound editor: Anne Sawyer; ADR editors: Gail Showalter, Deborah Wallach; Recording engineer: Alan Snelling; Stereo sound consultant (Dolby): Robert F Warren; Special effects: Dwight Benjamin-Creel; Stunt co-ordinator: John Robotham; Stunts: Mike Cassidy, Walter Robles, John Robotham, George P Wilbur; Unit publicist: Judy Arthur; Grip: Richard Aversa, Mick Lohrer; Production assistants: Jeffrey T Barabe, Monica Bielawski, Andre Blake, Becky Gibbs, Teri Hanson, Maria Alaina Mason, Paula Oliver, Ben Ramsey, Iane Ulan, 'Buz' Wasler, Gina White, Hyle White;

Additional casting (Pittsburgh): Donna M Belajac; Extras casting (Pittsburgh): Staci Blagovich; Music supervisor: Sharon Boyle; Assistant production co-ordinator: Lisa Bradley; Post-production assistants: Trish Breganti, Sam Bruskin, Priscilla Fleischman; Associate editor: Lisa Bromwell; Wardrobe supervisor: Mark Burchard; Electricians: Mike Burke, Ed DeCort, Peter Demme, Roswell Jones, James Petri; Art department co-ordinator: Francine Byrne; Apprentice film editors: Lynn Cassaniti, Nzingha Clarke, David Kirkman; Accounting assistant: Katie Clarke; Best boy electric: Kenny Conners; Location co-ordinator (Washington DC): John Crowder; Production auditor: Vicki Dee Rock; Orchestrator: Homer Denison; Dolly grip: John Donohue; Moth wrangler and stylist: Raymond A Mendez; Assistant moth wrangler and stylist: Leanore G Drogin; Gaffer: Rusty Engels; Dialect consultant: Richard Ericson; Assistant to Mr Utt: Robin Fajardo; Craft service: Richard Fishwick; Assistant costume designer: Kathleen Gerlach; Stage manager: Paul Giorgi; Location co-ordinator (Bimini, Bahamas): Gus Holzer; Additional assistant camera: Larry Huston, Jay Levy; Financial representative: Thomas A Imperato; Projectionist: Alan Jacques; Camera operator: Tony Jannelli; Stand-by dresser: C A Kelly; Continuity: Mary A Kelly; Assistant to Ms Foster: Patricia LaMagna; Transportation captain: John Leonidas; Locations: Annie Loeffler, Mike McCue; Entomological consultants: Sally Love, John E Rawlins; First assistant camera: Bruce MacCallum; Accounting assistant: Ann F Markel; Location projectionist (Washington DC): John Marston; Steadicam operator: Larry McConkey; Special production assistant: Kevin McLeod; Dog trainer: Christie Miele; Key grip: Billy Miller; Grips: Matt Miller, Calvin Price; Second assistant camera: Tom O'Halloran; Police consultant: Walter Oggier; Color timer: David Orr; Camera trainee: Brian Osmond; Special drawings: Paula Payne; Post-production supervisor: Marshall Persinger; Assistant to Mr Demme: Lucas Platt; Transportation co-captain: Dennis Radesky; Still photographer: Ken Regan; Assistant production co-ordinators: Andrew Sands, Alison Sherman; Assistant production auditor: Steven Shareshian; First assistant editor: Colleen Sharp; Second assistant editor: Alice Stone; Location manager: Neri Kyle Tannenbaum; Wardrobe supervisor: Hartsell Taylor; Assistant to Mr Saxon: Valerie Thomas; Video engineer: Howard Weiner; Wardrobe assistant: Benjamin Wilson.

Cast: Jodie Foster (Clarice Starling), Anthony Hopkins (Dr Hannibal Lecter), Scott Glenn (Jack Crawford), Ted Levine (Jame Gumb), Anthony Heald (Dr Frederick Chilton), Brooke Smith (Catherine Martin), Diane Baker (Senator Ruth Martin), Kasi Lemmons (Ardelia Mapp), Charles Napier (Lt Boyle), Tracey Walter (Lamar), Roger Corman (FBI Director Hayden Burke), Ron Vawter (Paul Krendler), Danny Darst (Sgt Tate), Frankie Faison (Barney), Paul Lazar (Pilcher), Dan Butler (Roden), Chris Isaak (SWAT Commander), Lawrence T Wrentz (Agent Burroughs), Lawrence A Bonney (FBI Instructor), Don Brockett (Friendly Psychopath), Frank Seals Jr (Brooding Psychopath), Stuart Rudin (Miggs), Masha Skorobogatov (Young Clarice), Jeffrie Lane (Clarice's Father), Leib Lensky (Mr Lang), Red Schwartz (Mr Lang's Driver), Jim Roche (TV Evangelist), James B Howard (Boxing Instructor), Bill Miller (Mr Brigham), Chuck Aber (Agent Terry), Gene Borkan (Oscar), Pat McNamara (Sheriff Perkins), Kenneth Utt (Dr Akin), Adelle Lutz (TV Anchor Woman), Obba Babatunde (TV Anchor Man), George Michael (TV Sportscaster), Jim Dratfield (Sen Martin's Aide), Stanton-Miranda (1st Reporter), Rebecca Saxon (2nd Reporter), Cynthia Ettinger (Officer Jacobs), Brent Hinkley (Officer Murray), Steve Wyatt (Airport Flirt), Alex Coleman (Sgt Pembry), David Early (Spooked Memphis Cop), Andre Blake (Tall Memphis Cop), Bill Dalzell III (Distraught Memphis Cop), Daniel von Bargen (SWAT Communicator), Tommy LaFitte (SWAT Shooter), Josh Broder (EMS Attendant), Buzz Kilman (EMS Driver), Harry Northup (Mr Bimmel), Lauren Roselli (Stacy Hubka), Lamont Arnold (Flower Delivery Man), John Hall (State Trooper) [uncredited], Ted Monte (FBI Agent #5) [uncredited], George A Romero (FBI Agent in Memphis) [uncredited], 'Darla' ('Precious').

HANNIBAL 2001

Scott Free/Dino de Laurentiis/Universal/Metro-Goldwyn-Mayer
Theatrical running time: 132 minutes

Executive producer: Branko Lustig; Producers: Dino de Laurentiis, Martha de Laurentiis, Ridley Scott; Director: Ridley Scott; Screenplay:

David Mamet, Steve Zaillian, based on the novel by Thomas Harris; Director of photography: John Mathieson; Production design: Norris Spencer; Art direction: David Crank; Editing: Pietro Scalia; Music: Klaus Badelt, Hans Zimmer; Set decoration: Cynthia Sleiter; Costume design: Janty Yates; Special makeup effects artist: Greg Cannom; Makeup artist for Julianne Moore: Elaine L Offers; Makeup effects producer: Keith VanderLaan, Captive Audience Productions; Casting: Stephanie Corsalini; Unit production manager: Pamela Hochschartner; Second assistant director: Alberto Mangiante; Second second assistant director: Joe Incaprera; Second second assistant director, Italy: Filippo Fassetta; Third assistant director: Emma Horton; Dialogue editor: David A Cohen; Sound editor: Peter Staubi; Sound effects editor: Jon Title; Special effects coordinator: Daniel Acon; Stunt coordinator, Italy: Franco Maria Salamon; Assistant stunt coordinator: Cal Johnson; Stunts: Carlo Antonioni, Cort Hessler, Cal Johnson, Stefano Maria Salamon; Stunt double for Julianne Moore: Cinda-Lin James; Video assist operator: Lester Dunton; Second video assist operator: Pete Albert; Seamstress, USA: Susan Antonelli; Production secretary: Simona Batistelli; Location manager: Charles Thomas Baxter; Assistant location manager: Dawn Blacksten; Location assistants: Troy Benjamin, Bradley E Herring; Assistant costume designer, Italy: Andrea Cripps; Production accountant: Cheryl A Stone; Payroll accountant: Michael Dorner; Assistant accountant: Tom Dames; Accounts runner: Bernardo Galli; Assistant production coordinator, Washington DC: Katherine Dorrer; Camera operator: David M Dunlap; Additional camera operator, Richmond, VA: Thomas Loizeaux; Set costumer: Catharine Fletcher Incaprera; Unit publicist: Rob Harris; Dimmer operator: Jeremy Knaster; Additional set production assistant: Stephanie Lovell; Operations manager, Captive Audience Productions Inc.: Harvey Lowry; Dialogue coach: Daniela Merlo; Dialect coach: Tim Monich; Music scoring mixer: Alan Meyerson; Gaffer: Bill O'Leary; Music production supervisor: Gretchen O'Neal; Production assistant: Ian Quiles; Focus puller: Marco Sacerdoti; ADR group coordinator: Burton Sharp; Key costumer: Amanda Trewin.

Cast: Anthony Hopkins (Hannibal Lecter), Julianne Moore (Clarice Starling), Gary Oldman (Mason Verger), Ray Liotta (Paul Krendler),

Giancarlo Giannini (Rinaldo Pazzi), Francesca Neri (Allegra Pazzi), Zeljko Ivanek (Dr Cordell Doemling), Frankie R Faison (Barney), Danielle de Niesse (Beatrice), Hazelle Goodman (Evelda Drumgo), David Andrews (FBI Agent Pearsall), Francis Guinan (FBI Director Noonan), James Opher (FBI Agent Eldridge), Enrico Lo Verso (Gnocco), Ivano Marescotti (Carlo), Fabrizio Gifuni (Matteo), Alex Corrado (Piero Falcione), Marco Greco (Tomasso), Robert Rieti (Sogliato), Terry Serpico (Officer Bolton), Boyd Kestner (Special Agent Burke), Peter Shaw (Special Agent Brignam), Kent Linville (FBI Mail Boy), Don McManus (Asst Mayor Benny Holcombe), Harold Ginn (Larkin Wayne), Ted Koch (BATF Agent Sneed), Wm Powell Blair (FBI Agent), Aaron Craig (Il Mostro Detective), Andrea Piedimonte (Agent Benetti), Ennio Coltorti (Ricci), Ian Iwataki (Young Boy In Plane), Bruno Lazzaretti (Dante), Spike Jonze (Donnie Barber), Ivano Marescotti (Carlo Deogracias), Ajay Naidu (Perfume Analyst), Gianina Facio (Fingerprint Consultant), Sam Wells (TV Anchorman).

RED DRAGON 2002

124 minutes
Universal Pictures/Dino de Laurentiis/Metro-Goldwyn-Mayer

Executive producer: Andrew Z. Davis; Producers: Dino de Laurentiis, Martha de Laurentiis; Associate producer: James M. Freitag; Director: Brett Ratner; Screenplay: Ted Tally (based on the book by Thomas Harris); Director of photography: Dante Spinotti; Production design: Kristi Zea; Art directors: Steve Saklad, Tim Glavin; Set design: Nancy Deren, Jeff Markwith, James F. Truesdale; Editing: Mark Helfrich; Music: Danny Elfman.; Costume design: Betsy Heimann; Sound: Kim H. Ornitz; Supervising sound editors: Gregory King, Darren King; Assistant director: James M. Freitag; Casting: Francine Maisler, Kathleen Driscoll-Mohler Assoc.

Cast: Anthony Hopkins (Hannibal Lecter), Edward Norton (Will Graham), Ralph Fiennes (Francis Dolarhyde), Harvey Keitel (Jack Crawford), Emily Watson (Reba McClane), Mary-Louis Parker (Molly

Graham), Philip Seymour Hoffman (Freddy Lounds), Anthony Heald
(Dr. Chilton), Ken Leung (Lloyd Bowman), Stanley Anderson (Jimmy),
Azura Skye (Bookseller), Frankie Faison (Barney), Tyler Patrick Jones
(Josh Graham), Lalo Schifrin (Conductor), Tim Wheater (Flautist), Bill
Duke (Police Chief), Mary Beth Hurt (Museum Curator) [uncredited],
Ellen Burstyn (Grandma Dolarhyde – voice) [uncredited], Frank
Langella (Voice of the Dragon) [role deleted].
US release: 4 October 2002; UK release: 11 October 2002.

HANNIBAL RISING 2007

120 minutes (cinema version)/130 minutes (home video version)
Metro-Goldwyn-Mayer/The Weinstein Company/Dino de Laurentiis/
Quinta Communications/Ingenious Film

Executive producers: James Clayton, Duncan Reid; Producers: Dino de
Laurentiis, Martha de Laurentiis, Tarak Ben Ammar; Co-producer: Chris
Curling; Director: Peter Webber; Screenwriter: Thomas Harris; Director
of photography: Ben Davis; Production designer: Allan Starski; Editors:
Pietro Scalia, Valerio Bonelli; Costume designer: Anna Sheppard; Music:
Ilan Eshkeri, Shigeru Umebayashi.

Cast: Gaspard Ulliel (Hannibal Lecter), Gong Li (Lady Murasaki),
Rhys Ifans (Vladis Grutas), Dominic West (Inspector Popil), Kevin
McKidd (Kolnas), Richard Brake (Dortlich), Aaran Thomas (Hannibal
aged eight), Helena-Lia Tachovska (Mischa Lecter), Richard Leaf
(Father Lecter), Michele Wade (Nanny), Martin Hub (Lothar), Ingeborga
Dapkunaite (Mother Lecter), Joerg Stadler (Berndt), Stephen Walters (Zigmas
Milko), Ivan Marevich (Bronys Grentz), Goran Kostic (Pot Watcher).

BIBLIOGRAPHY

Bernstein, Jill, 'But Dino, I Don't Want to Make a Film About Elephants...',
The Guardian, 9 February 2001.

Blake, William, *Poems and Prophecies,* Everyman (London),1975.

Boorman, John and Donohue, Walter (eds), *Projections,*
Faber and Faber (London) 1992:

David Thompson & Saskia Baron, *Demme on Demme.*
Graham Fuller, *Making Some Light: An Interview with Michael Mann.*

Boorman, John and Donohue, Walter (eds), *Projections 7,*
Faber and Faber (London) 1997.

Kate Hardie: *Scene by Scene: Brian Cox on Manhunter.*

Butlin, Martin, *William Blake,* Tate Gallery (London), 1978.

Callan, Michael Feeney, *Anthony Hopkins, In darkness and light: A Biography,*
Sidgwick & Jackson (London) 1993.

Christie, Ian (ed), *Gilliam on Gilliam,* Faber and Faber (London), 1999.

Chunovic, Louis, *Jodie: A Biography,* Plexus (London), 1995.

Crowe, Cameron, *Conversations with Wilder,* Faber and Faber, (London), 1999.

Evans, Robert, *The Kid Stays in the Picture,* HarperCollins (London), 1995.

Farson, Daniel, *The Beaver Book of Horror,* Hamlyn (London), 1977.

Foster, Buddy with Wagener, Leon, *Foster Child:*
An Intimate Biography of Jodie Foster, Heinemann (London), 1997.

French, John, *Robert Shaw: The Price of Success,*
Nick Hern Books (London), 1993.

Goodwin, Christopher, 'Back for seconds', *The Sunday Times,* 4 February 2001.

Gray, Beverly, *Roger Corman:*
An Unauthorized Biography of the Godfather of Indie Filmmaking,
Renaissance Books (Los Angeles), 2000.

Harris, Thomas, *Hannibal,* Arrow Books (London), 2000.
        Hannibal Rising. William Heinemann (London) 2006.
        Red Dragon. Arrow Books (London), 1993.
        Silence of the Lambs, The, Arrow Books (London), 1999.

Heston, Charlton, *In the Arena: The Autobiography,*
HarperCollins (London), 1995.

Holden, Anthony, *The Oscars:*
The Secret History of Hollywood's Academy Awards,
Little, Brown and Company (London), 1993.

Jackson, Kevin (ed), *Schrader On Schrader & Other Writings,*
Faber and Faber (London), 1990.

Karim, Ali S.. 'Hannibal Rising. Look Back in Anger', from Szumskyj,
Benjamin ed). *Dissecting Hannibal Lecter. Essays on the Novels of Thomas
Harris.* McFarland (Jefferson, North Carolina and London) 2008.

Katz, Ephraim, *The Macmillan International Film Encyclopedia,*
Macmillan (London), 1994.

Kennedy, Philippa, *Jodie Foster: The Most Powerful Woman in Hollywood,*
Macmillan (London), 1995.

Maltin, Leonard (ed), *Leonard Maltin's Movie and Video Guide, 1995,*
Signet (London), 1994.

Morris, Mark, 'Pleased to eat you...', *The Observer,* 4 February 2001.

Newman, Kim, *Nightmare Movies:*
A Critical Guide to Contemporary Horror Films,
Harmony Books (New York), 1988.

Newman, Kim (ed), *The BFI Companion to Horror,*
British Film Institute/Cassell (London),1996.

Pearce, Garth, Ridley Scott interview, *The Sunday Times,* 4 February 2001.

Peary, Danny, *Cult Movies,* Vermilion (London), 1982.

Pym, John (ed), *Time Out Film Guide, Ninth Edition,* Penguin (London), 2000.

Russell, Mark and Young, James, *Film Music,* Screencraft/ RotoVision (Hove), 2000.

Segaloff, Nat, *Hurricane Billy: The Stormy Life and Films of William Friedkin,*
Morrow (New York), 1990.

Shipman, David, *The Great Movie Stars 3: The Independent Years,*
Macdonald (London), 1991.

Smith, Adam, 'Signed, sealed, de-livered...', *Empire,* March 2001.

Walker, John, *Halliwell's Film & Video Guide 2001,*
HarperCollins (London), 2000.

Halliwell's Filmgoer's Companion, 10th Edition, HarperCollins (London), 1993.

DVD DOCUMENTARIES, INTERVIEWS AND COMMENTARIES

RED DRAGON (Universal)

HANNIBAL RISING (Momentum)

INTERNET

Internet Movie Database – www.imdb.co.uk

The Guardian and The Observer – www.guardian.co.uk

The Independent – www.independent.co.uk

The Telegraph – www.telegraph.co.uk

The Times and The Sunday Times – www.thetimes.co.uk

Variety – www.variety.com

The Hollywood Reporter – www.hollywoodreporter.com

The New York Times – www.nytimes.com

INDEX

NUMERICAL TITLES

8½: 87

10 Rillington Place 27

300: 211

1492: The Conquest of Paradise 163

2001: A Space Odyssey 104

2046: 210, 212

A

Aber, Chuck 123

Academy Awards 136-41

Accused, The 77, 95

Acid House, The 211

Adair, Gilbert 50, 69

Adam Adamant Lives! (series) 162

Adventures of Baron Munchaousen, The 139

Adventures of Sherlock Holmes' Smarter Brother, The 39

Adventures of Young Hannibal Lecter, The 200

AI: Artificial Intelligence 189

AIP Films 75

Air Force One 173

Alice Doesn't Live Here Anymore 95

Alien 162, 163, 184, 194

Alien 3: 165

Aliens 96

All That Jazz 93

Allen, Joan 44-5, 59, 64-5

Ally McBeal (series) 169

Altered States 111

Amadeus 91

American Gigolo 35

American History X 188

American Pie 25

American Psycho 142-3

Amistad 172

Amityville Horror, The 76

Amityville II: 40, 180

Ancient of Days, The (painting) 153

Anderson, Gillian 169-70

Andrew, HRH Prince 84

Andrews, Nigel 12

Angel of Vengeance 37

Angela's Ashes 189

Angels Hard as They Come 87-8, 105, 106

Anna and the King 169

Annie Hall 33, 137

Anniversary, The 75

anti-hero, appeal of 8

Anzio 173

Apocalypse Now 103

Armageddon 186

Arthur 91

As Good As It Gets 170

Assassins 171

Atkinson, Michael 196

Audrey Rose 100

Avalanche Express 26

Avanti! 35

Avengers, The (film) 188

Awakening, The 76

Awakenings 166

B

Backtrack 96

Bacon, Kevin 76

Bad Lieutenant 189

Badelt, Klaus 165

Badham, John 86, 96

Badlands 27, 94

Baker, Diane 109, 174

Bale, Christian 143

Balsam, Martin 135

Baltimore State Forensic Hospital 190

Baltimore Symphony Orchestra 192

Bamigboye, Baz 160

Band of the Hand 70

Barabbas 158

Barbarella 29

Barber, Donnie (character) 174

Barker, Clive 77

Barney (character) 109, 151-2,

153, 174, 190
Baron, Saskia 102, 112, 126, 161
Barry Lyndon 40, 77
Barrymore, John 74
Basic Instinct 107
Basic Instinct 2 164
Basic Instinct 2: 210
Batman 134, 187
Bay, Michael 186
Beatty, Warren 138-9
Beauty and Beast 138
Beethoven Secreet, The 102
Beetle Juice 187
Before and After 158
Before Sunrise 187
Behind the Mask 200
Being John Malkovitch 174
Beloved 158
Berenger, Tom 163
Berlusconi, Silvio 136
Bernstein, Jill 168, 169, 170,
174, 184
Betrayed 107
Beyond the Mask 199-200
Beyond the Valley of the Dolls 108
Bible, The 28, 180
Bibliography 227-30
Bierce, Ambrose 13
Big 94
Big Bad Mama 89
Big Lebowski, The 170, 189
Big Sleep, The (1977) 40
Billson, Anne 135
Billy Jack 89
Bimmel, Frederica (character)
123, 126
*Bird with the Crystal Plumage,
The* 27
bit parts played by production
team members 93, 110
Bitter Rice 28
Black Hawk Down 210
Black Mama, White Mama 88
Black Rain 138, 165
Black September movement 11, 23
Black Sunday (film) 23-4, 26
Black Sunday (novel) 10, 22-3, 82
Blade 165
Blade Runner 162, 162, 163,
177, 184
Blake, William 14-15, 18-20,
38, 57, 59, 153, 182, 195
Blanchett, Cate 170
'bleach bypass' technique 213

Blooding of Hannibal Lester, The 200
Bloody Mama 89
Blue Collar 188
Blue Thunder 86
Blue Velvet 39, 46, 68
'Blue-Eyes' (character) 204
Blues Brothers, The 108
Body of Evidence 157, 171, 180
Bone Collector, The 143, 169
Bonney, Lawrence A 110
Bonnie and Clyde 85
Boogie Nights 170-1, 189
Book of Revelations 18-19,57,61
Boorman, John 164
Boston Strangler, The 27
Boticelli 150
Bounty, The 40, 101-2
Bourne, Mel 33, 40, 45
Bowman, Lloyd 189
Boyle, Lieutenant (character) 130
Boys Don't Cry 169
Boyz N the Hood 138
Bozman, Ron 93, 138
Bradshaw, Peter 182, 197, 217
Bram Stoker's Dracula 165,
171, 173, 177
Brando, Marlon 140
Braveheart 43
Brazil 42, 55
Breaking the Waves 189
Brigade Criminelle 200
British actors and accents 43,
47, 103, 131, 138
British Board of Film
Classification 69, 133-4, 178
Broadcast News 179
Brooks, Mel 135
Brotherhood of the Wolf, The 210
Bruckheimer, Jerry 32
Brynner, Yul 158
Buffalo Bill (character)
see Jame Gumb
*Buffy the Vampire Slayer
(television)* 170
Bugsy 138, 138-9
Bullets Over Broadway 189
Bundy, Ted 81
Bunker, Eddie 31-2
Burke, Haydon (character)
110, 116
Burning, The 76
Burstyn, Ellen 189
Burton, Tim 187
Butler, Dan 109, 123

C

Caan, James 33
Cabinet of Dr Caligari, The 34
Cage, Nicolas 188
Caged Heat 88, 92, 93, 94,
108, 120, 131
Cagney and Lacey (series) 91
Caine, Michael 76
Callan, Michael Feeney 102,
104, 104, 115
Candleshoe 95
Candyman 109
Cannibal Holocaust 12
cannibalism 11,12, 167, 184
Cannom, Greg 165, 177
Cannonball 94, 110
Cape Fear (1962) 139
Cape Fear (1991) 215
Cape Fear (1992) 138-9
Captain America 174
Caravaggio 165
Carpenter, John 136
Carradine, David 86
Cassavetes, John 24, 75
Cat People 36, 109
CAT Squad: Python Wolf 85
'cat talking like James Stewart' 184
Catchfire 96
celebrity cameo parts 179
Challenge, The 25
Chaney, Lou 74, 101
Change of Seasons, A 101
Charbonneau, Patricia 57, 67
Cherry, Harry and Raquel 108
Chesapeake County Asylum 46
Chicago 211
Chilton, Dr Frederick
(character) 67, 83, 84, 98,
107-8, 116, 128, 132, 190, 193
Chilton's fiancée, Dr (character) 146
Chinatown 23
Christensen, Hayden 209
CHUD 42, 109
Cimino, Michael 66, 104,
113
Citizens Band 89, 108, 119
Civil Action, A 166, 174
Clear and Present Danger 166
Clockwork Orange, A 40
Code of Silence 45
Cohu, Will 207
Columbia-Tristar 133
Columbo (series) 90, 93

Compromising Positions 44-5
Conan the Barbarian 30, 67
Conan the Destroyer 180
Conformist, The 35
Connery, Sean 179
Contact 166
Cooper, Dominic 210
CopLand 174
Copycat 143
Corman, Julie 136
Corman, Roger 88-91, 94, 110, 116-17, 119
Corsalini, Stephanie 165, 173
Costner, Kevin 138
Cousins, Mark 63
Cox, Alex 50
Cox, Brian 43-4, 47, 85, 132, 172
    favourite scene 62
    Manhunter 47-8, 61
    Silence of the Lambs 98-9, 102-3
Crace, John 208
Crane, Marion (character) 171
Crawford, Bella (character) 151
Crawford, Jack (character) 15, 22, 25, 45, 51, 64, 75, 78-9, 79, 85, 98, 116-7, 122, 126, 151, 151, 167
Crazy Mama 89, 92, 94
Crime Story (series) 37, 45, 67, 107
Crimes of the Heart 40
Cronenberg, David 164
Cruel Intentions 170
Cruising 27, 41
CSI: Crime Scene Investigation 192
Culkin, Macaulay 179, 209
Curse of the Golden Flower 212
Curtis, Tony 76
Cushing, Peter 74

D

Damien - Omen II 76
Dance of the Vampires 75
Dancer in the Dark 174
Dances with Wolves 133, 138
Dancy, Hugh 210
Danger Man (series) 40
Dangerous Liaisons 96
Daniels, Jeff 90
Dante, Joe 136
Danton 211
Daumer, Jeffrey 137
Davis, Bette 75
Davis, Geena 139-40
Day Lewis, Daniel 138

de Laurentiis, Dino 12, 28, 29, 35, 45, 66, 68-9, 71, 72, 98, 101, 104, 141, 158-61, 169, 180, 199
de Laurentiis, Martha 164, 199, 215
De Niro, Robert 55, 138-9
De Palma, Brian 164
De-Lovely 211
Dead of Night 100
Dead Ringers 94
Dead Zone, The 30
Deal of the Century 41
Death in Venice 35
Death of a Salesman (play) 45
Death Race 2000 94
Death Wish 29
Deep, The 25
Deerhunter, The 66
DEG - De Laurentiis Entertainment Group 30, 45, 66, 68-9, 71, 104
Demme, Jonathan 96-8
    Academy Awards - Director 138
    background 77, 87-92
    beliefs and philosphy 91
    comparison with Manhunter and Hannibal 13
    enthusiasm for film of Hannibal 157, 160-1, 164
    loyalty to the text of Silence of the Lambs 119-20
    more background 87-90
    violence against women 92
    working with Jodie Foster 114-15
Dern, Bruce 23
Dern, Laura 140
Desert Hearts 67
Desperate Hours, The 104, 105, 113, 140, 180
Diamonds 34
Diaz, Cameron 169
directors of sequels 164
Dirty Harry 27
Dirty Mary, Crazy Larry 89
Do the Right Thing 109
Doctor Fell (character) 145, 150
Doemling, Dr Cordell (character) 150, 174, 184
Dog Soldiers 211
Dolarhyde - Dollarhyde spelling (character) 38, 44
Dolarhyde house 194
Dolarhyde, Francis (character)

82-3
    8-mm film 20
    background 17-18
    casting in Red Dragon 188
    goggles 17
    grandmother 17-18,
    Red Dragon finale 21
    scrapbook 20
    sympathetic figure 17
Dolarhyde, Grandma (character) 189, 194, 195
Dollarhyde, Francis (character)
    8mm home movies 63-4
    casting 44
    great psychopath 56
    lunar killing cycle 46
    tattoo 60-1
Donne, John 78
Donnie Brasco 174
Douglas, John 16, 106, 113, 132
Douglas, Kirk 76
Douglas, Michael 140
downlighting 129
Dr Jekyll and Mr Hyde (1920) 74
Dr Jekyll and Mr Hyde (1932) 74, 140
Dr Jekyll and Mr Hyde (1941) 74
Dracula (1930) 9
Dracula (1979) 76, 86, 189
Dracula, Count (character) 9
Dressed to Kill 76
Dreyfuss, Richard 25
Driller Killer 36
Drumgo, Evelda (character) 145, 182-3
Duellists, The 162, 188
Dune 28, 30, 45, 71, 162
Duvall, Robert 103, 131
Dylan, Bob 70

E

Ebert, Roger 196
Edge, The 165
Edward Scissorhands 187
Elephant Man, The 101, 101, 102
Elfman, Danny 187, 191
Elizabeth 170
End of the Affair, The 170, 188
Enduring Love 211
English Patient, The 188
Englund, Robert 76
Equus (play) 100
Europa, Europa 140
Evans, Robert 23, 26

Eve's Bayou 109
Excalibur 91
Exorcist II: The Heretic 164
Exorcist, The 41, 43, 75, 77,
 85, 189
Exterminator 2 109

F

Fabulous Baker Boys, The 96
Faison, Frankie R 109, 174-
 5, 190
 only actor in all the Lector
 films 190
Family Man, The 186, 187,
 188, 189
Family Plot 23, 25
Farewell My Concubine 210
Farina, Dennis 37, 45, 98, 188
Farrow, Mia 75
Fatal Attraction 136-7
FBI headquarters 46
FBI Quantico academy 78,
 113, 117, 122, 144, 176
Fear City 37
Fearless 212
Ferrara, Abel 36-7
Ferris Bueller's Day Off 94
Fiennes, Ralph 188, 194-5
Fifth Element, The 173
Fight Club 188
Fighting Mad 88, 93, 105
Filmography
 Hannibal 223-5
 Hannibal Rising 226
 Manhunter 218-19
 Red Dragon 225-6
 Silence of the Lambs, The 220-3
Fingers 188
Fischer, Tibor 207-8
Fisher King, The 138-9
Five Corners 95
Flash Gordon 30, 35, 40
Flesh Feast 73
Flockhart, Calista 169
Flora Plum 169
Florence 124, 150-1, 152,
 175-6, 182
Fly, The 94
Fonda, Jane 29
Food of the Gods 73
For the Boys 140
Force 10 from Navarone 26
Foster, Buddy 114, 156
Foster, Jodie 210
 Academy Awards - Best

Actress 139-40
 attitude to death 113
 background 86
 casting for *Silence of the
 Lambs* 95-8
 enthusiasm for film of
 Hannibal 157, 160-1,
 165-6, 168-9
 role in *Silence of the Lambs*
 122-7
 The Accused 77
 working with Anthony
 Hopkins 114-15
 working with Jonathan
 Demme 114-15
Francke, Lizzie 134
Frankenheimer, John 23, 24, 164
*Frankenstein and the Monster
 from Hell* 185
Frankenstein Unbound 87
Franklin (character) 149
Frasier (series) 109
Freejack 171
French and Saunders 135
French Connection II 23,
 104, 164
French Connection, The 41-2,
 85-6, 93
French, Philip 70, 131, 197, 217
Frida 188
Friday the Thirteenth 27, 49,
 76, 95, 129
Fried Green Tomatoes 189
*Fried Green Tomatoes at the
 Whistelstop Cafe* 140
Friedkin, William 41-2, 43-4,
 75, 85
Friend, Rupert 210
From Dusk Till Dawn 189
Fugitive, The 170
Fujimoto, Tak 93-4, 108, 117,
 119, 129
Fuller, Graham 71
Fury, The 76

G

Game, The 174
Gangs of New York 166
Garfield: A Tale of Two Kitties 211
Gattaca 187
Gein, Ed 81, 82
Gellar, Sarah Michelle 170
Gentlemen Prefer Blondes 44
Ghost of a Flea (painting) 182

Ghosts of Mississippi 173
GI Jane 163, 165, 174
Giannini, Giancarlo 173
Girl With a Pearl Earing 211
Gladiator 162, 163, 169, 180
Glaser, Paul Michael 36, 70
Glazer Safety Slugs 65
Glengarry Glen Ross (play) 164
Glenn, Scott 25, 105-6, 113, 188
*God Creating the Universe
 (painting)* 153
Godfather Part II, The 110
Godfather, The 119, 137, 139
Goetzman, Gary 93
Gold Coast 35
Goodfellas 174
Gosford Park 189
Gothard, Michael 185
Graham, Kevin (character)
 38, 53
Graham, Mrs Molly (character)
 15, 21-2, 22, 39, 42, 52, 53-4,
 53-5, 65, 189, 195
Graham, Will (character) 84,
 187, 195
 breaks into Dollarhyde's
 mindset 64
 character dropped 111
 dreams 53
 hero's role at the end 65
 key role in *Manhunter* 51-4
 opinion of Hannibal Lecter 148
 Red Dragon finale 21-2
 Red Dragon role 15
 references in *The Silence of
 the Lambs* 84
 scar 16
 three scenes with Hannibal
 Lektor in *Manhunter* 61-4
 videotape 38
Graham, Willy (character) 15, 38-9
Grant, Cary 75
Gray, Beverly 89
*Great Northfield Minnesota
 Raid, The* 103
*Great Red Dragon and the
 Woman Clothed with the Sun,
 The (painting)* 195
Great Red Dragon and the
 Woman Clothed with the Sun:
 The Devil is Come Down 57
Greggio, Ezio 135
Greist, Kim[berly] 42, 55-6
Griffith, Melanie 90

Grimm Brothers fairy tales 13, 201

Grosbard, Ulu 31-2

Grutas, Vladis (character) 202, 204, 205-6

Guinness, Sir Alec 121

Gumb, Jame aka Buffalo Bill (character) 81-3, 92, 106-7, 111, 124-5, 145

Gumb, Mrs (character) 82-3

Guns of Navarone, The 213

Gustavson, Victor(character) 204

Guthmann, Edward 196-7

Guttmacher, Peter 9, 61, 77

H

Hackman, Gene 85, 87

Halloween 9, 27

Hammer Film Productions 74-5

Handle with Care 89

Hanks, Tom 76

Hannibal (book)

changes in film to ending 175

climaxes and end 154-6

comparison with earlier novels 152-3

dinner party 155-6

film rights 157

Florence 150-1, 152

plot 144-8

rewritten climax for film 184

typographical errors 153

White House scandal 152

writing and sales 143-4

Hannibal (film)

alternative ending 185

alternative titles 157-8

atmosphere and setpieces 183-5

barn rescue sequence 177

bloody set-pieces 183-4

budget 158, 175

casting for role of Mason Verger 173

censorship classifications 178

changes from book 168

closed set 175-6

comparison with *Manhunter* 12-13

dinner party sequence 184

disputes over rights 159-60

ending 172

Filmography 223-5

finale 165, 168

finale and publicity ban 184-5

Florence scenes 175-6, 182

gross takings 180

horror atmosphere 177

leading lady possibles 169-70

legal actions 178

pig barn scene 176, 184

previews 178

producers 161-4

production in USA 176

production team 165

publicity 180

publicity build-up 178-9

release 180

reviews 181

rewrite 166-7

screenplay 165, 166-7, 183-5

supporting cast 173-5

supporting characters 184

teaser trailer 178-9

Hannibal 4: 200

Hannibal IV: 200

Hannibal Lickter 135

Hannibal Rising (book)

alternative titles 199-200

comparison with film 212, 213-14

errors 205, 208-9

Lithuanaia setting 200-1

'novelisation' of film 202

reviews 207-8

writing and plot 199-207

Hannibal Rising (film)

advanced publicity misleading 217

american TV trailer 217

budget 212

casting for Hannibal Lecter 209-10

casting for other roles 210-11

comparison with book 212, 213-14

comparison with *Hannibal* and *Red Dragon* 212-13

Filmography 226

Lecter-Kolnas fight 215

location 212

releases 217

reviews 216-17

screenplay 212

supporting actors 214-15

takings 217

teaser trailer 216

visual style 213

'Hannibal the Cannibal' 8

Hansel and Gretal 214

Hardie, Kate 63, 99, 132

Hardy, Rebecca 85

Harrelson, Woody 142

Harris, Thomas

background 9-11

Black Sunday (novel) 10, 22-3, 82

body parts fixation 205

classical allusions and quotations 78

comparison between three novels 152-3

contacts with Michael Mann 46

declines to preview *Silence of the Lambs* 121

enthusiasm for film of *Hannibal* 157

Florence visit 175

Hannibal (book) 143-4

Hannibal (screenplay) 167

Hannibal Rising (book) 199-207

liking for symbolism 79

literary allusions 201

Manhunter 68-9

possible further writings 218

real-life serial killers 81

script writing 199

seeming liking for loathsome appearance 149

Silence of the Lambs (book) 77

supposed minimal interest in films 13

Harry and Walter Go to New York 33

Hartlaub, Peter 216-17

Harvey, Dennis 216

Haunting, The 100

Hawke, Ethan 187

Hawn, Goldie 90

Hayek, Salma 188

He Knows You're Alone 76

Heald, Anthony 108, 190

Heartbeat (song) 65

Heat 40, 107

Heaven's Gate 33, 44, 66

Heche, Anne 171

Heidnick, Gary 81

Helfrich, Mark 187

Hendrickson, Benjamin 98

Henry: Portrait of a Serial Killer 92

Hercules Unchained 87

heroic female characters 143
Heston, Charlton 24, 76
high-class serial killer films 142
Hilary and Jackie 189
History Boys, The 210
Hobbs, Garrett (character) 38
Hoenig, Dov 33-4, 40
Hoffman, Philip Seymour
  189, 195
Hohimer, Frank 32
Holden, William 76
Hollywood Wives 101
Holocaust 2000 76
Home Alone 209
Home Alone 2: *Lost in New
York* 209
Home for the Holidays 168
Home Invaders, The (novel) 32
Hopkins, Anthony 40, 45, 77,
  86, 99-100, 113
Hopkins, Anthony
  Academy Awards -
    Best Actor 139-40
  accent for Hannibal Lecter 131
  background 102-3
  casting as Lecter in *Silence
    of the Lambs* 102-3
  enthusiasm for film of
    Hannibal 157, 160-1
  enthusiasm for *Hannibal*
    (film) 171-2
  Hannibal Lecter as
    favourite role 172
  last film as Lecter 198
  Red Dragon 187, 193-4
  role in Silence of the Lambs
    127-32
  views on Hannibal character 146
  working with Jodie Foster
    114-15
Hopper, Dennis 76
horror films 73-4
Hot Box, The 88, 92, 108
Hotel New Hampshire, The 95
House of Flying Daggers 212
House of Games 165
House of Usher 75
Howards End 137, 171
Howling, The 110
Humanoids from the Deep 92
Humperdinck, Engelbert 214
*Hunchback of Notre Dame, The
  (1923)* 74
Hunchback of Notre Dame, The

(1939) 74, 101
*Hunchback of Notre Dame, The
  (1982)* 101
Hunger, The 40
Hunger, The (series) 165
Hunt for Red October, The 106
Hunt, Helen 170
Hunter, Holly 76
Hunting Party, The 85

I

I Just Called to Say I Love You
  (song) 63
*I Know What You Did Last
Summer* 143, 170
Ideal Husband, An 170
Ifans, Rhys 211, 212, 214-15
In Dreams 143
In the Belly of the Beast (play) 41
In the Mood for Love 212
In-A-Gadda-Da-Vida (tune)
  41, 64, 68
Ingle, Doug 64
Insider, The 40
Insurrection 31
Into the Night 91
Invisible Man, The 74
Iron Butterfly 64-5
Irons, Jeremy 138
Isaak, Chris 110
Island of Dr Moreau, The 76
Island of Lost Souls 74
It Happened One Night 140
Ivanek, Zeljko 174

J

Jackson, Michael 190
Jacob's Ladder 179
Jacobi family (characters) 20, 57
Jacobi family (charactrs) 67
Jade 107
Jagged Edge 107
Jakov, Mr (character) 202
Jason and the Argonauts 28
Jaws 23, 25
Jaws 2: 161
Jennifer 8 142
Jericho Mile, The 32, 33
Jewel of Seven Stars, The 76
JFK 138, 140, 165
Johnson, Don 35
Jolie, Angelina 169
Jonze, Spike 174
Ju Dou 210
Judd, Ashley 169

Julia 39
Juror, The 158

K

Kalifornia 142
Karim, Ali S 201, 205
Karloff, Boris 74, 103
Keep, The 34-5, 36, 46, 106
Keeping the Faith 189
Keitel, Harvey 188-9
Keller, Marthe 23
Kestner, Boyd 174
Kilgore, Colonel (character) 103
King and I, The 25
King Arthur 210
King Kong (1976) 29-30, 104
King of the Gypsies 28
King, Stephen 14, 76, 144
Kingdom of Heaven 211
Kiss the Girls 143, 169
*Kiss the Girls and Make Them
Die* 180
Kojak (series) 31
Kraus, Mary Ann 113, 132
Krendler, Paul (character) 117,
  145-6, 149-50, 150, 155, 174
Kubrick, Stanley 76
Kuffs 159
Kung Fu (series) 86

L

LA Confidential 50
Lady in the Lake, The 117
Lake, Veronica 73
Lancaster, Burt 76
Landis, John 136
Lang, Fritz 164
Lang, Stephen 45, 58, 70
Langella, Frank 86, 189
Larkin, Philip 201
Last Embrace 90, 108
Last Emperor, The 137
Last of the Mohicans, The 35,
  40, 50
*Last Temptation of Christ,
  The* 189
Laughton, Charles 74, 101
Lauter, Ed 103-4
Lazar, Paul 109, 123
Le Carré, John 121
Le Mat, Paul 90
Le Roux, Lambert (character) 104
Lecher, Dr Hannibal 135
Lecktor and Lecter roles compared 132
Lecktor, Dr Hannibal

(character) 43, 47-9, 61-4
'Lecter brand' 199
Lecter family pennant 201
'Lecter fatigue' 198
Lecter Variations, The 200
Lecter, Dr Hannibal (character)
  cannibalism 8
  Clarice Starling fixation 146
  downlighting 129
  entrance in Silence of the
    Lambs 128-9
  eyes 17
  facial restraints 129
  gourmet dinner in cell 193-4
  Hannibal scenes   183-5
  impact on moral decline 13
  indoor exercise 193
  insane hospital 16
  Italian theme 80
  Memphis jailbreak 130-2
  polydactyly 80, 110-11,
    146, 205
  role in Silence of the Lambs
    127-32
  Senator Ruth Martin 130
  six fingers 80, 110-11, 146, 205
  souvenirs 145
  Starling-Lecter relationship
    124, 154-6
  website 145
Lecter, Mischa (character)
  148-9, 154, 202-3, 204-5, 213
Lecter, Robert (character) 203-4
Lecter, Simonetta (character)
  202, 213
Lecter-Lecktor spelling 43,
introductooy note
Lee, Christopher 74
Leeds family (characters) 16,
  20, 38-9, 52, 57, 64
Leeds, Valerie (character) 191
Legend 162-3, 163
Lehman, Ernest 25
Lemmons, Kasi 109
Leon 173, 215
Leoni, Tea 189
Lepke 34
Leung, Ken 189
Levine, Joseph E 87, 100
Levine, Ted 107, 113, 124-5
Levinson, Barry 138
Lewis, Juliette 142
Li, Gong 210, 214
Libertine, The 210

Lindbergh Kidnapping Case,
  The (series) 105
Lion in Winter, The 99
Liotta, Ray 90, 174, 184
Little Girl who Lives Down the
  Lane, The 95
Little Man Tate 140, 168
Little Mermaid, The 138
Little Nicky 211
Lloyd Wyman (character) 132
Longest Yard, The 104
Los Angeles morgue 113
Lost in Space 173
Lost World: Jurassic Park,
  The 170
Louis Friend (character) 112
Lounds, Freddie (character)
  17, 45, 51, 52-3, 56-7, 58, 62,
  189, 195
Love at Large 107
Lucky Lady 86
Lugosi, Bela 9, 74
Lumet, Sidney 118
Lupino, Ida 73
Lustig, Branko 165
Lynch, David 162

M

M 27
*M*A*S*H (series)* 31
M. Butterfly (play) 86, 103
Mad About You (television) 170
Mad Movies (magazine) 50, 56, 66
Madonna 43
Magic 100, 104, 131
Magician of Lublin, The 34
Magnolia 189
Mahler 102
Malcolm, Derek 134
Mamet, David 164, 166, 170
Man of Iron 211
Man of Marble 211
Manchurian Candidate, The 24
Mandingo 180
Mangano, Silvana 28
Manhunter
  awards 71
  bit parts played by prison
    inmates 32
  box-office results 68
  British Board of Film
    Classification 69
  climactic ending 64-5
  coda 65
  comparison with *Hannibal*

    12-13
  cuts 55-6, 67-8
  Dollarhyde-Reba lovescene
    59-60
  8mm cinefilm 38, 54
  FBI team analysing
    Dollarhyde note 50
  Filmography 218-19
  French release as
    Le Sixieme sens 70
  German release as
    Roter Drache 70
  Hannibal Lektor three
    scenes 61-4
  lighting 49-50
  locations 45
  London Film Festival 69
  mistakes 51
  music 41
  other titles used 70
  overview starts 28
  plot ending 65
  pre-credit sequence 49
  pressbook 30
  promotional campaign 68-9
  release in USA 68
  re-release in UK 72
  reviews in UK 69-70
  screenplay 191
  slide show 57, 59
  star-free cast 41
  suspense creation 49
  tension between police and
    FBI 52
  title change from
    Red Dragon 66
  uncut versions 71-2
  videotape 38
  visual style 33, 48
  voyeurism at heart of film 54
  wheelchair 57, 58
  wide-screen process 46
  Will Graham character 51-2
Manhunter 3 158
Manhunter 3: 164
Manitou, The 76
Mann, Michael 56, 190
  background 30-1
  British Actors 47
  comparison with Hannibal 12
  contacts with Thomas Harris 46
  no interference 161
  other 1986 films 70
  title change reasoning 66-7

visual flair 49
Mannlein Steht Im Walde, Ein (song) 214
Mapp, Ardelia (character) 109, 151, 167
Marathon Man 23
March, Frederic 74, 140
Marnie 109
Married to the Mob 87, 91, 93, 94, 96, 103, 110
Mars Attacks! 187
Martin, Senator Catherine (character) 78, 81-2, 111-12, 120, 125, 145
Martin, Senator Ruth (character) 109, 130, 147
Mask of Zorro, The 171
Mask, The 165
mass murderers 11
Masters of the Universe 189
Masters, Brian 135
Mathieson, John 165
Maverick 166
McCarthy, Todd 196
McClane, Reba (character) 20, 59, 59, 64-5, 64-5, 189, 191
McKay, Craig 94, 108, 120
McKidd, Kevin 211
Mean Streets 188
Medavoy, Mike 87, 92, 92, 96, 97, 103, 131
Meet Joe Black 172
Mellville, Jean-Pierre 213
Melvin and Howard 90, 94, 119
Memoirs of a Geisha 210, 212
Mendez, Agent (character) 174
Merchant-Ivory productions 137, 171, 183
Metro-Goldwyn-Mayer 159
Metromedia Company 160
Miami Blues 108
*Miami Vice (*2006*)* 210, 212
Miami Vice (series) 31, 35-6, 42, 49-50, 69
Midler, Bette 140
Midnight Cowboy 93
Midsummer Night's Sex Comedy, A 91
Miggs, Multiple (character) 80, 120, 146
Milius, John 67
Mimic 173
Miracle Worker, The 33
Mirage 109

Miss Scaremento 1948 82-3
Mission: Impossible 166
Mission: Impossible 2 164
Mission: Impossible 2: 165, 171
Mississippi Burning 85-6, 109
Mona Lisa Smile 211
Moonstruck 137
Moore, Demi 73
Moore, Julianne 188
  background 170
  sensitiveness 176-7
Morbidity of the Soul 158
Moriarty, Professor (character) 9
Ms.45: 37
Munich Olympic Games 23
Music Lovers, The 102
My Left Foot 138

Nanny, The 75
Napier, Charles 108, 130
National Inquisitor, The 112
National Lampoon's Loaded Weapon 1 135
National Tattler, The 8, 17, 43, 52, 58, 66, 84, 112, 144, 146
Natural Born Killers 142
Natural, The 33
NBK 142
necrophilia 20
Nell 50, 166
Neri, Francesca 173-4
New York Stories 173
Nicholas and Alexander 43
Nicholson, Jack 76-7, 179
Nightmare Before Christmas, The 187
Nightmare on Elm Street (series) 27, 76
Nights of Cabiria 180
Nixon 45, 172
No Beast So Fierce (novel) 31
Nolte, Nick 138-9
Noonan, Tom 44, 56, 60-1, 107
Noonan, Tommy 44
North By Northwest 25
Norton, Edward 187-8, 191-2
Nosferatu 34
Notting Hill 211
nurse-biting incident 168

Oldmam, Gary 171, 173, 177, 179, 184
Oldman, Gary 215
Oliver Twist 211

Olivier, Laurence 76
Omen, The 18, 75
Once Upon a Crime 173
Once Upon a Time in America 173
One Flew Over the Cuckoo's Nest 77, 88, 140
One Little Indian 95
Orca - Killer Whale 28, 180
Orion Films 116
Orion Pictures 85, 87, 90-1, 133, 137-8, 141, 159-60, 168
Outland 39

Pacte des loups, Le 210
Paltrow, Gwyneth 143, 169
Parasite 73
Parker, Mary Louise 189
Pat Garrett and Billy the Kid 71
Patterson, John 181
Paul the Butcher (character) 203-4
Payne, Tom 210
Pazzi, Laura (character) 173
Pazzi, Rinaldo (character) 150-1, 166, 173, 177
Pearce, Garth 173
Pearl Harbor 186
Peck, Gregory 75
Pee-wee's Big Adventure 187
Peeping Tom 20
Penn, Sean 188
People versus Larry Flynt, The 188
Perkins, Anthony 103
Petersen, William L 41-2, 47, 54-5, 68, 188
Peterson, William L 192
Pfeiffer, Michelle 87, 91, 96-7
Phantom of the Opera, The (1925) 74
Phantom of the Opera, The (1943) 74
Phantom of the Opera, The (1962) 75
Philadelphia 118, 158
Pianist, The 211
Piano, The 189
Pilcher, Noble (character) 84, 109, 123
Pitt, Brad 142
Piven, Jeremy 188
Platoon 91
Plunkett and Macleane 165
Poe, Edgar Allan 74
Polanski, Roman 75

Police Story (series) 31
Pollock, Tom 159
Poole, Steven 208
Popil, Inspector (character) 204, 206-7
Porcellinno, Il (statue) 175
Portnoy's Complaint 25
Possession, The 40, 180
Postcards from the Edge 108
Pravda (play) 104
Predator 187
Price, Jimmy (character) 109
Price, Vincent 74
Pride and Prejudice 210
Primal Fear 188
Primarvera (painting) 150
Prime Cut 85
Prince of Tides, The 136, 138, 139, 140
Prisoner, The (series) 40
Prize, The 109
Projections 7 (magazine) 47
Promises, Promises 44
Prophecy 25
Psycho 194
Psycho (1960) 9,11, 17, 27, 82, 103, 135
Psycho (1998) 171
Pulp Fiction 189
Punch-Drunk Love 189

Q

Quick and the Dead, The 50
Quiz Show 188

R

Rafferty, Terrence 207, 217
Raging Bull 139
Ragtime 109, 164
Rains, Claude 74
Raise the Red Lantern 210
Rambaldi, Carlo 30
Rambling Rose 140
Rambo: First Blood Part II 108
Rambo: First Blood Part II: 187
Rampage 54
Randall, June 46
Rashomon 87
Raspail, Benjamin (character) 81, 120
Rat in the Skull (play) 44
Ratner, Brett 186-7, 195
Record Releasing 69
Red 7: 65
Red Dragon (book)

changes made when filmed as *Manhunter* 66
changes when filmed 37-9
film rights 28
plot 15-16
publishing history 14
screen adaptation 23
Red Dragon (film)
budget 186
closing scenes 191, 195-6
comparison with other Hannibal films 190-1, 194, 198
crew 187
faithful to book 190
fidelity to novel 192
Filmography 225-6
Hopkins, Anthony 187, 193-4
locations 190
museum tri[p 195
Norton, Edward 192
pre-credits sequence 192
project 186
releases 197-8
reviews 196-7
screenplay 191
slide show 195
style 190-1
takings 198
tiger scene 191
title change to *Manhunter* 66
Red Dragon, The (Mah Jong piece) 61
Red Dragon: The Pursuit of Hannibal Lector 72
Red Sonja 180
Red Sorghum 210
Remains of the Day, The 171
Repo Man 50, 108
Repulsion 75
Reservoir Dogs 32, 189
Ressler, Robert K 16
Return of Frank James, The 164
Reversal of Fortune 138
Reynolds, Sled 177
Rich, Frank 26
Richard III: 211
Right Stuff, The 106
Rising Sun 165
Road to Wellville, The 171-2
Rob Roy 43, 172
Robards, Jason 90
Robin Hood: Prince of Thieves 134, 179

Robocop 133
Robson, Mark 26
Rock, The 186
Roden (character) 109, 123
Rogers, Mimi 163
Rolling Stone (magazine) 68
Romeo is Bleeding 173
Romero, George 110, 114
Romney, Jonathan 197
Ronin 165
Rosemary's Baby 75
Roter Drache 70
Roth, Richard 39, 42
Roth, Tim 172
Rourke, Mickey 66
Rubini, Michel 40-1, 70
Rufin, Dr (character) 203
Running Man 70
Rush Hour 186, 187, 189
Rush Hour 2: 186, 187, 188
Rushmore 43
Ryan, Meg 97-8

S

Safe 170
Samourai, Le 213
Sarandon, Susan 93, 139-40
Sardinia 175
Saturday Night Fever 86
Saturday Night Live (television) 94
Saving Private Ryan 213
Saxon, Edward 92, 93, 108, 120, 138
Scalia, Pietro 165, 212
Scanners 94
Scarface 36
Scarfiotti, Ferdinando 35-6
Scheider, Roy 25
Schindler's List 166, 188, 211
Schrader, Paul 35-6
Score, The 188
Scott, Jake 165
Scott, Ridley 12-13, 138, 162-5
Scott, Tony 165
Scream (trilogy) 143
Scream 2: 165, 170
Scream and Scream Again 185
Scully, Dana (character) 169-70
Seconds 24
Secrets of a Door-to-Door Salesman 88
Sender, The 174
serial killers films 26-7, 92

Serpico 29
Seven Beauties 173
Seven Days in May 24
Se7en 142-3, 169
Shadowlands 171
Shaw, Robert 23, 25
Sherman family (character) 57
Sherman family (characters) 59, 67-8
Shikibu, Lady Murasaki
(character) 203, 204, 205,
206, 213, 214
Shining, The 76-7
Shipping News, The 211
Shore, Howard 94, 118, 129
Short Circuit 86
Short Cuts 170-1
Sierra, High 73
Silence of the Hams, The 135
Silence of the Lambs 2: 158, 164
Silence of the Lambs, The (book)
as sequel to *Red Dragon* 98
changes made for film 111-12
conclusion 84-5
film rights 85
flaws in plot 83-4
plot and storyline 77-83
problems inherent in
adaptations 126-7
reviews 77
supporting characters 83
Silence of the Lambs, The
(film) 63, 67
Academy Awards 136-41
Academy Awards -
Best Actor 139-40
Academy Awards -
Best Actress 140
Academy Awards -
Best Picture 138
Academy Awards -
Director 138
Academy Awards -
Nominations 137-8
Academy Awards -
Screenplay 140
Academy Awards sweep 140
american tv version 120-1
as sequel to *Manhunter* 98
autopsy scene 123
awards 136
budget 92
cable television release 137, 141
Clarice Starling casting 95-8
comparison with *The Shining* 76

cuts 116-17, 175
ending 132
entrance of Hannibal Lecter
128-9
Filmography 220-3
flashback scenes 118
graphic gore 119-20
horror movie with class 77
mistakes 121
music 118
parodies 135-6
pivotal film 12
post-production changes 116
poster campaign 73
previews 120
producers 92-3
production and locations 113-14
production team 93-4
promotion 133-4
publicity 133-4
release 133
reviews 133-5
screen rights 96
screenplay 93, 111-12
set for Lecter's cell 112-13
subjective camera 117
supporting roles 105-10
takings 134
video release 137, 141
visual style 119-20
Silenzio dei Prosciutti, Il 135
Silkwood 108
Silver Bullet 180
Silverado 106
Simpsons, The (series) 64, 135
Singleton, John 138
Sixieme sens, Le 70
Skins (series) 210
slasher films 76
Sleepy Hollow 187
Smiley's People 121
Smith, Adam 171, 183-4
Smith, Graham 179
Snider, Stacey 166, 167
Soldiers and Sailors Memorial
Hall, Alleghenny 129
Someone to Watch Over Me 163
Something Wild 90, 93, 108, 174
Sommersby 166
Sorcerer 41
Sound of Music, The 25
Spader, James 93
Spanish Prisoner, The 165
Spartacus 71

Spice World 211
Spider 188
Spiegel, Adam 174
Spielberg, Steven 161
Spinotti, Dante 40, 48, 50, 63,
129, 187
Stakeout 86
Star 80 93
Star is Born, A 44
Star Wars 94
*Star Wars Episode 2 -
Attack of the Clones* 209
*Star Wars Episode 3 -
Revenge of the Sith* 209
*Star Wars Episode I -
The Phantom Menace* 211
Starling, Clarice (character)
casting for *Silence of the
Lambs* 95-8
Hannibal scenes 182-5
name 79
plot of *Silence of the Lambs*
(book) 77-81
positive resolution 84-5
role contrast betwen *The
Silence of the Lambs* and
Hannibal 156
role in *Hannibal* (book)
144-6, 149-51, 154-6
role in *Silence of the Lambs*
122-7
seen by Demme as key to
Silence of the Lambs 92
Starling - Gumb relationship
124-5, 126-7
Starling - Lecter relationship
124, 154-6
treated with respect in
Silence of the Lambs 117
Starling, Mr (character) 78, 118, 154
Starski, Allan 211
Starsky and Hutch (series) 31, 36
State and Main 165
Steele, Barbara 88
Steiger, Rod 75, 76
Stone Killer, The 180
Stone, Oliver 138
Stop Making Sense 90, 93
Strada, La 29
Straight Time 31-2, 93
Strait Jacket 110
Strasberg, Susan 76
Sturridge, Tom 210
subjective camera 117

Summer of 42 39
Summer of Sam 142-3
Super Bowl game 22, 23, 24
Superman 86
Supervixens 108
Surviving Picasso 172, 184, 211
Swank, Hilary 169
swans, black 201
Swashbuckler 25
Sweet Smell of Success 25
Swimming to Cambodia 90
Swing Shift 90, 110
Szwarc, Jeannot 161

T

Tai-Pan 30, 46, 72
Tally, Ted 85-6, 92, 92-3, 96,
  102, 111, 119-20, 128, 158,
  161, 186, 191, 192
  Academy Awards -
  Screenplay 140
Tangerine Dream 33
Taxi Driver 95, 96, 139, 188
Temptress Moon 210
Terminator 96
Terminator 2: Judgment Day 134
Texas Chain Saw Massacre,
The 12, 119, 125
Texas Chain Saw Massacre
Part 2: 76, 131
The Reds 40-1
Thelma and Louise 139-40,
  139-40, 163, 165, 189
There's Something about Mary 25
Theron, Charlize 169
Thief 32, 33, 36, 41-2, 42, 49
Thinner 165
Thomas, Melissa 182-3
Thomas, Philip Michael 35
Thompson, David 89, 91, 110, 119
Three Days of the Condor 29
Three Kings 174
tiger scene 191
Timlin, Mark 209
Timmerman, Bonnie 41
Tinker, Tailor, Soldier, Spy 121
Titus 172
To Live and Die in LA 41-2
Tonkin, Boyd 208
Tooth Fairy (character) 16, 48,
  50, 52, 56, 58
Topsy-Turvey 211
Tracy, Spencer 74
Trainspotting 211

True Grit 103
True Romance 165, 173
Twin Town 211
Two Minute Warning 24
Tyger, The (poem) 59

U

U-571: 157, 159, 162
Ulliel, Gaspard 210, 212,
  214, 215
Ulysses 28-9
Umebayashi, Shigeru 211-12
United Artists 33
Universal 169
Universal Pictures 159, 186
Universal Studios 74, 166
Unlawful Entry 174
Untouchables, The 165
Utt, Kenneth 93, 108, 138

V

Vadim, Roger 29
Vanity Fair 210
Vanya on 42nd Street 170
Vawter, Ron 117, 174
Vega$ 31
Verdict, The 164-5
Verger, Margot (character) 153-4
Verger, Mason (character) 148,
  153, 166, 173, 177-8, 184
Very Long Engagement, A 210
Videodrome 94
Violent Streets 33
Virgin Suicides, The 209
Von Richtofen and Brown 87

W

Wag the Dog 164-5
Wagner, Erica 208
Walk in the Clouds, A 173
Walker, Alexander 11, 69-70, 134
Walking Tall 89
Walter, Tracey 108
War and Peace 29
War Games 86
Waterloo 28
Watson, Emily 189, 191
Watts, Peter 197
Way We Were, The 39
Weale, Sally 181
Weaver, Fritz 23
Weaver, Sigourney 162
Webber, Peter 211, 212
Weinstein Company 212
Welcome to the Dollhouse 189

Welk, Lawrence 201
West Side Story 25
West, Dominic 211
Whatever Happened to Baby
  Jane ? 75
When a Man Loves a Woman 98
When Eight Bells Toll 99
When Harry Met Sally 97
Where Eagles Dare 213
White Buffalo, The 28
White Palace 93
White Squall 163, 165, 174
Who's Afraid of Virginia Woolf? 25
Wild Angels, The 87
Wild Thing (pop song) 204
Wilder, Billy 36
Williams, Bernard 40
Williams, Robin 138-9
Wilson, F Paul 34
Windbag the Sailor 12
*Winslow Boy, The (*1999*)* 165
Wire, The (series) 211
Wolf Man, The 74
Wolfen 44
Woman in Red, The 63
women in prison film genre 88, 92
Woo, John 164
Woods, James 173
Wrentz, Lawrence T 110

X

X Files, The (series) 169-70

Y

Yates, Janty 165
Year of the Dragon 46, 66,
  68, 104
York, Susannah 76
Young Frankenstein 200
Young Guns 55
Young Guns II 54
Young Hannibal 200
Young Winston 100

Z

Z Cars (series) 162
Zaillian, Steven 166-7
Zardoz 164
Zea, Kristi 94, 119, 125, 187
Zimmer, Hans 165